BUCKNELL REVIEW

John Cage
at Seventy-Five

STATEMENT OF POLICY

BUCKNELL REVIEW is a scholarly interdisciplinary journal. Each issue is devoted to a major theme or movement in the humanities or sciences, or to two or three closely related topics. The editors invite heterodox, orthodox, and speculative ideas and welcome manuscripts from any enterprising scholar in the humanities and sciences.

This journal is a member of the Conference of Editors of Learned Journals

BUCKNELL REVIEW
A Scholarly Journal of Letters, Arts, and Sciences

Editors
RICHARD FLEMING
MICHAEL PAYNE

Associate Editor
DOROTHY L. BAUMWOLL

Assistant Editor
STEVEN W. STYERS

Editorial Board
PATRICK BRADY
WILLIAM E. CAIN
JAMES M. HEATH
STEVEN MAILLOUX
JOHN WHEATCROFT

Contributors should send manuscripts with a self-addressed stamped envelope to the Editors, Bucknell University, Lewisburg, Pennsylvania, 17837.

BUCKNELL REVIEW

John Cage
at Seventy-Five

Edited by
RICHARD FLEMING
and
WILLIAM DUCKWORTH

LEWISBURG
BUCKNELL UNIVERSITY PRESS
LONDON AND TORONTO: ASSOCIATED UNIVERSITY PRESSES

Associated University Presses
440 Forsgate Drive
Cranbury, NJ 08512

Associated University Presses
25 Sicilian Avenue
London WC1A 2QH, England

Associated University Presses
P.O. Box 488, Port Credit
Mississauga, Ontario
Canada L5G 4M2

The paper used in this publication meets the requirements
of the American National Standard for Permanence of Paper
for Printed Library Materials Z39.48-1984.

Library of Congress Cataloging-in-Publication Data

John Cage at seventy-five.

(Bucknell review ; v. 32. no. 2)
Includes bibliographies.
1. Cage, John.   I. Fleming, Richard.   II. Duckworth,
William.   III. Series.
AP2.B887   vol. 32, no. 2 [ML410.C24] 051s   88-47817
ISBN 0-8387-5156-3 (alk. paper) [780'.92'4]

(Volume XXXII, Number 2)

PRINTED IN THE UNITED STATES OF AMERICA

Contents

Recent Issues of BUCKNELL REVIEW

photograph GENE BAGNATO

Introduction

THE present issue of the *Bucknell Review* is a seventy-fifth birthday tribute to the American composer John Cage. Unlike many such projects this one did not begin with ambitious intentions. As editor, I had become convinced that the *Bucknell Review* needed to renew its contact with its immediate University surroundings and needed firmer grounding in the strengths and interests of the Bucknell community. To recover such contact I thought it appropriate to seek out members of the faculty and ask for their help on a special topic that could comprise part of a particular issue of the *Review*. My first choice of such an individual was Bill Duckworth, and my hope was for a special section of the *Review* devoted to John Cage. My choice of Cage was in part a result of his visit to Bucknell in 1986 and the enjoyable conversations I was able to have with him at that time. My reasons for approaching Bill Duckworth were simpler. He embodies intellectual qualities that Bucknell University can be justly proud of—his music has been performed on four continents, and he has received national recognition as one of the leading teachers of music—but (most importantly) he is a friend. Only a friend would have considered accepting the workload and anxieties generated by the project I was proposing. Not only did Bill accept my proposal, but he expanded it and developed it to the grand scale that it has now assumed. It is not fulsome praise to say, therefore, that without his efforts the present issue of the *Review* would not be.

It is not just my friendship with Bill, however, that made this issue possible. Just as important was Bill's friendship with John Cage. Without Bill's personal relationship to Cage and without John's suggestions and help, this book would have been impossible. To relate but one instance of his help, John gave us access to hundreds of personal photographs (photographs he had stored in several chests of drawers) which we carefully combed in order to create the photo essay at the center of this issue. Only because of John's friendship with Bill was an issue, devoted completely to the work of Cage, pursued.

Similar stories of friendship can be told about each of the selections in this volume. Over the last two years Bill has contacted

9

numerous people concerning the "Cage project." He and I have
discussed its possibilities between ourselves and with others for
hundreds of hours, and we have worried individually for many
more hours about how to structure and present the material.
Thus, while *John Cage at Seventy-Five* does correctly title this issue
of the *Bucknell Review,* I hope its pages in some way reflect the
friendships that made it possible.

The issue begins with Gene Bagnato's commissioned portrait of
John Cage, taken at John's home in 1987, just a few months before
Cage's seventy-fifth birthday. The rest of the issue is bracketed by
two interviews. The first is Bill Duckworth's interview, which presents a general introduction to Cage's music, while the second
interview and last piece in the volume is by Richard Kostelanetz
and specifically addresses Cage's works involving radio. Following
Duckworth's interview are two pieces on the most important influences on Cage's music: Eastern philosophy and the American
thought of Henry David Thoreau (and by implicit implication the
influence of Charles Ives). Margaret Leng Tan's essay looks at the
Eastern influences on Cage's work, while William Brooks writes
about Cage and Thoreau. The important influence that Cage's
own work has had is examined by Arthur Sabatini with specific
attention given to how a reading of Cage's writing is itself "a silent
performance."

At the center of the issue are the photo essay mentioned above,
a lecture on Cage by Norman O. Brown, and a new piece by Cage
entitled "Anarchy." These are then followed by a reproduction of
a Neil Anderson painting, especially done for Cage's seventy-fifth
birthday. The remaining three essays of the volume all concern
the single most significant long-term contribution made by Cage
to music: chance. Deborah Campana's piece addresses how
chance originally became a part of Cage's music, while James
Pritchett's essay discusses how one can analytically approach
chance in Cage's work. Finally, Tom Johnson discusses how to
perform Cage's chance pieces of music.

I hope that a reading of this special issue of the *Bucknell Review*
will allow those moments of the last seventy-five years, on which
the individual selections of the issue are based, to find a new life in
our present time.

RICHARD FLEMING

Letter to the Editor
March 25, 1955

E DITOR, the *Argus:*
       The John Cage Recital at last night's assembly provoked a
number of questions. Would you please print the following, with
my answers?

Q: Was it a hoax? A: No.

Q: Is Cage a serious artist? A: Yes.

Q: Is this music? A: Although it is obviously so far removed
from our norm, as to be almost in another category, it could only
be conceived and executed by musicians.

Q: Is this typical of contemporary music? A: No.

Q: Was the audience rude? A: Partly. I think I was partly
responsible through failure to publicize the thing properly.

Q: How can you listen to such stuff? A: The great problem is to
listen to it without the expectation of hearing something "normal."
Until you can listen with a vacant mind, you'll be hearing Cage's
music not for itself but as an unwanted distortion of something
else.

Q: Why bother to listen? A: Why give up the codpiece?

Q: Was any of it meant to be funny? A: Yes.

Q: Will this music become common? A: More and more is being
done with sound possibilities outside our particular tradition.

Q: Wasn't it awfully haphazard? A: One of Mr. Cage's goals is to
exploit the charms of chance—to make of art a play which can't be
"psychoanalyzed"—to work without "purpose." (May I remind the
students who have read the *Bhagavad Gita* that this is a familiar
concept expressed in the command "Act without coveting the
fruits of action.")

Those who were antagonized by the performance and who have
run out of descriptive terms for it, can find a variety of fresh
insults in a book called *Lexicon of Musical Invective* by Nicolas
Slonimsky (Olin Library), a compilation of on-the-scene reactions
to the music of, e.g., Beethoven, Bach, Mozart, Verdi, etc. I do not
by this remark suggest that Cage is a major prophet—though he

11

may be. I do infer that, faced with something you don't understand, humility is in order.

Sincerely,
R. K. Winslow
Associate Professor of Music

Editor's Note: This "Letter to the Editor" appeared in the student newspaper at Wesleyan University, Middletown, Connecticut, a few days after the first appearance of John Cage and David Tudor on that campus. They had been brought there by Richard Winslow to give a two-piano recital of the music of Cage and Stockhausen. Although no one remembers the exact program they performed, it is believed that the second half of the concert consisted of Cage's *34'46.776"*, a piece for two prepared pianos written in 1954. In describing this program at the recent "John Cage at Wesleyan" festival in honor of Cage's seventy-fifth birthday, Richard Winslow, now the John Spencer Camp Professor of Music Emeritus, wrote: "The place started to go mad. I saw people, red faced with anger, punching one another. I saw people stuffing handkerchieves in their mouths. And I sensed that the audience was polarizing into two camps—those who felt they were in the presence of Art and those whose risibilities had become unhinged." Today, thirty-three years later, his responses at the time still stand as one of the clearest explanations of Cage's intentions ever written.   **WD**

BUCKNELL REVIEW

John Cage
at Seventy-Five

Anything I Say Will Be Misunderstood: An Interview with John Cage

William Duckworth

T HE windows, the skylight, and the forest of plants—some four hundred of them—give a sense of a simpler, rural life in the midst of the city. Although at first impressed by the names on the walls—Robert Rauschenberg, Jasper Johns (Cage's friends from the fifties)—a visitor soon recognizes that life in this Chelsea apartment centers on the open kitchen, crowded with macrobiotic foods and jars of all sizes, and on the large, round table by the windows. The windows completely cover two walls. An unavoidable presence, they offer both sunlight and a panoramic view of traffic rushing up Sixth Avenue.

We began our conversation, however, away from the windows, at a small table against a wall at the edge of the kitchen. Although I had visited a number of times before, this was our first talk "for the record," and I confessed to John that I was a little nervous about it. He said not to worry; he'd think of something to say.

DUCKWORTH: It occurs to me that I don't have a very good understanding of what your early musical training was like. Is that because you've been intentionally vague about it?
CAGE: No. I've told everything I can think of. I've told, for instance, about studying piano with my Aunt Phoebe and my love of music "the whole world loves to play." And loving the music of Grieg, and being kept away from the music of Bach and Beethoven, and so forth.
D: I guess what I don't understand is: Were you a good pianist?
C: I was never interested in the scales. I had what was called a beautiful touch, which means that you have a sense of continuity. I hated scales and anything like that. And I still do. I'm not interested in virtuosity, per se. I was always, and still am, interested in the variety and nature of musical activity outside my own tastes and inclinations. So I did a great deal of sightreading—first of the

15

nineteenth century, and later of earlier music, and later of modern music.

D: Was this before you went to Europe, before you started composing?

C: The interest in nineteenth century was. It was in Europe that the teacher I took one lesson with, Lazare Lévy at the Conservatoire, sent me to a Bach festival because he learned that I knew nothing of Bach. I had found out about Beethoven, but not about Bach or Mozart. I went to a whole festival of Bach's music, and found it very interesting. At the same time, I heard John Kirkpatrick play Scriabin and Stravinsky. I went to visit him, and through him I became aware of that collection called *Das neue Klavierbuch* of other modern composers. And I began writing music in response to all that music.

D: What was your first music like?

C: It was mathematical. I tried to find a new way of putting sounds together. Unfortunately, I don't have either the sketches or any clearer idea about the music than that. The results were so unmusical, from my then point of view, that I threw them away. Later, when I got to California, I began an entirely different way of composing, which was through improvisation, and improvisation in relation to texts: Greek, experimental from *transition* magazine, Gertrude Stein, and Aeschylus. Then, becoming through Richard Buhlig and others aware of my disconnection with musical technique or theory, I began studying the books of Ebenezer Prout. I went through them just as though I had a teacher, and did all the exercises—in harmony, primarily. I don't think I did counterpoint. It was later, with Schoenberg, that I studied that.

D: If you studied primarily romantic music with your aunt and you had gone through those harmony books, why do you suppose you had such a lack of feeling for harmony that Schoenberg talked about?

C: I don't have an ear for music, and I don't hear music in my mind before I write it. And I never have. I can't remember a melody. A few have been drummed into me, like "My Country 'Tis of Thee," but there will come a point in even those songs that I'm not sure of how the next note goes. I just don't have any of those things that are connected with solfège and with memory and with what you might call, imagination. I don't have any of those things. I have other qualities which are, I would say, more radical than those. But all those things which most musicians have, I don't have.

D: Well, most of the people I know who would admit that would have never gone into music.

C: I know that. Demosthenes wouldn't have gone into ⌐
he'd told you his experience beforehand. He was the⌐
who overcame stuttering by speaking with stones in his ᵐᵘᵘ
But I didn't have the desire to overcome those absences in my
faculties. I rather used them to the advantage of invention.

D: Early, though, in your training, did you see them as problems?

C: Oh, yes.

D: Real problems?

C: No. I saw them always as perfectly good for what I could offer
to the musical world—namely, invention. I knew that from my
father, because I had the example every day of a person in the
house inventing. And I knew that that was the only thing I would
be able to do in the field of music.

D: How do you think about your early pieces now—*A Metamorphosis* and the *Sonata for Clarinet?*

C: I don't think *A Metamorphosis* is an interesting piece. It's the
least interesting of them all. But I think the others are very
interesting.

D: In those early works, were you beginning to envision that being
a composer was something beyond what you were doing at the
moment, or were you still being influenced by your teachers, and
writing in the style of your teachers?

C: None of those pieces are written in the style of my teachers.

D: No, but they show influences of them.

C: No, they don't, really. What? How do they?

D: Well, if you think about the *Sonata for Clarinet,* there's a lot of
twelve-tone work there.

C: No, it's not twelve-tone.

D: I know what you're saying; you're saying that it's not the
traditional way of dealing with twelve-tone.

C: And I hadn't yet studied with Schoenberg when I wrote it.

D: That's true, but *A Metamorphosis* you had. But again, that's a
totally different way of dealing with twelve-tone.

C: Um hum. So it doesn't show his influence.

D: Is there any influence of Schoenberg on your work?

C: I would say not, in that sense. I would say in a radical sense
there is. Because of his insistence upon the importance of structure and harmony and tonality as a structural means in music, I
devised the macro-micro-cosmic rhythmic structure for a music
which wouldn't have its basis in pitches and frequencies, but rather
in time.

D: Do you have a favorite piece from among your early works?

C: Every time anyone has asked me what is my favorite piece from
the past, I've consistently said I don't have any favorites. Anytime

you say that something is your favorite, you're negating all the things that are not.

D: What's the difference, then, between saying that you don't have any favorite pieces and saying that *A Metamorphosis* is not a good piece?

C: I think not having any favorites is seeing each thing as unique and being at its own center. Then, when you look at the *Metamorphosis* and see the nature of its center, you see that for certain reasons it was not interesting, and really would have been better not written. It had no life in it. It had something else in it, but not a real life. If something has life in it and is at its center, it's very hard and useless to say that you prefer it to something else which also has life and is at its own center. But if something doesn't have any life in it, and is nothing but a set of relationships that are so forceful that the things that are being related cannot be heard apart from the relationship, then what you have is an intellectual situation that has no, I will say, physicality. And the thing about that piece is that it has no physicality. It's not a piece of music worth listening to. We could think about it, and we could teach people how to write another one like it, but we wouldn't want to listen to it.

D: How about the transition, then, to percussion music?

C: It wasn't a transition, Bill; it went on at the same time.

D: Simultaneously?

C: Yes. I thought that when I was writing for instruments the music should be chromatic rather than diatonic. And when I was writing for noises that the music should have a rhythmic structure. Those were my thoughts. And those were going on simultaneously. Instead of a transition, there was a dialogue between those two attitudes that brought about a number of changes. It brought about the invention of the prepared piano, on the one hand, and then the application of rhythmic structural ideas to instrumental works, that is to say, nonpercussion instrumental works. So that all those ideas that were, at first, in two different parts of my work came together.

D: How did it come about that writing for noises was musical in your mind?

C: I was introduced by Galka Scheyer to Oskar Fischinger, the film maker, and he was making films—abstract films—to the *Hungarian Dances* of Brahms. Galka thought, I think rightly, that his work would be more interesting if he used modern music. And she thought that my music could get more interesting through some connection with his work. He, in fact, made a remark to me which dropped me into the world of noise. He said: "Everything in the world has a spirit, and this spirit becomes audible by its being set into vibration." He started me on a path of exploration of the world around me which has never stopped—of hitting and scratching and scraping and rubbing everything, with anything I can get my hands on. I don't seem to be doing it as much as formerly; but when I was first doing it, I was doing it constantly.

D: When you were developing the percussion orchestra, did you know Varese's work in percussion music?

C: Yes. I heard Nicolas Slonimsky conduct the *Ionization* at the Hollywood Bowl, and that experience, together with Fischinger's remark, confirmed my decision to work with percussion instruments.

D: For a number of years you used rhythmic structure based on duration. Then, all of a sudden, you seemed to stop and you went in another direction.

C: It wasn't all of a sudden. The gradual renunciation of those things is recounted in the essay in *Silence* called "Composition as Process." Rhythmic structure was characteristic of composition as object. And what I'm talking about in those three lectures is composition as process. That's why the notion of rhythmic structure was gradually dropped. It didn't happen all of a sudden. The *Music of Changes*, and even the timelength pieces for percussion and voice and stringed instruments, are all written in rhythmic structures, but structures that have become so flexible through the admission of acclerandos and ritards that the time is no longer fixed. At that point, then, where you introduce accelerando and ritard into a structural principal based on time (in other words, when it becomes flexible), it's on its way to no longer being necessary and it's moving into process. Had it remained fixed, without accelerandos and ritards, there would have been no reason to drop it. When David Tudor worked on the *Music of Changes*, he learned a kind of mathematics to translate the notation of accelerandos and ritards into clock time—stopwatch time. His copy of the *Music of Changes* has all the exact timelengths for the appearance of each event.

D: Your early comments about the *Bacchanale* and the reason you invented the prepared piano all center on the fact that you didn't have space for percussion, and that the piano, in essence, gave you a percussion orchestra. When did you become aware that the prepared piano was more than a percussion orchestra?

C: It was through the social problems here in New York City. You can't get a group of people to work together in New York for any length of time, because they're all too busy making money. So that when I had to give a concert of percussion music at the Museum of Modern Art, I found that I couldn't get a full rehearsal—ever. Even for just a short time. So I threw my energy and everything into the prepared piano. I had already written *Amores* and some other pieces, *Bacchanale* and some dance pieces, but then I began to write *A Book of Music* for two pianos and the dances and then the *Sonatas and Interludes* and, finally, the *Concerto for Prepared Piano and Chamber Orchestra.*

D: When you were writing *Sonatas and Interludes* did you understand the full possibilities of that piece as you were writing it, or is it only as it developed that it became such a major piece in your life?

C: It's not in my life; it's in *its* life. Many people have been attracted to playing it. And I think anyone will have to remark eventually on the fact that all of the performances are different, because my table of preparations is not precise, and only suited the piano that I was actually working on. So that the result is that everyone's performance of the *Sonatas and Interludes* is a fresh experience. And this is a feather in the hat of indeterminacy, I think. Or it could be a black eye on indeterminacy, according to how you look at it. I think David Tudor feels that the *Sonatas and Interludes* only existed when I played them on the piano for which they were composed. I think he thinks that the work has disappeared in the various transformations that have taken place.

D: But I would think that you'd like the idea that they change every time they're played. Is that not true?

C: I didn't like it when I first wrote it. I was persuaded to like it through what I call practicality and circumstances. And it was one of the things that committed me to indeterminacy and chance operations.

D: Was your interest in Indian and oriental philosophy simultaneous with this move toward indeterminate music, or did one lead to the other?

C: No, they were coexisting.

D: Are they two sides of the same coin?

C: No. I think it has more than two sides. I think it's different aspects of a changing mind, which I was trying to describe in a variety of ways in that essay in *Silence,* "Changes."

D: How do you feel now compared to the way that you felt then? For instance, is self-expressive art, art since the Renaissance, still radical?

C: I would say so, yes. Some of it is very beautiful, but I think it's ineffective. I mean to say that the self is not really expressed when it expresses itself. It takes the mind of the person who's doing the work off his proper work.

D: Which is what?

C: Either the imitation of nature in her manner of operation, or the sobering and quieting of the mind making it susceptible to divine influences. Those are the two reasons for making music that are traditional.

D: If you're doing one, aren't you doing the other, at least to some extent?

C: I think probably.

D: Let me ask you a few questions about *4'33"*. Is it true that it was actually conceived of in the late forties and just not presented until the fifties?

C: Yes. I knew about it, and had spoken about the possibility of doing it, for about four years before I did it.

D: Why were you hesitant?

C: I knew that it would be taken as a joke and a renunciation of work, whereas I also knew that if it was done it would be the highest form of work. Or this form of work: an art without work. I doubt whether many people understand it yet.

D: Well, the traditional understanding is that it opens you up to the sounds that exist around you and . . .

C: . . . and to the acceptance of anything . . .

D: yes . . .

C: . . . even when you have something as the basis. And that's how it's misunderstood.

D: What's a better understanding of it?

C: It opens you up to any possibility *only* when nothing is taken as the basis. But most people don't understand that, as far as I can tell.

D: Is it possible that instead of being taken as too foolish, it's now taken too seriously?

C: No. I don't think it can be taken too seriously.

D: What I mean is that it's approached too intellectually. My own feeling is that it's not a piece to approach intellectually—maybe not even a piece to approach, in the traditional sense.

C: Well, I use it constantly in my life experience. No day goes by without my making use of that piece in my life and in my work. I listen to it every day. Yes I do.

D: Can you give me an example?

ιn't sit down to do it; I turn my attention toward it. I realize ..ɔ going on continuously. So, more and more, my attention, as now, is on it. More than anything else, it's the source of my enjoyment of life.

D: But it seems to me that when you focus on that piece it becomes art silence rather than real silence. And that the understanding of real silence is what that piece is about. But that the only way you can get to real silence is through artistic silence. Is that accurate?

C: Thoreau came to this same attitude of mind and use of his faculties without my being anywhere around.

D: Yes, but you'd be hard-pressed to name another one who came to that attitude, wouldn't you?

C: Well, I would think quite a lot of people in India feel that music is continous; it is only we who turn away. This is a cliché in Indian thinking and, surely, in Indian experience. My affirmation of this is within the context of twentieth-century art music. But the important thing, surely, about having done it, finally, is that it leads out of the world of art into the whole of life. When I write a piece, I try to write it in such a way that it won't interrupt this other piece which is already going on. And that's how I mean it affects my work. But I don't mean by the silent piece, or any other, that I accept all the intentional self-expressive actions and works of people as suitable interruptions of this other activity. I don't believe that a bad, thoughtless, undevoted performance of one of my works is a performance of it.

D: So that even in indeterminate, nonintentional music value judgments still play a part?

C: Oh, certainly.

D: How do you, how does anyone, distinguish between appropriate and inappropriate value judgments?

C: This is our problem, and one that we can't set down in any strict way. You'll have to study the situation thoroughly to find out what needs to be done at the time.

D: So it's different for every situation?

C: Yes, I think so. That's what the critics don't understand. I mean just because my name comes up doesn't make a failure a success.

D: No, that's true. But you've suffered from performances like that forever.

C: Oh, yes.

D: How. . . ?

C: How do I manage?

D: And overcome it?

C: Well, I take as primary to the whole thing the purpose of music,

which is to sober and quiet the mind, thus making one susceptible
to divine influence. So that when I find myself being taken away
from that purpose, I veer back toward it. It is more important for
me to be at home with the silent piece than it is for me to get
irritated by what some critic says, for instance, or how badly
somebody plays something.

D: From all I've read, it appears that those early meetings on
Monroe Street with Feldman and Wolff and Tudor were very
significant meetings. The image that comes out is one of daily
activity and daily changes of attitude. Is that true?

C: Yes.

D: How long did that last?

C: It lasted at least a year, maybe two years. Then I went to
Colorado and met Earle Brown and Caroline Brown, and they
became so interested in the work that they decided to leave Colorado and come to New York and live here. I, meanwhile, had
started a tape music project with Louis and Bebe Barron and
David Tudor. And Earle went into this. Well, the appearance of
Earle Brown on the scene infuriated Morton Feldman, so that the
closeness that I had had with Morty and David and Christian was
disrupted by the advent of Earle Brown. Later, that whole problem was resolved by our raising the money to present a concert of
the music of Brown and Feldman at Town Hall. Then both Earle
and Morty became friends, and had a truce.

D: Did the intensity of that group of people extend outside of the
group?

C: Oh, yes. There were other people who wanted to enter the
group and enjoy the exchange of ideas and so forth, but Morty
refused to let that happen. He insisted upon its being a closed
group. It was through my acceptance of Earle Brown that Morty
then left. The group then dissolved. Morty was literally furious
that anyone else was allowed into the group. Another one who
might have been in it but wasn't was Philip Corner. And I don't
know, but I imagine Malcolm Goldstein and James Tenney. However, the fact that they weren't brought into it made it come about
that they formed their own group, which was called Tone Roads.
And they did beautiful work.

D: Do you think everything works out for the best?

C: Maybe not the best, but everything works out to something.

D: What is your current relationship with the members of the
group?

C: The closeness that I had with Morty, even though it was always
revived when I saw him again, didn't go from day to day. It only

bloomed again briefly when we were together. We loved one
another very much, but each life had gone in its own direction.
And that's true of Christian too.

D: Is that less true of David Tudor?

C: No, I don't know David Tudor really anymore either in that
close way that I knew him to begin with, though we're more
frequently together than the others. But we're together through
the circumstances of being musicians for the Cunningham Dance
Company. If we weren't that, I would never see David anymore.
Not because I don't enjoy seeing him, but because circumstances
just don't bring us together. He's doing such beautiful work in
electronic music that I have no desire to do any in that field. And
that's because I'm an inventor. He's doing all the inventing that's
necessary in that field. Where invention is required now, it seems
to me, is in the field of piano, the violin, and possibly the flute,
which I intend to work on.

D: Even after all of the flute pieces from the sixties? Every composer in the world had to write an obligatory flute piece in the
1960s. Does it still need invention?

C: I think so.

D: What direction is it?

C: I'll have to find it out.

D: Have your ideas about the function of notation changed recently?

C: I use notation in a variety of ways, all the way from the
explicitness of the *Freeman Etudes* to the indeterminacy of the
Variations. I'm not concerned with one particular kind of notation,
but with many. I've done also a number of things in which there
isn't any notation except verbal directions. Those things have been
done by other people, but I continue to work in all those ways
rather than in one of them exclusively. When I write, for instance,
for orchestra, I'm writing for strangers and so I tend to write very
conventionally. I'm careful to make something that can be understood without spending too much time.

D: But that hasn't always been true, has it? I'm thinking about
something like the *Concert for Piano and Orchestra*.

C: No, that was always true. I developed that notation with the
players themselves, so the notation was not strange to them, but
arose out of our conversations.

D: But you worked with people who were in some way interested
in and dedicated to new music. When that piece is handed to
orchestra musicians, who are more dedicated to music of the past,
it becomes very confusing for them.

C: The people I wrote it for were the first ones. The subsequent ones are a result of circumstances over which I have no control. But when I made the notation, it was made with people who knew its meaning. Since then, the ambiguity that you speak of is certainly present, and sometimes it works and sometimes it doesn't. But that's true of any notation. The classical notation sometimes works, and sometimes it doesn't. I've heard Beethoven played very badly . . . and Mozart too.

D: Well, I was thinking also about that seven- or eight-minute performance of *Atlas Eclipticalis* with the New York Philharmonic in the sixties.

C: So what relation does the notation have to that? The rehearsal was seven minutes long. You can scarcely say that they could tell you what the notation was.

D: So intent and commitment transcend notational problems?

C: I wouldn't say intent and commitment; I would say spending time with something. It's that simple. I mean, even a desultory spending of time over a thirty-hour period would result in something different than paying no attention during a seven-minute period.

D: Are your experiences with orchestras getting better now that you've become more well known?

C: Yes. I'm now more demanding of what happens in the way of rehearsal. And I've refused to work with them unless they will give time. That, of course, is not always in my control. It's only in my control at the time of the first performance, in the case of a commissioned work. I can't, for instance, demand of an orchestra with which I have no connection, who gets the music from Peters, I can't demand anything of them. I don't even come into the picture.

D: Does that worry you?

C: It doesn't worry me at all.

D: Your piece has a life of its own at that point?

C: It has to have a life of its own, because I don't wish to be a policeman in the society. I have too many things to do to add to them the police function, which I'm not interested in, in any case.

D: But it must be worrisome, if not painful, to know about bad performances.

C: I don't have time to be worried, and I have little occasion to be pained, because the people who are not caring about something are not apt even to invite me to the performance. And worrying accomplishes nothing. So I try, in my life and in relation to my work, to do the things that are useful (and I frequently use that word) rather than to spend my energy and time in a way that results in nothing. You might say that worry could result in a change of attitude, but I'm too old to do that.

D: And you never worried about it? There was never concern?

C: I do my work as well as I can, and as practically as I can. And I've always done that. I've always advised certain people who ask me for advice to keep their feet on the ground. I don't like it when people write large works for orchestra when they have no commission from an orchestra. The reason I don't like that is because my early teacher, Adolph Weiss, had a stack of music that was never played, and he became embittered in the society. And so he was an example to me of how not to behave. I don't think I have any pieces that haven't been performed.

D: Of course you're in the situation now where any piece you write is going to be performed.

C: That was always the case. And the reason it was the case was because I had the example of Adolph Weiss, for whom it wasn't the case. He was such a bitter, ugly-tempered man as a result that I knew I didn't want to become that way.

D: Was Schoenberg bitter?

C: No, never. Everything he wrote was performed. He organized the society in Vienna which played all the music that he was interested in, including his own, without the audience knowing what was being played.

D: But his work was questioned and ridiculed at times.

C: That didn't bother him. But everything was played. He was a fighter from the word go.

D: Did you pick that up from him?

C: No, I think I picked all of these qualities up from my father.

D: Wasn't there a point, say in the late fifties, where the actual look of the music that you were writing made performances difficult?

C: No. Are you thinking of the *Concert for Piano and Orchestra?*

D: I was thinking of the pieces around that, yes, and then beyond. The *Variations.*

C: No. Those were all written for David Tudor.

D: And you had very little concern beyond David Tudor? I mean, I'm sure you were aware of the controversy.

C: If you knew David Tudor, and worked with him as I did over a long period of time (I would say we worked closely together for between fifteen and twenty years), he's one of the greatest musical . . . I was going to say minds. I would say that of Schoenberg. But David Tudor is not so much a musical mind as he is a musical . . . At that time, he was, as Busotti said, "a musical instrument." And when Busotti wrote a piece for him, he didn't say for piano, he said for David Tudor, meaning him as an instrument. David still has that aspect in the society. I noticed him recently in California after a concert with the Cunningham Dance Company, and the young composers of the Bay area flocking around him because of his technical knowledge and technical experience in the field of live electronics. And formerly, it was in the field of piano. And before that, it was in the field of the organ. But he was such an extraordinary musician that if you were near him, and even now if you're near him, you don't need anything else. The world is immense through him, has no limits, has only inviting horizons.

D: Why do you suppose David never played any Ives?

C: I asked him why he didn't play Ives, because that's the remarkable thing that is missing in his history. He said: "It's too difficult." And I didn't know what that meant. This is why he's so fascinating. At first, I didn't know what that meant, because it was not too difficult from the point of view of his hands. He played the Boulez Second Sonata, which is more difficult. Either he told me or I then realized that he would have had to change his mind over into that of a transcendentalist, which he didn't wish to do. When he played the Boulez sonata, he read all the poetry that Boulez was reading at the time—René Char. He learned the French language in order to read that poetry; he didn't know it until then. He became, insofar as he could, the composer. And he said it would be too difficult to do that in the case of Ives. Had he done it, we would have had performances of Ives that we haven't yet had. This sounds very elitist, and I think I am actually an elitist. I always have been. I didn't study music with just anybody; I studied with Schoenberg. I didn't study Zen with just anybody; I studied with Suzuki. I've always gone, insofar as I could, to the president of the company.

D: Yes, but now you're the president of the company.

C: I have tried to indicate that there is no company. And I don't teach. So it makes it difficult. It obliges people to do what I think is finally important, and that is to work from their own centers. This is what I keep writing about.

D: But unless you're dealing with extraordinary people, their own centers aren't well enough defined to understand how to work from them.

C: But Bill, I think they are. I don't believe in education. I don't believe in things being explained or understood. I believe in things that are inexplicable.

D: That statement might be misunderstood if we leave it at that.

C: And the elitist business. All of those things can easily be misunderstood, because people don't think clearly. I think, for the most part, people don't think. I don't know how they do what they do, but I guess it's that they're on the lookout for some advantage and that when one thing gives them an advantage they go in that direction rather than in the one where they don't get an advantage.

D: Yes, but I think you do believe in education. You've been educating yourself all of your life.

C: That's different.

D: What's different about it?

C: Well, the difference is that when I was in school I learned very little. When I was thirty-five years old, I began to learn what school had not taught me, and I did it through my own efforts and through my own studying.

D: Could you have done it without school?

C: Yes. In fact, I'm a dropout you know. The question arises: Why didn't I drop out sooner?

D: Is there an answer?

C: I think there may be one. I've never tried to find it. But there was something about the things that I did in high school that seemed to me to be challenging. They filled up my life, and I was able to expend my energy on them with interest. In high school, I studied Greek and geometry (I didn't get as far as calculus) and literature and botany. In addition to which I won a cup for the school in oratory—giving speeches. After hours in high school, I conducted the boy scout radio program which I arranged each week. I had some speaker from the Protestant, Catholic, or Jewish community give an inspiring ten-minute talk, and then the rest of it was jokes and stories and music. It went on for an hour over KNX for two years. Those were my two years in high school.

D: You were valedictorian; you must have believed in education at that point.

C: No, that was through my interest in oratory that I did that. It wasn't education. My valedictorian speech was on international patriotism, the devotion to the whole world, which I was not taught in school. I was taught only the patriotism part—swear allegiance to the American flag—and I was saying we must swear allegiance to the whole world, which no one taught me in school.

D: Are you positive now or negative about the state of the world?

C: I'm positive. I think the world is only part of creation, and that creation is going to continue willy-nilly. That if we destroy this earth, which we may very likely do, it would be like destroying one leaf of a tree. So why should I feel pessimistic about that?

D: So where in high school you were talking about the family of the world . . .

C: International patriotism, I would say.

D: . . . now you're talking about . . .

C: . . . the universal creation, I would think. We all cling to what we have done, and others have done, on this planet. But we surely know, as well as any Buddhist or any Jewish mind, the futility of placing faith in anything of this earth. Doesn't the prophet say: "Vanity of vanities, all is vanity."? We're well aware that at any moment we may go out of existence. We already know as individuals that death can take us at any moment, that we live, in fact, in a mystery where each one of us is the central character in a mystery that's going to end with death. And we don't know who killed us. But the one thing we're certain of is our death.

D: Where do you put your faith then?

C: You don't put it outside of yourself; you put it inside of yourself and in your energy. And you put that as close to zero as you can.

D: Do you pay much attention to current events?

C: I think more and more people, like Thoreau, just don't read the newspapers. I don't even bother looking at the television anymore. I don't even listen to the radio. You could say, perhaps, that I'm not a proper member of the twentieth-century society. On the other hand, I'm aware that we are very close to destroying ourselves. And I think when that news arrives, one way or the other, I'll be aware of it.

D: Most people seem only to read the headlines.

C: Recently, I found myself, because of airplane travel and so forth, reading more than usual. And I must say the best newspaper I picked up in the course of the last month was the *Christian Science Monitor*. It was so amusing to see that even *they* were not able to make sense out of current events. They actually had an article that said that it was important for there to be a balance between the United States and Russia, and that we had to keep up the defense. I mean they actually said that. Whereas if one of the countries would be willing to approach zero and open itself to attack, the other would immediately. We know from Thoreau, from Martin Luther King, from Ghandi, and everything, that defenselessness is the best protection against attack. Daniel in the lion's den. Throw us in there where the Russians can *really* get us! The other thing that the newspapers have headlines about is unemployment, because it's going up very high. Instead of being

seen as the nature of the future, unemployment is seen as some
horror. None of the jobs that anyone is offered is of any interest.
No one wants a job. What everyone needs in order to do his best
work is, as you know very well now, self-employment. Here we are
almost halfway toward self-employment, and all we do is complain
about the fact that we have this big unemployment problem. It's
stupid. It's as stupid as believing in God.

D: That statement's going to be misunderstood too.

C: Almost anything I would say is going to be misunderstood.
And if we say that, then maybe somebody will understand.

D: How do you handle your critics, and I don't mean professional
critics, but people who profess a love for music, who have trouble
with what they consider the feeling that anything goes in your
music?

C: They don't understand it. And mostly they don't understand
anything. So I don't handle them, and I stay as far away from
them as I possibly can. I don't even object to their idiotic statements.

D: Did you ever pay attention to the professional critics, and
worry about what they said?

C: I worried about their liking my work.

D: What is your current feeling about critics?

C: I've just returned from a month in Europe, and I met one of
the most brilliant music critics who's living now. His name is Heinz
Klaus Metzger. He was a pupil of Adorno; so he comes, as I came,
from the president of the company. He said to me, when we were
in Frankfurt together recently, speaking of my *Etudes Australes,*
that it was not composed by me but by God. And the reason he
said God was because he's witty, and because the piece used star
maps. That, theoretically, God's heaven is somewhere close to the
stars, I think is what he meant. Also, *The New York Times* critic
recently said that if the *Etudes Australes* lasts beyond my life that it
will be not because of me but because of the stars from which it
was derived. Now, neither Heinz Klaus Metzger nor *The New York
Times* know what they're talking about when they make such
statements. We know, for one thing, that God doesn't exist; therefore he didn't write the music. I know perfectly well that I wrote
it. God had no more to do with writing that music than you did
. . . or than Heinz Klaus Metzger did.

D: That brings up a. . .

C: So what does this bring up? It brings up the fact that I am
working in a way in the field of music that does not correspond to

the way critics are working in the field of music criticism. They don't know what I'm doing, so they make such stupid remarks as that. The brightest critic I know of says that God wrote my music. I really think that a form of music criticism has not yet been practiced which is suitable for chance-determined or indeterminate music—or even process music; you can put it that way. I don't think any critic has come up with a valid way of approaching that work, including Heinz Klaus Metzger.

D: How would they go about coming up with something like that though? What's the process?

C: They would have to place themselves where the composer placed himself: at a point which was indifferent to the end result. If I use chance operations, it's evident that I don't care whether this sound, this, this, this, this, or this comes up, that I will welcome any one of them. Or as they put in the program of the Bremen festival: "I welcome whatever happens next." The critic has to put himself at that point, rather than at the point of attacking what happened as being earth shaking. He has to change his mind from seeing what he's actually hearing (as being what he's writing about) to finding out the source of that as what he's writing about. I don't know whether you understood what I just said. How would you say it?

D: Oh, you're putting me on the spot. I'll come at it from a different direction: that certain basic things have changed in the way a composer looks at the process of writing a composition and, in fact, what that composition is. And that critics continue to bring. . .

C: No, the composition, you see, becomes sounds, and so appears to the critic that it's a piece of music like any other piece of music.

D: Right. But it's not.

C: It's not.

D: And the critic comes to it like he comes to other pieces of music. . .

C: . . . and attacks it from the old-fashioned point of view, and finally comes to the conclusion that God created it, which is stupid.

D: For a long time you've talked about the fact that we've got to put memory and values and all of that in its proper place. How do people go about doing that though? How do you weaken taste and memory?

C: The Zen method is by sitting cross-legged.

D: But the majority of Western civilization doesn't feel it can do that.

C: No. The way I have chosen to do that is to compose by means of asking questions rather than making choices, and to use chance operations to determine the answers.

D: And how should the listeners do that?

C: The listeners and the critics have a problem. And I would like to find out how to solve that or how to indicate where that is. I know that I may be able to answer it, because instead of hearing music in my head before I write it, I write in such a way as to hear something that I have not yet heard. Therefore, I'm in the position that the listener is in, and the critic is in with respect to my music. How do I approach it? How do I hear it, is the answer. Not because I know anything that they don't know, but because I haven't heard it anymore than they've heard it.

D: Do you think resistance to change is the problem?

C: No, because people love new automobiles and new refrigerators. They have no resistance to change.

D: What is it then?

C: They have preconceptions and likes and dislikes, and memories from which they are not free.

D: Are there any underlying concepts that continue throughout all of your music?

C: I recently made a text. It's mesostics on what seem to me to be the most important things in my work. The way I found out those things was by giving ten lectures, improvised lectures, at the University of Surrey in Guildford for a group of professional composers. What I did was I took all of my work and divided it into twelve areas. Then I said I would sit down and attempt to write mesostics on the subject of the improvised lecture. So I tried to find the most important word or idea in my work in order to write the mesostics on that word. So there were ten lectures, and the first was on the subject of METHOD; the second was on the subject of STRUCTURE; the third was INTENTION; then DISCIPLINE fourth, fifth and sixth; then NOTATION, then INDETERMINACY, then INTERPENETRATION, and then IMITATION, DEVOTION, finally CIRCUMSTANCES. Those seem to me to be the most important things, and they omit, curiously enough, the word *invention,* and the word *nonintention,* or even such things as chance and so on, which mostly come in under the word *discipline.*

D: What's your current feeling about what seems to be necessary?

C: Well, what I'm searching for is what the next step is in any field. What next step is implied. My father said he always got his best ideas while he was sound asleep. Other people say that ideas come to them from out of the air. That's what I'm trying to say—that we must be open if we're interested, as I am and still am, in what is called the avant-garde. We must then remain open to what seems to be necessary not to us as persons but to us as members of the musical society.

D: Do you like recordings of your music?

C: I don't use them.

D: Would you just as soon they didn't exist?

C: Yes. I don't listen to any of them. I really don't believe that that's where music is. And yet, for many people that's all that music is . . . even some people I love. And I myself, more and more, have to concern myself with records. I made a recording of all of *Empty Words*. I think it's fourteen sides.

D: But you're not enthusiastic about that?

C: I'm not enthusiastic about it. On the other hand, I made it. I know that many people want it, so I not only don't stand in its way but I further it.

D: Isn't that contradictory?

C: Yes.

D: You're not bothered by that?

C: No. I'm not bothered by contradictions. Inconsistency, we know from Emerson, is not a bad thing.

"Taking a Nap, I Pound the Rice": Eastern Influences on John Cage

Margaret Leng Tan

> When silence, generally speaking, is not in evidence, the will of
> the composer is. Inherent silence is equivalent to denial of the
> will. "Taking a nap, I pound the rice." Nevertheless, constant
> activity may occur having no dominance of will in it. Neither as
> syntax nor structure, but analogous to the sum of nature, it will
> have arisen purposelessly.
>
> John Cage, *Silence*

IN the span of four decades, John Cage has emancipated contemporary American culture from the shackles of European
domination and given American artists the confidence to be themselves. Even more to the point, the directional trend of influence
has been reversed whereby Cage's ideas, as transmitted via the
Cage-Boulez/Stockhausen connection, have made an irrevocable
impact on European avant-garde art. Furthermore, in place of
traditional European influences, Cage has introduced to American sensibilities traditional influences from yet another source,
namely the Far East. To further compound these cultural
crosscurrents, Cage has, in the past two decades, become the
galvanic element in contemporary Japanese musical life to the
extent that he is accorded the reverence and acclaim customarily
reserved for Japan's National Living Treasures.

Ever since 1945, John Cage has drawn upon the ancient teachings of India, China, and Japan to evolve an enviable personal
philosophy which eschews the labyrinthian pathways of Western
psychoanalysis for the illusively simple "no-mindedness" of Zen
(not to be confused with the Western notion of "mindlessness").

What are these Eastern concepts which have, in the course of
the years, become Cage's raison d'être? The following attenuated
chronology will serve as a guide for the ensuing discussion.

1933: Studies Asian, folk, and World music with Henry Cowell at the New School for Social Research in New York.

1934: Returns to Los Angeles. Studies counterpoint and analysis with Arnold Schoenberg for two years.

1937: Moves to Seattle as composer-accompanist for Bonnie Bird's dance classes at the Cornish School. Becomes increasingly involved with writing percussion music using found objects and invented instruments. Organizes percussion ensembles and collects a vast array of instruments. Meets Merce Cunningham.

1938: Presents his first percussion concert. Invents the prepared piano in order to compose *Bacchanale* for dancer Syvilla Fort.

1939: Moves to San Francisco. Gives concerts of percussion music with Lou Harrison with whom he collaborates to write *Double Music* (1941).

1939–41: Composes his *Construction in Metal* series of percussion works (three in all). Writes *Living Room Music* using objects found in a living room.

1942: Moves to New York.

1942–45: In addition to writing for percussion, composes many works for the prepared piano, mostly for dance.

1945: Encounters the writings of Ananda K. Coomaraswamy and attends his lectures at the Brooklyn Academy of Music. Meets Gita Sarabhai with whom he studies Indian philosophy and traditional Indian music daily for six months.

1946–48: Composes the *Sonatas and Interludes,* dedicated to the pianist Maro Adjemian, and *The Seasons,* a commission from the Ballet Society.

1948–51: Attends Dr. Daisetz Teitaro Suzuki's lectures in Japanese Zen Buddhism at Columbia University. Delivers "Lecture on Nothing" and "Lecture on Something" at the Artists' Club in New York (1950). Meets David Tudor (1950). Composes the *Concerto for Prepared Piano and Chamber Orchestra* and *Sixteen Dances* using the Magic Square (1950–51).

1951: Christian Wolff introduces Cage to the I Ching (Chinese Book of Changes). Over the next nine months, Cage composes *Music of Changes* for David Tudor, followed by *Imaginary Landscape No. 4* for twelve radios, both based on I Ching-determined chance operations.

1952 (July): Conceives and organizes an untitled "event" at Black Mountain College, North Carolina with Merce Cunningham, Robert Rauschenberg, David Tudor, Charles Olson, M. C. Richards, and Cage himself participating simultaneously in independent artistic activities. (August): First performance of silent piece *4'33"* with David Tudor at the piano in Maverick Concert Hall, Woodstock, New York. Composes *Water Music* for a pianist using the radio and an assortment of whistles as ancillary instruments.

1952–56: Uses chance operations to compose works in varying degrees of indeterminacy. These include the *Music for Piano* series (pieces one through eighty-four), *31'57.9864"* for a pianist, *34'46.776"* for a pianist, *26'1.1499"* for a string player, and *27'10.554"* for a percussionist.

1957–58: Creates works fully indeterminate in nature: *Winter Music* for one to twenty pianists, *Concert for Piano and Orchestra* consisting of solos for piano and thirteen instruments to be played in whole or part in any combination, *Variations I* for any number of players and any instruments. From this point on, chance operations and indeterminacy remain basic to Cage's work.

1960–61: Fellow at the Center for Advanced Studies at Wesleyan University, Middletown, Connecticut, where he completes *Silence*, his first anthology of lectures and writings.

1961–63: Composes a trilogy based on the symbolic meaning of the three lines in haiku poetry as interpreted by Japanese musicologist Hidekazu Yoshida: 1) *Atlas Eclipticalis* (Nirvana); 2) *Variations IV* (*Samsara*, the Wheel of Life); 3) *0'0"* (specific happening). In 1962, embarks on a six-week concert tour of Japan with David Tudor, the first of many visits in the course of which Cage's reputation evokes increasing reverence in Japanese contemporary music circles.

1963: Directs the premiere performance of Erik Satie's *Vexations* with eight-hundred and forty repetitions involving a relay of pianists.

1964: Invited by the University of Hawaii music department to participate in an East/West exchange with Toru Takemitsu from Japan. As musical director, Cage travels with the Cunningham company on a world tour including Japan and India.

1967: For the composition of *HPSCHD* in collaboration with La-jaren Hiller, the coin tossing procedure of the I Ching is pro-grammed into a computer resulting in computerized hexagrams which make the hundreds of required chance operations possible.

1971: Begins study of the writings of Mao Zedong.

1973: Begins writing *Empty Words* based on Thoreau's *Journal* which takes him over a year to complete. Increasing involvement with nonsyntactical "demilitarized" language spurs his interest in ancient Chinese.

1976: Commissioned by the Boston Symphony Orchestra to com-pose *Renga* based on the elaborate Japanese poetic structure of that name, to be performed with *Apartment House 1776*.

1977: On the advice of Yoko Ono, consults *shiatsu* therapist Shizuko Yamamoto for his arthritis and adopts the macrobiotic diet.

1982–85: Creates *Ryōanji* series of works (both graphic and musi-cal) inspired by the Japanese stone and sand Zen garden of that name.

1986: *Vis-à-Vis*, a collaborative work between Cage, Takemitsu, and the ensemble [THE], is commissioned by the Pacific Ring Festival (University of California, San Diego).

> Man is a thinking reed but his great works are done when he is not calculating and thinking. "Childlikeness" has to be restored with long years of training in the art of self-forgetfulness. When this is attained, man thinks yet he does not think.

I have chosen these words by the Zen Buddhist scholar, Dr. D. T. Suzuki,[1] as an apt and eloquent depiction of his pupil, John

Cage. Since midcentury, Cage's life and work have been the apotheosis of his own personal approach to Zen philosophy, replete with all its paradoxes and culminating in *4'33"* (silence), the keystone summation of Cage's Zen experience, the ultimate manifestation of the "artless art."

The events leading to this landmark occurrence in Cage's career trace a distinct path of evolution within a personal philosophy that has always been markedly susceptible to influences from the East. From the preceding chronology of events, the roots of these influences can be seen to stem from the early 1930s when Cage, after his return from Europe, was initiated into the then obscure byways of Asian and other world musics through Henry Cowell's classes at the New School in New York. (It was Cowell, in fact, who coined the phrase "world" music.)

In his explorations of Asian music, familiarity with the highly sophisticated *gamelan* (percussion orchestra) ensembles of the Far East no doubt contributed to Cage's growing involvement with percussion music by the mid-thirties. At this time, Cage returned to the West Coast, a move not only coincidental but propitious in that the West Coast, facing Asia, lies open to whatever influences may be borne on cross-cultural currents.

Until this time, percussion music did not exist in the West as an independent genre, but served merely to enhance with touches of exotic coloration within a conventional orchestral context. With the exception of Varese's revolutionary *Ionisation* (1930), it was the rugged individualists of the 1930s "West Coast Group" (Cowell, Lou Harrison, Harry Partch, Cage, and later Alan Hovhaness, all of whom had had contact with Asian music cultures) who were responsible for imbuing percussion instruments with an identity, respectability, and, most significantly, a repertory they could call their own. This pioneering effort in percussion music Cowell referred to as "Drums along the Pacific."

Having rejected the Schoenbergian notion of harmony as the structural underpinning of a musical composition, Cage turned to rhythmic structure based on time lengths as the fundamental principle underlying his percussion works of the mid-to-late 1930s. For Cage, the system of *talas*, or rhythmic cycles, in Indian music became a viable alternative to traditional Western rhythmic concepts for his organization of unconventional sounds, pitched and nonpitched, drawn from invented instruments and found objects as instruments. His application of the *tala* approach meant dividing a work into small cohesive segments, each of which had a mathematical relation to the whole. The underlying consideration for Cage's initial reliance on structural rhythm was a pragmatic one; in the course of his earlier studies with Schoenberg, he discovered that he had no ear for harmony. Asian music, conceived linearly on rhythmic and melodic planes, is essentially nonharmonic; in turning to the conventions of a non-Western musical system, Cage was able to circumvent what, in Western terms, might be regarded as a serious shortcoming for a composer.

In his prophetic 1937 lecture, "The Future of Music: Credo," Cage writes: "Percussion music is a contemporary transition from keyboard-influenced music to the all-sound music of the future. Any sound is acceptable to the composer of percussion music; he explores the academically forbidden 'non-musical' field of sound insofar as is manually possible."[2] With the admittance of these "non-musical" sounds into the realm of serious composition, Cage became, along with Edgard Varese, the perpetrator of a new music where there was no longer a distinction between noise and music as *yin-yang* opposing forces. By the integration of noise into the domain of music, Cage redefines the latter as "arising from an acceptance of all audible phenomena as material proper to music."[3] At this juncture, albeit prior to his study of Zen, Cage, by letting "sounds be just sounds" (*Silence,* p. 170), had, through the admission of noise into music, admitted life into art; the sacrosanct walls of the ivory tower had begun to crumble.

During this period of heightened percussion activity, the prepared piano was born out of necessity when Cage was asked to compose percussion music for dance within a restricted space. Encouraged by Cowell's forays into the piano's interior, Cage hit upon the idea of objects wedged between the strings of a grand piano (often at predetermined points) acting as mutes which drastically altered the timbral characteristics of the instrument. In so doing, Cage had transformed the piano into "a percussion ensemble under the control of a single player" (RK, p. 76). The resultant *gamelan*-like coloration of the prepared piano works has often been commented on although Cage refutes any direct association with *gamelan* influences: "Rather I was making a music not based on Western tonality and including noises. The strangeness of what I was doing led many to think of it as Oriental."[4] On the other hand, Calvin Tomkins remarks that Cage's "music for the prepared piano was so Eastern in quality that the OWI, during the war, used to beam it on short wave to the South Pacific 'with the hope,' Cage wrote, 'of convincing the natives that America loves the Orient.'"[5]

The creation of individual tones, each endowed with a unique timbral identity, is the distinctive feature of the prepared piano. This is in accord with the inherently Chinese concept of the living essence of every tone. Moreover, the Chinese classification of instruments into the "eight sounds" system according to the materials of which they are made (earth, wood, stone, metal, bamboo, gourd, skin, and silk) is one that Cage was not unaware of in his "found-objects-as-instruments" approach. Some examples which come to mind are wood blocks and pod rattle in *Amores,* sounds from instruments in four categories: metal, wood, skin, and all others in *27'10.554"* for a percussionist, and later the conch shells of *Inlets* and amplified plant materials in *Child of Tree.*

The percussion and prepared piano works of the forties continue to explore Cage's adaptation of the *tala* system and this approach to organizing rhythm will be maintained until 1952. In the mid-forties, Virgil Thomson expressed great enthusiasm for Cage's rhythmic originality: "Cage has developed the rhythmic element of composition . . . to a point of sophistication unmatched in the technique of any other living composer" (RK, p. 72). Cage's own historical view of rhythm is, as usual, a provocative one: "Harmonic structure in music arises as Western materialism arises, disintegrates at the time that materialism comes to be questioned, and that the solution of rhythmic structure, traditional to the Orient, is arrived at with us just at the time that we profoundly sense our need for that other tradition of the Orient: peace of mind, self-knowledge" (RK, p. 84).

The prepared piano works up to 1945 are characterized by an emotional subjectivity often associated with personal experiences as in the love triangle of *Amores* (1943) and *The Perilous Night* (1944) which depict "the loneliness and terror that comes to one when love becomes unhappy" (Tomkins, p. 97). It is music that seeks to communicate, prompting Virgil Thomson to remark that Cage "writes for expressive purposes; and the novelty of his timbres, the logic of his discourse, are used to intensify communication, not as ends in themselves" (RK, p. 72).

From 1945 onward, a radical shift begins to take place in Cage's thinking, brought about by contact with two individuals who were to become his mentors at a critical time when he was seriously considering giving up composing and availing himself of psychoanalysis. They were an Indian musician, Gita Sarabhai, and Dr. D. T. Suzuki. In 1944, Cage had completed two piano compositions, *Root of an Unfocus* and *Four Walls,* both of which reflected his preoccupation with disturbances of the mind. Through Gita Sarabhai, he learned that the traditional Indian reason for making a piece of music is "to sober and quiet the mind and thus make it susceptible to divine influences" (*Silence,* p. 158). Cage elaborates: "We learned from Oriental thought that those divine influences are, in fact, the environment in which we are. A sober and quiet mind is one in which the ego does not obstruct the fluency of the things that come in through our senses and up through our dreams. Our business in living is to become fluent with the life we are living, and art can help this" (RK, p. 77). Thus music would achieve by external means what psychoanalysis attempted to accomplish from within. Through Indian philosophy and, later, Zen, Cage would discover alternatives to Western psychoanalysis, other means of freeing the psyche to experience a heightened awareness of everyday life.

The years 1946–48 saw the creation of two important works, the lengthy *Sonatas and Interludes* and *The Seasons.* The *Sonatas and Interludes* depict the nine permanent emotions of Indian tradition, four white (love, mirth, wonder, the heroic) and four black (fear, anger, sorrow, disgust) with their common tendency toward tranquillity in the middle. In *The Seasons,* Cage looks to their symbolic meaning as interpreted through Indian philosophy: spring as regeneration, summer as preservation, fall as destruction, and winter as quiescence. In both these works as well as in the *String Quartet in Four Parts* of 1949–50, a shift in perspective begins to take place from the highly personal involvement of the earlier prepared piano works to a more detached view of the creative process which, in Indian terms, is merely to "imitate nature in her manner of operation" (*Silence,* p. 194). Cage was particularly taken with this idea through his contact with Ananda K. Coomaraswamy's teachings in the mid-forties. Paul Griffiths has made some perceptive observations about the music of this period:

> A flat purposelessness . . . was gaining ground in Cage's output in the later 1940's. He had begun this period, in such works as the *First Construction* and *Bacchanale,* by filling his pre-arranged time schemes with dynamism, but now there was a tendency to leave a vacuum of silence or of empty repetition. It was as if he was intentionally showing up the passive nature of his rhythmic-structure technique, which asks for time simply to be filled and not necessarily engaged: where earlier his ostinatos had made the technique work in an active manner, now he was sometimes content to let his ideas loose in music having no such directing impulse.[6]

The abnegation of ego and will implied in this statement as well as in Cage's choice of piano preparations in his *Sonatas and Interludes,* "chosen as one chooses shells while walking along a beach" (*Silence,* p. 19), is not unrelated to Cage's studies in Zen Buddhism with Suzuki, begun during this period of personal and creative transitions.

Also around this time, Cage had a sobering experience regarding the prepared piano that brought with it implications of great consequence. On hearing a performance of *The Perilous Night* by a pianist who had prepared the piano very poorly, Cage's initial reaction was that he wished he had never written the piece. Further reflection brought with it, however, important realizations eloquently recaptured by Cage twenty-five years later:

> When I first placed objects between piano strings, it was with the desire to possess sounds (to be able to repeat them). But, as the music left my home and went from piano to piano and from pianist to pianist, it became clear that not only are two pianists essentially different from one another, but two pianos are not the same either. Instead of the possibility of repetition, we are faced in life with the unique qualities and characteristics of each occasion. . . . And so my work since the early fifties has been increasingly indeterminate.[7]

The prepared piano, "a feather in the hat of indeterminacy,"[8] thus marked the first step for Cage along the Zen path of nonintention and noncontrol.

The years 1950–51 represent a transitional period where, prior to Cage's discovery of the I Ching, he composes the *Concerto for Prepared Piano and Chamber Orchestra* along with the *Sixteen Dances* using a chart which he called the "Magic Square" to determine the gamut of pitches, chords, and noises used. This approach is indicative of Cage's first attempts to free himself from subjective involvement with the compositional process and constitutes the first use of chance procedures. In 1951, the Magic Square is superseded by the I Ching, the Chinese oracular guide from which answers are obtained by throwing forty-nine yarrow sticks or tossing three coins. Hereafter, Cage's work processes will be based entirely on chance operations; the I Ching has become the essential tool for composing, writing texts, and printmaking. Together with the late Morton Feldman, Christian Wolff, and later, Earle Brown, Cage works to disassociate the ego from the creative process, to free sounds from memory, taste, experience, and any preconceived relationship to each other. Cage and his colleagues have become the first aleatory composers.

While the percussion and prepared piano works of the forties express a concern with structure through the organization of rhythm, the early works composed with the help of chance operations—such as *Imaginary Landscape No. 4* (1951) and the tape collage *Williams Mix* (1952)—begin to reflect a changing attitude where *process* has become the prime consideration. In contrast to music as *object*, Cage now regards his work as "music made essentially without intention in opposition to music of results" (RK, p. 10); this approach will lead to further self-distancing in his later work which he will come to describe as "a process set in motion by a group of people" (RK, p. 204).

In this identification with process, goals, success, and value judgments all lose their meaning. Value judgments, according to Cage, "are destructive to our proper business, which is curiosity and awareness" (RK, p. 27). In the first performance of *Imaginary Landscape No. 4*, the twelve radios did not come up with particularly interesting results owing to the lateness of the hour, exacerbated by some extremely low volume levels which had been established by the chance procedures. The rehearsals had, in fact, yielded far more exciting effects. Cage, however, was quite indifferent to the outcome of the performance since, as Henry Cowell states, Cage believes "the concept to be more interesting than the result of any single performance" (RK, p. 97). To quote Shōji Hamada, the great Japanese potter: "I am not interested in the pot; I'm interested in the process of making it."[9] This emphasis on the act itself is a distinctly Asian trait whereas in the West the focus would be unequivocally on the outcome of the act.

In this scheme of things then, error becomes yet another irrelevant issue. By Cage's definition, it is "simply a failure to adjust immediately from a preconception to an actuality" (*Silence*, pp. 170–71). This being the case, "there is no need to cautiously proceed in dualistic terms of success and failure or the beautiful and the ugly or good or evil but rather simply to walk on 'not wondering' to quote Meister Eckhart, 'am I right or doing something wrong'" (*Silence*, p. 47). Cage often cites the classic example of the Zen archer who has yet to succeed in hitting the bull's-eye but, nonetheless, is highly esteemed in Japan. "The 'Great Doctrine' knows nothing of a target. . . . It only knows of the goal, which cannot be aimed at technically, and it names this goal, if it names it at all, the Buddha" (*ZAA*, p. 63).

In 1950, Cage delivered his famous "Lecture on Nothing," which represents his personal interpretation of Zen philosophy. Centered primarily on the Zen logic (or nonlogic) of the empty circle, the text obsesses on

```
              the reali-zation            that we possess     nothing

                      Anything                therefore       is a delight

(since we do not      pos-sess it)       and thus             need not fear its loss
```

[*Silence*, p. 110]

One of the reasons why Cage's writing so often communicates with a seemingly effortless spontaneity is that it conveys what Jill Johnston calls "a quicksilver transaction between thought and word" (RK, p. 149). This is a phenomenon peculiar not only to the ideographs of the Chinese language (the components of a single character imparting an instantaneous wealth of information in block format as opposed to the linear perception of meaning presented through the Western script) but is also common to haiku poetry as well as to the other arts governed by the Zen aesthetic. In ink painting, for instance, "the hand that guides the brush has already caught and executed what floated before the mind at the same moment the mind began to form it, and in the end the pupil no longer knows which of the two—mind or hand— was responsible for the work" (*ZAA*, p. 46). Similarly, in the martial arts, there is "not a hair's breadth between perceiving the extended thrust and evading it, so now there is no time lag between evasion and action" (*ZAA*, p. 84). In his "Lecture on Nothing" Cage writes:

```
                                                       I began to see

that the separation of   mind and ear    had spoiled        the sounds

,---                            that a clean slate    was necessary.   This made me

not only contemporary    ,                    but "avant-garde."  I used noises

.                    They had not been    in-tellectualized;   the ear could hear t

directly    and didn't have to go through any abstraction       a-bout them


.
```

[*Silence*, p. 116]

That peculiar quality of aimlessness or purposelessness that begins to appear in Cage's music in the late forties finds its literary counterpart in the following refrain:

re we are now   at the beginning of the thir-

enth unit   of the fourth large part   of this talk.

re and more   I have the feeling   that we are getting

where.   Slowly   ,   as the talk goes on

                    we are getting   nowhere   and that is a pleasure

          It is not irritating   to be where one is   .   It is

ly irritating   to think one would like   to be somewhere else.   Here we are now

          a little bit after the   beginning of the   thir-teenth unit   of the

urth large part   of this talk   .

                    More and more   we have the feeling

                    that I am getting   nowhere   .

                    Slowly   ,   as the talk goes on

                    slowly   ,   we have the feeling

                    we are getting   nowhere.   That is a pleasure

          which will continue   .   If we are irritated

          it is not a pleasure   .   Nothing is not   a

easure   if one is irritated   ,   but suddenly

          it is a pleasure   ,   and then more and more

          it is not irritating   (and then more and more

          and slowly   ).   Originally

                    we were nowhere   ;   and now, again

                    we are having   the pleasure

being   slowly   nowhere.   If anybody

sleepy   ,   let him go to sleep   .

[*Silence*, p. 123]

This last sentence is, in fact, a direct spin-off from the "everyday mind" of Zen which Suzuki says is no more than "sleeping when tired, eating when hungry" (*ZAA*, p. vii). The advice contained in the above refrain is a sound one when applied to the complete performance of Satie's *Vexations* which Cage organized. *Vexations* is also the perfect illustration of one of Cage's favorite Zen anecdotes: "If something is boring after two minutes, try it for four. If still boring, try it for eight, sixteen, thirty-two, and so on. Eventually one discovers that it's not boring at all but very interesting" (*Silence*, p. 93).

For Cage's career, 1952 was a milestone year, the historical repercussions of which are still reverberating today. In retrospect, Cage relates the creative occurrences of that year to events he had observed in his life: "This testing of art by means of life was the result of my attending the lectures of [D. T.] Suzuki for three years" (RK, p. 23).

The untitled event which Cage staged at Black Mountain College that summer (actually the prototype for "Happenings" in the sixties) contained many germinal ideas which would come to fruition time and time again in subsequent works. Most significant were the dissolution of boundaries between the various artistic disciplines, the notion of art spilling over into life, and that life and theater are synonymous. These premises are also present in the highly concentrated *Water Music* of the same year while *Musicircus, Reunion,* and *HPSCHD,* "environmental extravaganzas"[10] from 1967–69, are more ambitious sequels to the Black Mountain College event. These large-scale works are symptomatic of Cage's "continuing interest in simulating a lifelike chaos of sounds and sights, or building an artful universe within the larger world."[11]

In promulgating a philosophy in which every man will become continually aware of the art surrounding him, Cage is merely reiterating that which is, or at least was present in many Asian cultures, notably Japan and Bali where "the making without the noticing"[12] is a fact of everyday life. When temples serve as sets for the reenactment of ancient dramas, the fine line of distinction between theater and life becomes all but nonexistent. Furthermore, the various arts are not regarded as separate entities in the East; rather, they are complementary components within a traditional "theater of mixed-means," to quote Richard Kostelanetz. "Mixed-media," "interdisciplinary"—terms in vogue in the seventies—are but humble newcomers alongside the centuries-old traditions of the East.

Cage's mixed-media presentations are concrete manifestations of his "global mind" theory. Once an advocate of the Eckhartian belief that "a person cannot be more than single in attention" (*Silence,* p. 64), Cage concedes that "nowadays everything happens at once and our souls are conveniently electronic (omniattentive)" (RK, p. 167). The resultant, indeterminate chaos of these works embodies the Cagean/Zen paradoxes of ordered disorder, controlled noncontrol, and purposeful purposelessness—ordered, controlled, and purposeful because the parameters are rigorously determined by chance operations; disordered, noncontrolled, and purposeless because the composer as "simply someone who tells other people what to do"[13] has abdicated in favor of disciplined creative anarchy on the part of the participants. Cage says, "I used to think of five as the most things we could perceive at once, . . . when you use the word 'chaos,' it means there is no chaos, because everything is equally related—there is an extremely complex interpenetration of an unknowable number of centers" (RK, p. 175).

This brings us to two tenets central to Cage and Zen—unimpededness and interpenetration. Cage paraphrases Suzuki thus: "Unimpededness is seeing that in all of space each thing and each human being is at the center and furthermore that each one being at the center is the most honored one of all. Interpenetration means that each one of these most honored ones of all is moving out in all directions penetrating and being penetrated by every other one no matter what the time or what the space" (*Silence,* p. 46). For Cage, interpenetration and unimpededness occur not only within a musical context, but also between the various artistic disciplines and, in the broadest sense, between art and life and within society at large. In this last, Cage is no less influenced by the writings of Mao Zedong as by the ideas of Buckminster Fuller. By allowing for the interpenetration and nonobstruction of sounds, he is further able to renounce the dictatorial nature of harmony and its effect of fusing sounds into a fixed relationship. In his collaborations with Merce Cunningham, they have established, since 1952, an independent but cooperative relationship between music and dance based on nonobstruction and interpenetration in time and space. This principle will come to underlie all Cage's indeterminate works from the late fifties on.

The multifarious bombardment of the senses experienced in the Black Mountain College event and its successors raises yet another fundamental issue of Zen. It is the age-old question of "What is Reality?" A film which Cage admires, Akira Kurosawa's *Roshomon*, tells us that reality is merely that which is perceived by the beholder. For those who were present at *HPSCHD*, Richard Kostelanetz reports: "While everyone saw the same thing in general, each one registered a specific experience particularly his own" (RK, p. 174). For Cage, the meaning of a composer's work is determined by each person who sees and hears it. He wishes the listener to understand that the hearing of a piece is the listener's own action and responsibility. Furthermore, if there are several sound sources distributed in a space, each person will actually hear something different from what someone else hears. Nonetheless, "Each person is in the best seat. . . . Each now is the time, the space" (*Silence*, p. 97).

In stark contrast to the "omniattentive" demands of the Black Mountain College event, Cage staged in the month following an event of singular austerity. This was his infamous silent piece, *4'33"*, where David Tudor sat at the piano for that duration of time without playing, implying by the opening and closing of the keyboard lid that the work had three movements. The piece may be performed by any instrumentalist or combination of instrumentalists and last any length of time. As can be imagined, Cage's audacity in presenting such a "performance" sparked off a barrage of outraged indignation as well as admiration of the highest order, depending on whether one perceived it as the ultimate Dada joke or the ultimate Zen statement.

In a 1974 interview, Cage considered *4'33"* not only his most important contribution but perhaps his best piece, at least the one he likes the most.[14] He had initially come up with the idea back in 1948 but thought it would be "incomprehensible in the European context."[15] Cage reminisces, "I was just then in the flush of my contact with Oriental philosophy. It was out of that that my interest in silence naturally developed: I mean it's almost transparent. If you have, as you do in India, nine permanent emotions and the center one is the one without color—the others are white or black—and tranquillity is in the center and freedom from likes and dislikes, it stands to reason, [tranquillity is also] the absence of activity which is characteristically Buddhist."[16]

Robert Rauschenberg's all-white paintings exhibited at the Black

Mountain College event gave Cage the impetus necessary to present his silent piece. Of these paintings Cage wrote: "The white paintings caught whatever fell on them" (*Silence,* p. 108); "there is nothing in these paintings that could not be changed . . . they can be seen in any light and are not destroyed by the action of shadows" (RK, p. 112).

Just as Rauschenberg's all-white canvases provided the perimeter defining the space within which the "art" of nature could be appreciated, Cage's *4'33"* provided the temporal frame for the inherent "music" of nature, or the environment, to enter. "There is no such thing as an empty space or empty time. There is always something to see, something to hear. In fact, try as we may to make a silence, we cannot. Sounds occur whether intended or not" (*Silence,* p. 8). One of Cage's best-known anecdotes is a recounting of his experience in the anechoic chamber at Harvard University: "In that silent room, I heard two sounds, one high and one low. Afterward I asked the engineer in charge why, if the room was so silent, I had heard two sounds. He said, 'Describe them.' I did. He said, 'The high one was your nervous system in operation. The low one was your blood in circulation.' "[17] Cage, in an act of breathtaking courage, then redefines silence as "all of the sound we don't intend" (RK, p. 166).

4'33" is an exercise in Zen meditation, experiencing the "now" moment, encouraging us to listen and explore the entire gamut of sound contained within its spatial and temporal boundaries. For Cage, the frame is no longer necessary for the music is now ongoing, just as in the Zen approach to archery, "bow and arrow are only a pretext for something that could just as well happen without them, only the way to a goal, not the goal itself, only helps for the last decisive leap" (*ZAA,* p. 8).

Living above one of the busiest thoroughfares in Manhattan, Cage finds the kaleidoscopic variety of sounds in the environment a continuous source of fascination. He has achieved that Zen state of supreme spiritual alertness where the music never stops. "If you want to know the truth of the matter," says Cage, "the music I prefer, even to my own or anyone else's, is what we are hearing if we are just quiet" (RK, p. 12).

In *4'33"* Cage has moved beyond the acceptance of noise as music, through the synonymity of life and art to the acceptance of silence, not as the opposite of sound, but the encompassing of all sound. This is in keeping with the Zen paradox that everything contains its opposite and therefore opposites are, in a sense,

identical. *4'33"* is the quintessential experience in Cage's Zen
odyssey and, as such, it abounds in a multitude of paradoxes
unique to Zen.

Concurrent with the frame which is empty yet not empty, the
most obvious paradox is that Cage's nonintentional piece is actually filled with intent—the intent to heighten our perceptive faculties in order that we may perceive of silence as the unmoved
center through which all the music of the environment flows in an
unbroken stream. This is akin to the "purposeful purposelessness" expressed in Cage's statement that "the highest purpose is to have no purpose at all. This puts one in accord with
nature in her manner of operation" (*Silence,* p. 155). And so, we
come to the Zen state of "no-mindedness" where, in becoming
purposeless, the doing occurs ("it" happens) beyond the need of a
controlling or reflecting intelligence.

When "it" happens, there is also the identification of activity
with inactivity. In nondoing, something continues to happen:
"Life goes on very well without me and that will explain to you my
silent piece *4'33"*" (RK, p. 118). "Taking a nap, I pound the rice"
(*Silence,* p. 53). In *4'33"* the audience has become, simultaneously,
the creator (composer), performer, and listener. The integration
of these hitherto distinct, active and passive roles into a single
indivisible experience is tantamount to the instantaneous transformation of thought-into-word, perception-into-reaction phenomenon so characteristic of the Zen arts.

Finally, Cage's *4'33"* is a living testimony to the "artless art." "He
who can . . . hit the center without bow and arrow, he alone is
Master in the highest sense of the word—Master of the artless art.
Indeed, he is the artless art itself and thus Master and No-Master
in one. At this point archery, considered as the unmoved movement, the undanced dance, passes over into Zen" (*ZAA,* p. 73).

And so, in John Cage's performance without means, we hear at
last the sound of one hand clapping.

In contrast to how they are perceived in the West, time and
space have never been regarded as separate entities in Japanese
thinking. Pertaining to both time and space, the Japanese word *ma*
refers to the interval or the natural distance between two or more
events existing in a continuity. It is the coincidental conceptualiza-
tion of these elements which is perhaps the main feature dis-
tinguishing Japan's artistic expression from that of the West. More

important, *ma* implies that the space is a *living* one. For the Zen disciple there is no fear of The Void that envelops, yet is at the core of all things, ever present yet intangible.

That Cage has absorbed this aspect of the Japanese mind is evident in his writings which make constant reference to the time-space principle. It is, however, his silent piece which is his most vivid and dramatic illustration of *ma* where "all that is necessary is an empty space of time and letting it act in its magnetic way" (*Silence,* p. 178). In his "Lecture on Nothing," Cage reassures us that

```
        This space of time                                      is organized
.                       We need not fear these        silences,--
we may love them        .
```

[*Silence,* pp. 109–10]

The collaborative process between Cage and Merce Cunningham further embraces the simultaneity of these elements where the music and the dance are bound only by their common occurrence within the same space and the same time span.

Cage's initial experiments with magnetic tape in the late forties and early fifties emphasized the fact that duration (time length) is synonymous with tape length (space) and it is the application of this principle which forms the basis for the space-time proportional notation used in the *Music of Changes* and the *Two Pastorales* of 1951. In his *Music for Piano* series, begun the following year, the notes have been reduced to points without stems, representing a further refinement in space-time notation. This notational approach will be used again in several later works including the *Etudes Astrales* of 1974–75 and in *ASLP* (1985).

The pitches for the *Music for Piano* series were derived from imperfections in the paper while chance operations determined the number of sounds for each page. The duration of the notes is free, as are the dynamics; moreover, the pieces may be performed as solos, or combined in any way by any number of pianists. The four highly demanding timelength pieces written during this same period (detailed in the chronology) may again be freely combined with each other, with or without excerpts from Cage's lecture, "45' for a Speaker," while *Radio Music* calls for one to eight performers, each at one radio. (Ever since the early forties the radio has remained a consistently recurring "instrument" in

Cage's oeuvre, for its nonpredictable nature lends itself ideally to indeterminacy and the removal of taste and memory.)

All these works written between 1952 and 1956 show an evolution from the rigid performance strictures of the early I Ching-determined "determinate" works (e.g., *Music of Changes, Imaginary Landscape No. 4*) to a new freedom involving varying degrees of indeterminacy in performance. Cage explains the essential difference between chance operations and indeterminacy: "In the case of chance operations, one knows more or less the elements of the universe with which one is dealing, whereas in indeterminacy, I like to think . . . that I'm outside the circle of a known universe and dealing with things I literally don't know anything about" (RK, p. 141).

By 1957 and 1958, Cage is writing fully fledged indeterminate works which he defines as "processes, essentially purposeless."[18] "The only structure which permits of natural activity is one so flexible as not to be a structure; I write in order to hear; never do I hear and then write what I hear. Inspiration is not a special occasion" (*Silence,* p. 169). Unlike other composers whose ears are "walled in with sounds of their own imagination" (*Silence,* p. 155), "I never imagine anything until I experience it" (RK, p. 133).

In *Winter Music, Variations I,* and the monumental *Concert for Piano and Orchestra,* Cage has not only succeeded in freeing himself from the dictates of taste, memory, will, and intention, but he has also achieved for himself that optimum condition of disorganization, noncontrol and noninterference—in short, the Zen state of "no-mindedness." In so doing, he must accept with equanimity whatever is the outcome of a performance: "the important questions are answered by not liking only but disliking and accepting equally what one likes and dislikes" (*Silence,* p. 133).

In *4'33",* the performer as artist has been absorbed into the larger context of the environment as artist. In the indeterminate works that follow, Cage not only reinstates the performer in a key role but invests him with ever-increasing responsibility to the extent of establishing him as cocreator in the *Concert for Piano and Orchestra.* Having freed him from the dictates of the composer, Cage now presents the performer with an entirely different set of challenges: to explore a whole new range of extended notational and instrumental techniques, to liberate himself from preconceived ideas of taste and aesthetic considerations of structure and form, and to adopt a fresh approach to discipline which goes hand in hand with an unprecedented freedom of choice, all this in order to produce a performance of "utopian anarchy" whereby the individual centers may radiate out in unimpeded inter-penetration.

Cage says his biggest problem lies in finding "a way to let people be free without their becoming foolish,"[19] and he has, in recent years, insisted on ample rehearsals prior to the performance of his indeterminate works whose "success" depends to a very great extent on what the players contribute. To construe these works as open invitations to improvisation is to misunderstand totally the whole Cagean concept of indeterminacy. On the contrary, im-provisation as essentially an edification of the ego, would be a total refutation of Cage's philosophy. Cage believes that "chance ought to be very controlled" (*Silence,* p. 186), and he himself has always used chance operations in a highly systematic, disciplined fash-ion—a discipline for him "as strict as sitting cross-legged."[20]

This brings up a rather intriguing paradox: since 1951, Cage has relied exclusively on his bible, the I Ching, to free himself from making personal choices. In so doing, he has made himself virtually a prisoner of the system (albeit willingly) to the extent that the I Ching now completely controls all aspects of his work and life.

For the past twenty years, Cage has been using a computerized version of the I Ching to describe the parameters of his indeter-minate works. This presents an ironic contradiction in that the computer has to be programmed with complete determination (i.e., intention) to assist in the making of a nonintentional process whose outcome cannot be foreseen.

Yet another paradox arises with regard to Cage's indeterminate compositions: while the outcome of an indeterminate work can always remain an unknowable surprise for Cage, can it ever be so for the performers themselves, given Cage's emphasis on respon-sible preparation and discipline? Can the results ever transcend the level of a predetermined performance of an indeterminate work to achieve a truly indeterminate performance? In other words, is it realistic to expect a performer to internalize the parameters at his disposal to the extent that he can spontaneously give different performance renditions of the same indeterminate work?

These are but a few of the many provocative issues which come to mind. On close examination, John Cage's philosophy is fraught with contradictions, but is that not inevitable and true to the highest traditions of Zen?

In retracing the path of Cage's long career, we observe that with the exception of the macrobiotic diet and his adoption of Indian metrical concepts into the early percussion and prepared piano works Cage's indebtedness to the East lies exclusively within the realm of its ideas and not its practices. At the same time, he has been quick to acknowledge that coterie of seminal Western thinkers and artists who have become his heroes—among them James Joyce, Marshall McLuhan, Marcel Duchamp, Erik Satie, and Charles Ives. In the minds of Meister Eckhart, Henry David Thoreau, Buckminster Fuller, and Norman O. Brown, Cage finds sympathetic reverberations of ideas rooted in those ancient Eastern civilizations to which he has been particularly drawn—a true interpenetration of East and West, unimpeded by time and space.

In turn, John Cage himself has become the *spiritus rector* of twentieth-century avant-garde art. The predictions spelled out in his "The Future of Music: Credo" have long since been fulfilled and Cage the prophet has turned Cage the patriarch, gently, by example, guiding the gaze of the avant-garde Eastward. There were those composers who had the privilege of direct contact with him—the late Morton Feldman, Christian Wolff, Earle Brown, David Behrman, Gordon Mumma, La Monte Young, Pierre Boulez, Karlheinz Stockhausen, Toshi Ichiyanagi, and Takehisa Kosugi, among others, but Cage's sphere of influence extends well beyond musical horizons into all of the major contemporary art movements of the sixties and seventies where his writings and lectures have penetrated the sensibilities of yet another generation of avant-gardists in the choreographic, visual, and interdisciplinary arts.

Cage's silent piece foreshadowed the Conceptual art movement no less than his emphasis on "art-is-life-is-theater" set the stage not only for Fluxus and Performance art, but for Pop art and Environmental art as well. His Experimental music classes at the New School in the late fifties were attended by George Brecht, Al Hansen, Dick Higgins, Allan Kaprow, and Jackson MacLow, all of whom subsequently became key figures in experimental art developments from multimedia Happenings to Visual poetry.

While Cage's contribution to the development of Minimalist art and music might be less apparent than his direct influence on the development of aleatoric music both in the United States and abroad, the detachment of Minimalist art and the nondirectional processes of Minimalist music find a common source in Cage's attitude of deliberate distancing and "purposeful purposelessness."

In proposing a philosophy where anything is possible, Cage has wiped the slate clean even for those who do not necessarily subscribe to his theories, as is the case with the British artist, Hamish Fulton, who realizes that "if John Cage hadn't existed and done the work he has done, it would never have been possible for me to be doing the work I am doing today."[21]

Then there are those who have not heard of John Cage and those who would rather not have heard of John Cage, but it is undeniable that Western art culture has been irreversibly altered by his presence. He has radically broadened our tolerance for sounds; synthetically made music of every conceivable ilk flourishes along with World music where pitches formerly considered out of tune we now accept as microtones. "Our ears are in excellent condition" (*Silence*, p. 49). He has affected our perception of time, so much so that we can now indulge ourselves in Minimal music of maximal proportions, and withstand with grace, Peter Brook's nine-hour rendition of the *Mahabharata* as a concomitant to the ongoing theater of life. In short, John Cage has given us that ultimate freedom

to Become

fRee:

nOt

to knoW

whether we kNow or not.

[*Empty Words*, p. 131]

POSTSCRIPTS

			But beware of
that which is	breathtakingly	beautiful,	for at any moment
	the telephone	may ring	or the airplane
come down in a	vacant lot		

["Lecture on Nothing," *Silence,* p. 111]

The New York Times ®

THE NEW YORK TIMES, FRIDAY, NOVEMBER 13, 1987

Arson at the Frankfurt Opera

Special to The New York Times

BONN, Nov. 12—The Frankfurt Opera House was badly damaged today by a fire started by an unemployed and homeless East German refugee, officials said.

The damage was estimated at 3.5 million marks, about $2.1 million, and the officials said it would take two to three years to repair. The modern opera house, opened in 1963, was extensively renovated last summer.

Gary Bartini, who took over as director of the Frankfurt Opera this season, said that after a short break the company would resume performances at other sites. The company is known for its un-conventional stagings; this season it plans to offer a premier of John Cage's "Europeras I and II."

The Frankfurt city prosecutor, Jochen Schroers, said at a news conference that a 26-year-old man identified only as Michael W. had been picked up at a public telephone booth from which he called to confess setting the fire.

Mr. Schroers said the man had told the police that he entered the building through an open window about 2 A.M., looking for food. When he found none, the suspect reportedly said, he started a fire in the stage area with newspapers.

Notes

I wish to thank the following individuals for their kind assistance: Don Gillespie, Heiner Stadler, Richard Kostelanetz, William Duckworth, Eric Salzman, Grete Sultan, Joshua Pierce, Rosemarie Fava, Anne Tardos, Lilah Toland, Bennet Ludden, and Chean Eng Ooi.

1. In the preface to Eugen Herrigel, *Zen in the Art of Archery* (New York: Random House, 1971); hereafter *ZAA,* with page numbers cited parenthetically in the text.

2. John Cage, *Silence: Lectures and Writings* (Middletown, Conn.: Wesleyan University Press, 1961), p. 5; hereafter *Silence,* with page numbers cited parenthetically in the text.

3. Jill Johnston, "There Is No Silence Now," in *John Cage,* ed. Richard Kostelanetz (New York: Praeger, 1970), p. 146. Hereafter, references to the varied offerings in Kostelanetz's book will be cited as RK, with page numbers in parentheses in the text.

4. Letter from John Cage to Margaret Leng Tan, 17 May 1982.

5. Calvin Tomkins, *The Bride and the Bachelors* (New York: Viking Press, 1965), p. 98.

6. Paul Griffiths, *Cage* (London: Oxford University Press, 1981), p. 18.

7. John Cage, *Empty Words: Writings '73–'78* (Middletown, Conn.: Wesleyan University Press, 1979), p. 8.

8. In "Anything I Say Will be Misunderstood," William Duckworth's interview with John Cage in this issue of the *Bucknell Review.*

9. John Cage, in an interview with Tom Darter, *Keyboard* (September 1982), p. 27.

10. Richard Kostelanetz, preface to "Re. Musicircus" by John Cage, RK, p. 171.

11. Richard Kostelanetz, "Environmental Abundance," RK, p. 177.

12. Marcel Duchamp, in an interview (1963), quoted in the preface to RK, p. xvii.

13. John Cage, *A Year from Monday: New Lectures and Writings* (Middletown, Conn.: Wesleyan University Press, 1967), p. ix.

14. John Cage, in an interview with Jeff Goldberg (1974), excerpted in *Perspectives of New Music* 25, no. 1 (Winter 1987): 97.

15. John Cage, overheard by Michael Nyman (1973), in *Perspectives of New Music* 25, no. 1 (Winter 1987): 99.

16. John Cage, in an interview with Stephen Montague (1982), excerpted in *Perspectives of New Music* 25, no. 1 (Winter 1987): 97–98.

17. Cage, *Year from Monday,* p. 134.

18. Ibid.

19. Ibid., p. 136.

20. John Cage, in an interview with Stuart Smith (1983), excerpted in *Perspectives of New Music* 25, no. 1 (Winter 1987): 92.

21. In Kathan Brown, "Changing Art: A Chronicle Centered on John Cage," in *John Cage: Etchings 1978–1982* (Oakland, Calif.: Crown Point Press, 1982), p. 6.

Bucknell Review gratefully acknowledges Wesleyan University Press for its permission to reproduce selections from its publications by John Cage.

About Cage about Thoreau

William Brooks

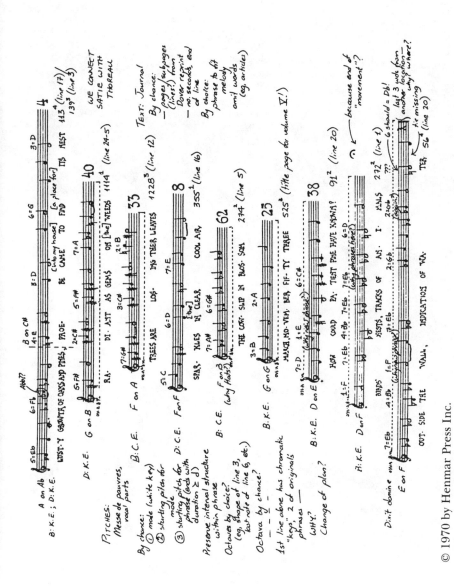

I

About Thoreau

"Simplicity, simplicity, simplicity." [*Walden,* p. 33]

(This in the midst of a five-hundred-word paragraph embedded in a hundred-thousand-word book extracted in part from a two-million-word journal.)

About Cage

"Nothing is accomplished by writing a piece of music. Our ears are now in excellent condition." [*Silence,* p. xii]

(This in 1952, after twenty years and sixty-six compositions, and before thirty-five and more than one hundred more.)

About Cage about Thoreau

Where is the simplicity? What is the purpose?

Talk. "We live in a complex world." (NYC, DNA, BBC) "There's too much to keep track of." (CIA, ART, DOS) "Twenty years ago things were simpler."

Sure they were.

Twenty years ago, on a bus, on the way to Albany, Neely Bruce observed, with the force of revelation, that human activity necessarily simplifies the world. Cities are less complex than forests; thermostats, simpler than the weather; music, less intricate than cornfields in August. That which simply occurs is, inevitably, richer than that which is planned.

But we aspire to complexity, seek always to become (not to imitate) nature. (AI, FM, GE) Our aspirations suggest two tactics: 1) increase quantity; 2) decrease predictability. In the domain of language: 1) use complex principles (syntax) to make so many simple objects (sentences) that the totality cannot be grasped. Or 2) use simple principles (chance) to make complex objects that are intrinsically ungraspable.

The *Journal* . . . "Empty Words."

What is simpler than flipping a coin? What more purposeful than a daily account? Cage/Thoreau: symbionts, doppelgänger, com-

plements. From both, an art, unnatural, which returns us to
nature; a purpose, unyielding, which precipitates the unexpected.

II

Thoreau

"The truest beauty was that which surrounded us but which we
failed to discern . . . the forms and colors which adorn our daily
life . . . are our fairest jewelry." [*Journal*, 11: 166]

Cage about Thoreau

"*Journal* is filled with illustrations . . . Amazed 1) by their beauty,
2) by fact I had not . . . been seeing 'em as beautiful." [*Empty
Words*, p. 11]

About Thoreau

On page 47 we learn to make bread.

Thoreau's recipe was prepared and eaten several nights in succes-
sion on stage at the old Depot Theatre, some seventeen years
ago—a curious context, but with successful results. *Walden* is, in
the end, a do-it-yourself book.

Utility is everything, and everywhere. As a rule of thumb: if it's
useful, and if it's needed, then use it; if not, enjoy the encounter
and leave it undisturbed. Thoreau's accounts, his economy, his
resolute self-scrutiny, all bespeak a minimalist ethic: do what
needs to be done; use what is there.

About Cage

And for Cage, what is there? Thoreau is there, to be used to make
the music that is needed. The visible Thoreau ("That government
is best . . .") is used visibly *(Song Books)*; the unnoticed Thoreau
(the illustrations), unnoticeably *(Renga)*.

What has been rejected? What discarded? What has decayed? Use
it: music from noise; art from accident; food from fungi. *Silence*,
too, is do-it-yourself: just listen.

Thoreau

"They impress me like humors . . . pimples on the face of the earth . . . A sort of excrement they are." [*Journal*, 5: 374–5]

Cage about Thoreau

"There's no indication in any of his writings that Thoreau ever ate a mushroom." [*Empty Words*, p. 88]

Thoreau

"Only that day dawns to which we are awake." [*Walden*, p. 221]

III

Cage about Thoreau

"Reading Thoreau's *Journal*, I discover any idea I've ever had worth it's salt." [*M*, p. 18]

Cage about Cage about Thoreau

> Devote myself
> to askIng
> queStions
> Chance
> determIned
> answers'll oPen
> my mind to worLd around
> at the same tIme
> chaNging my music
> sElf-alteration not self-expression
>
> thoreau saiD the same
> thIng
> over a hundred yearS ago
> i want my writing to be as Clear
> as water I can see through
> so that what i exPerienced
> is toLd
> wIthout
> my beiNg in any way
> in thE way

[*X*, 132–33]

About Cage about Thoreau

Scholarship. Accuracy. Footnotes. Let's face it: to quote is to misrepresent. What I do here is worse than futile; it's fiction.

"Thoreau said the same thing . . .". Did he? *I* can't find it (though probably it's there). Thoreau *did* say that "it is considered a ground for complaint if a man's writings admit of more than one interpretation . . . I do not suppose that I have attained to obscurity, but I should be proud if no more fatal fault were found with my pages on this score than was found with the Walden ice. Southern customers objected to its blue color, which is evidence of its purity, as if it were muddy, and preferred the Cambridge ice, which is white, but tastes of weeds. The purity men love is like the mists which envelop the earth, and not like the azure ether beyond" (*Walden*, p. 216). Thoreau also said "how can the language of the poet be more expressive than nature? He is content that what he has already read in simple characters, or indifferently in all, be translated into the same again" (*Journal*, 1: 149). But did he say "i want my writing to be as Clear as water I can see through"? Beats me.

Everything changes. To use again is to make anew. Scholarship is art.

Cage (about Thoreau?)

"Spent several hours searching through a book trying to find the idea I'd gotten out of it. I couldn't find it. I still have the idea." [M, p. 15]

Cage about Cage

My

mEmory

of whaT

Happened

is nOt

what happeneD

[X, p. 123]

IV

Cage about Cage

"A transition from language to music . . . Nothing has been worked on: a journal of circa two million words has been used to answer questions." [*Empty Words,* p. 65]

About Cage about Thoreau

A distinction: let "abstract" works be those which establish connections; let "concrete" works simply present, leaving connections to their users. Music by Webern, then, is abstract, as is "Sweet Suffolk Owl"; a river, *Winter Music,* a recording of crickets, are concrete. (Musique concrète, usually, is abstract.)

Then writing "about writing" (expressing thought) is abstract; "writing about" writing (glossing a tradition) is less so; "writing through" (recording, listing) is still less so. More concrete yet is writing incomprehensibly.

Empty Words makes Thoreau's *Journal* concrete. The corruption (the perfection) is gradual: part I: phrases, words, syllables, letters; part II: words, syllables, letters; part III: syllables, letters; part IV: letters. From

```
notAt evening
          right can see
             suited to the morning hour
```

to

```
        i           k v    ooa e.
```

But: Is this necessary? What of uncorrupted, imperfect Thoreau?

A small study: examine every sentence which falls halfway down every twenty-fifth page in volumes 2, 7, and 14 of the *Journal.* Classify each of these entries as "abstract" (concerned with thought) or "concrete" (a record, usually of nature). In Volume 2 are 9 concrete entries, 11 abstract (45% concrete); in volume 7, 12 concrete, 8 abstract (60%); in volume 14, 14 concrete, 3 abstract (82%).

Too subjective? Well, then: at its most concrete, writing is ideographic. And so for Thoreau: volume 2 contains 15 drawings; volume 7 contains 72; volume 14 contains 96. The *Journal* itself, then, grows concrete; words, from the beginning, grow ever more empty.

In the beginning, to write "about" means literally that:
words placed *about* someone else's words; glosses, marginalia,
interpolations. Source and commentary are inseparable;
texts are three-dimensional, time being measured by layers
of script. History simply accumulates; art illuminates,
embellishes, accompanies.

Then comes type: modular script, infinitely and easily
reproducable. "Writing about" is stood on its head:
rather than wedging one's words into crevices in the
source, bits of the source are wedged into one's words.
Texts are no longer "writing about", but "about writing."

Thence comes discursive history, criticism, art. From the
past, that vast tip, one sifts a few castaways, embedding
these like stones from the road in a necklace of one's own
design. That done, the necklace itself is cast away,
itself to be found, borrowed, fragmented. History made
fresh; history discarded.

Texts "about writing", then: logics which link fragments
filtered from the past. The logic lives in the links, not
the fragments, just as a path which connects thirty different
towns may become an east-west highway. A road to knowledge:
scholarship, essays, theses. An art full of purpose,
conviction: inspirational, suggestive, contentious.

And after this, and overlapping it, is simple sorting:
first lists, then card files, then data bases. Using an
arbitrarily large number of criteria, sort and distinguish,
but leave logic out. (What's logical about the alphabet?)
Let writing (when it exists) be simply a collection, to be
ordered by the user: a map, not a highway. History lives
in our midst, a conversation held with and between fragments
we select. "Writing about" becomes "writing with," "writing
through"; art wanders off, into fields, attics, crossroads.

Cage gives us a digest, writing about, writing through. The plot,
the characters, the outcome? All the same.

Thoreau about Thoreau

"No page in my *Journal* is more suggestive than one which includes a sketch." [Quoted in *Empty Words,* p. 11]

V

About Cage

How do we divide up the work? (There's too much for one person
alone.) Genres don't work; too many pieces are for unspecified
instruments. Pieces themselves can not always be distinguished,
being "to be performed in whole or in part, together with . . ."

Nor is the line between music and writings always clear (is the "Lecture on Nothing" a text or a score?).

There remains the old standby: time. We could, for example, divide the work into pre- and post-Thoreau (that is, essentially, pre- and post-1967). Before Thoreau: the inclusion of that which had been refused (noise, silence, happenstance). After Thoreau: the inclusion of what was then refused (staff notation, repetition, harmony). "No difference, only the feet are a little bit off the ground." [Silence, p. 88]

So is Thoreau responsible? Is the turn to Thoreau a turn inwards, backwards? Concord, not Japan; past, not future; observation, not creation?

About Thoreau

How shall we divide up Thoreau? By years? But how distinguish 1853 from 1852 from 1860? When is *Walden*?

The seasons are better: winter differs from spring far more than from a previous winter. *Walden* presents two years in one: "Thus was my first year's life in the woods completed; and the second year was similar to it" (*Walden*, p. 212). There is no pre-, no post-, in Thoreau; only the seasons, spiraling cyclically on.

About Cage about Thoreau

And for Cage? The writings, pre-Thoreau, are about writing: linear, syntactic, expositional. Chance may determine the order, performances may confound the sense, but the writings are linear: sentence to sentence, year to year. Time marches on.

Post-Thoreau begins the writing through: first the *Song Books*, then *Mureau*, then *Empty Words* (all writing through the *Journal*); then *Writing through Finnegans Wake* (four, five times by now). In each of these, a collection made into a list by means of an index: research and replication, nothing more. The source is available in its entirety all of the time; no marching, no cycles; all is present.

Is Thoreau responsible? All Cage's *Seasons (Winter Music,* the *String Quartet)* came much earlier. Not guilty, then (but an accomplice).

VI

Thoreau

" 'That government is best which governs not at all;' and when
men are prepared for it, that will be the kind of government
which they will have" ("On the Duty of Civil Disobedience," p. 222;
quoted in *Song Books,* passim, *A Year from Monday,* p. 166, *M,* p. 24,
Empty Words, p. 183).

About Cage about Thoreau

Both are observers; both devote themselves to noticing. They do
not judge; they record and accept, gratefully and with pleasure.

Cage

"Suddenly a clam rose to the surface directly, remained there a
moment, then descended slowly, leaf-like, tipping one way, then
the other, arriving at the bottom to produce a disturbance, such
that clam after clam did likewise, sometimes several, sometimes
many, sometimes not one at all, producing a dance that completely
involved us." *[A Year from Monday,* pp. 55–56]

Thoreau

"The sky is two-thirds covered with great four or more sided
downy clouds, drifting from the north or northwest, with dark-
blue partitions between them. The moon, with a small brassy halo,
seems travelling ever through them toward the north. The water
is dull and dark, except close to the windward shore, where there
is a smooth strip a rod or more in width protected from the wind,
which reflects a faint light. When the moon reaches a clear space,
the water is suddenly lit up quite across the meadows, for half a
mile in length and several rods in width, while the woods beyond
are thrown more into the shade, or seen more in a mass and
indistinctly, than before." *[Journal,* 3: 387–8]

About Cage about Thoreau

Both protest, both complain. Both require discipline; both refuse
indulgence.

Thoreau

"How does it become a man to behave toward this American government today? I answer that he cannot without disgrace be associated with it." ["On the Duty of Civil Disobedience," p. 224]

Cage

"Revolution remains our proper concern. But instead of planning it, or stopping what we're doing in order to do it, it may be that we are at all times in it." *[Empty Words,* p. 182]

About Cage about Thoreau

Thoreau went to jail; not so Cage. Cage composes, speaks, travels, tirelessly; not so Thoreau. Whence comes the difference? Temperament? Tactics? Time?

Thoreau is an activist. Refusing to pay his taxes, he is sent to jail. Sent to jail, he writes a defense which inspires Gandhi, Martin Luther King, others. Changes occur.

Cage is a saboteur. March to a different drummer? No; corrupt the drum itself: *Imaginary Landscape No. 4 (March No. 2),* for twelve radios. March with the feet of a sentence? Corrupt the language: "Lecture on the Weather." Not change, but the possibility of change.

A proposition: the nineteenth century (which extends at least to 1917 in the West, to the present elsewhere) requires change by revolution, by action. The twentieth century (which we've barely entered) permits change by dissolution, inaction.

Thoreau's world, then, is split: nature (to be observed), government (to be confronted). For Cage (for us), no such comfort: "humanity and nature, not separate, are in this world together" *(Silence,* p. 8). We observe, we subvert, in the same realm. In this realm is the past; in the past is Thoreau. Observe Thoreau; subvert Thoreau. Empty words: about Cage about Thoreau.

Cage

" 'World's O.K. as is': 'Work to make the world O.K.' " *[A Year from Monday,* p. 57]

Acknowledgments

The page of music is "Solo 27," page 93 from volume 1 of John Cage's *Song Books*, published by C. F. Peters, New York, 1971.

John Cage's writings *(Silence,* 1961; *A Year from Monday,* 1967; *M,* 1973; *Empty Words,* 1979; *X,* 1983) are published by Wesleyan University Press, Middletown, Connecticut.

The Journal of Henry David Thoreau was reprinted by Dover Publications, Inc., New York, in 1962, in two volumes, from the edition first published by Houghton Mifflin Company in 1906 in fourteen volumes.

Walden, or Life in the Woods and "On the Duty of Civil Disobedience" were printed in 1960 in the paperback series of "Signet Classics" by The New American Library, New York.

Permission to reproduce extracts from these is hereby gratefully acknowledged.

Index: Cage about Thoreau

A Year from Monday: 166

M: "Mureau", 35-56; "Song", 86-91; in passing, [ix],
[xii], [xiii], [xiv], 3, 8, 18, 24, 59, 61, 70, 77, 80,
114, 122, 127, 133, 145, 147, 156, 158, 161, 166, 167,
175, 178, 180

Empty Words: "Preface to 'Lecture on the Weather'", 3-
5; in passing, 88, 95, 133, 136, 183, 186-7

X: "Another Song", 103-7; in passing, 69-70, 133, 155,
163, 164

Silent Performances: On Reading John Cage

Arthur J. Sabatini

> At any rate, my musical words, strictly speaking, have managed to arouse either indignation or sympathy—nothing compared to my books. You can't imagine how many people were touched by *Silence!* I received many letters, sometimes extremely lucid, always interesting. Next to that, the reactions to my music are predictable.
>
> Cage to Daniel Charles

THE writings of John Cage are destined to provoke more varied, and ultimately more enduring, responses than his music. This is no doubt a chancy proposition, but since Cage's aesthetic is most widely known because of theories founded upon his concept of "silence," it is not unreasonable to argue that his art and practice are most dramatically experienced in the context of that realm where silence has reigned most inviolable: reading. Moreover, because nearly everything in Cage's writings directs reading into performance, his texts have the potential to create increasingly unpredictable readerly responses and generate an abundance of "touched" and touchy reactions.

Each reading of Cage is, in effect, a silent performance. The silence associated with reading, however, differs from the silence, or nonsilence, of music. It is a self-induced, private silence, drawn between consciousness and the page. Though occurring over time, reading is not bound by time measured as in music; nor has anyone ever suggested that the silence that surrounds the trance of reading is pure. The French poet Stephen Mallarmé, who wrote about reading, elegantly described the silence "between the sheets and the eye" as "the condition and delight of reading," an authentic, luxurious state.[1]

But since Mallarmé, Joyce, and a long list of others, the art of reading has undergone a great transformation. As texts broke out of the cages of linear narrative, closed forms, generic definitions, typographic constraints and physical structure, readers assumed and were forced to adopt new roles. Reading evolved from a passive, reactive phenomena to an active, performative state. It also acquired its own elaborate poetics, theoretical formulations, and romance. "Let others boast of the pages they have written," Jorge Luis Borges announced in a poem titled "A Reader," "I take pride in those I've read."[2] John Cage has echoed that sentiment in practice by often referring to authors and books and by writing on names, in mesostics, and "through" the books of Thoreau, Joyce, Pound, and Merce Cunningham. Cage has even taken Borges a few steps further, for the next lines of the poem are

> I may not have been a philologist,
> or gone deeply into declensions or moods or those
>   slow shifts of letter sounds—
> the *d* that hardens into *t*.
> the kinship of the *g* and *k*—
> but through the years I have professed
> a passion for language.

Since his days at Black Mountain, and perhaps before, Cage's attention to language, writing, and writing-as-process has set the stage for performative readings—by himself and others. He has written lectures and works that were specifically for performance. In numerous instances, he has "composed" texts as he composed music for use in performance situations. A 1979 work, *Circus On,* is a score "for translating a book into a performance without actors, a performance which is both literary and musical or one or the other." Finally, when compiling his books, Cage has given careful consideration to their style, structure, and the effect on the reader. In many ways, he has "prepared" readers and insured that whoever chooses one of his texts is never a mere page turner.

Cage has not only written, performed, composed, typed, copied, printed, Letrasetted, plexi-glassed, and framed his texts, but, in *Themes and Variations,* the mesostic "Composition in Retrospect," and other pieces, he has subjected them to rereadings and rewritings. His more recent writings are, in fact, glosses and reductions of earlier work. Employing a surface of sounds and letters, in mesostics and the "writings through" (*Finnegans Wake*) Cage seems to be in search of an Ur-language, another form of silence, or not. And, with each new writing—which, of course, reflects off and through all previous writings—the reader warily accompanies Cage. Or not.

For, by now, to read Cage is to knowingly pass (kick, fall, run?)

into a galaxy where performance is everywhere influenced by a physics that mixes aesthetics with psychology and politics. The features of Cage's universe are clearly documented. Philosophically and in practice, Cage is concerned with *indeterminancy, purposeful purposelessness, nonintention, uncertainty, anarchy, meaninglessness as ultimate meaning,* and various states of presence and absence (silence/nonsilence, mobility/immobility, art/life). These unsteady states (of mind and being) are plentiful and unavoidable because of the very structure, intention, and thematic interrelationships among all the writings. In order to pursue any vector within the Cagean system, a reader must negotiate Cage's thought and come to grips with his methods and directives. Where reading Cage was once a matter of "seeking" information or playing with a text's descriptions and formulas, the immensity of his oeuvre now seems to impose other considerations. There are simply too many demands, explicit and implicit, prompted by a Cagean text. The allusions, practices, and sheer density of meaning (encompassing, as it does, nonmeaning) that have accumulated around Cage's every gesture—at this point in his long career—transform reading into a self-conscious and reflexive performative behavior.

Inevitably the dynamics of Cage's discourse entangle and perhaps threaten the reader. Then, as Cage quotes Sri Ramakrishna, the plot thickens. For a reader's silence, though active, is above all circumscribed by the need for security and affirmation. Reading is a one-on-one game which flows toward resolution, order, and meaning. Yet, with Cage, reading becomes risky, unpredictable. Readers are confronted with the possibility of a reading/performance that results in the production of a text that is the very antithesis of the agenda of reading. Stated directly, reading Cage creates the conditions for the production of nonmeaning, purposeful purposelessness, uncertainty, etc.—and the reader is an adjunct to the process. As an aesthetic gesture—or a social one—conspiring to produce nonmeaning, even within the privacy of the readerly cocoon, is an act of some consequence. At the very least, nonmeaning is a noise neither desired nor easily accommodated in the silent orbit of a reader's journey and, at its farthest reaches, nonmeaning is a notion (Cagean, Zen-like, nature-like) that is problematic with regard to reading and consciousness.

Reading through the works of John Cage raises these and other issues. Cage's texts, and his performance theories (of music, writing, reading) are elaborate and complex. In this essay I want to wander/wonder through the near and far territories of Cage's writings. I will begin by surveying the multiplicity and character of

Cage's texts, since the sheer quantity and variety of them poses questions for any would-be reader. (For the most part, I will focus on writings in books and collections.) The second matter I'll address is the physical structure and composition of the writings, with particular attention to Cage's use of mesostics and open formats. The third part of the essay is more speculative and referential, as I gauge Cage's work according to schemes of reading/writing that are simultaneously ancient and postmodern.

I believe Cage's writings will eventually gain more attention than his music because, McCluhan notwithstanding, we remain a culture of print and the book. The writings are, unarguably, stunning repositories of original insights, aesthetic theory, and poetries. They include valuable critical commentaries on musicians, composers, artists, dancers, and social theorists as well as an intriguing personal history of the avant-garde from the 1930s to the present. And they are plainly fun to read.

As an author, Cage has been prolific. He has written, coauthored or contributed to twelve published books under his own name. Several books are collections of previously published material; three *(For the Birds* and Kostelanetz's books) include extensive interviews and articles by others; a few books, usually collaborations *(Another Song, Mud Book),* are primarily photographic or graphic. In addition, he has written innumerable pieces for periodicals, catalogues, and other sources which have yet to be collected.

The most striking and obvious facts about Cage the writer is that he is stylistically consistent, ceaselessly inventive, and never at a loss to meet the demands of the occasion or the page. The hybrid quality of his writing—part essay, part narrative, part word/text play, part score—is always maintained. All of which poses the first question to any would-be reader: what, precisely, is a Cagean text? Is it to be read as diversion, as instructions, as a continuation or development of theses? Do the writings in a given collection add up to a "statement" or "position"?

Throughout his career, Cage's range has been astonishing. He has written reviews, program notes, essays, lectures, diaries, scripts, sound/text pieces, scores, mesostics, letters, books, and more. Scattered among the work are biographical notes, anecdotes, commentaries, dialogues, forewords, afterwords, and explanations concerning methods of composition or the circumstances that surrounded a particular writing. When editing collections, as he does periodically, Cage augments his books with fillers, minutiae, photographs, and etchings.

Amidst this plethora of texts, a reader's first questions echo titles of some of Cage's early lectures: where to begin? what order to follow? where to go next? how to read? and what am I reading for?

If one's impulse, or method, is to "read in order," a first question is what type of order? Cage's writings, it is true, are scrupulously identified chronologically, but reading pieces according to their dates quickly reveals little in the way of a systematic development of ideas. Cage often wrote essays or delivered lectures on specific subjects to fulfill commissions. On given occasions he repeated himself; or reused serviceable anecdotes or comments as a source for continuing a thought. In "45' for a Speaker," for example, he notes that "the text itself was composed using previously written lectures together with new material."[3] After reading any number of pieces, the same material about his teachers reappears: D. T. Suzuki ("Before studying Zen, men are men and mountains are mountains), Satie ("You'll see when you're fifty, I'm fifty and I've seen nothing"), Schoenberg ("The eraser is more important than the point of the pencil"). By the time Cage writes *Themes and Variations,* he acknowledges "fifteen men who have been important to me in my life and work" and "one hundred and ten ideas" he "listed in the course of a cursory examination of my books."[4] The repetitiousness of Cage's thoughts and sources in different types of texts thus belies reading in "order."

Nevertheless, it is possible to approach at least one of Cage's efforts chronologically. The "Diary: How to Improve the World (You Will Only Make Matters Worse)" dates from 1965 and numbers eight sections (to 1982, as published in *X*). It is a remarkable documentation of Cage's interests, travels, readings, friendships, and enthusiasms. The nominal "theme" of the Diary is "improving the world." For Cage, this involves observations of daily events, incidental notes and remarks on the way things ought to be, according to his "teachers" (Norman O. Brown, McLuhan, et al.) and his own good uncommon sense.

Although wonderfully engaging and diligently kept, the Diary remains more of a listing than a reliable chronicle. It details Cage's activities but does not disclose a reasoned development of his thinking. Cage, for instance, often quotes Fuller or McCluhan, but (intentionally) refrains from analyzing or reviewing issues. He cites Mao Tse-tung, but never considers Mao in the context of the negative, often murderous circumstances of the Cultural Revolution. The chosen abbreviated form of the Diary, which Cage calls a "mosaic," prohibits elaboration on his part. Reading the Diary offers a chronological glimpse of Cage's life and times, if that, but little else.

Surveying Cage's entire output as a writer, any "order" for reading would be arbitrary. Cage's writings do not handily fall into genres or categories. Lectures are simultaneously performance works, essays are rewritten interviews or radio transcriptions; and what of the mesostics? They are at once formal structures and about a variety of subjects. As in the case of any number of Cage's compositions (*Fontana Mix* comes to mind), the materials for performance are available ultimately for the reader to select and define.

And the materials are abundant. But, even as one chooses, say, to proceed through the Diary, or only read lectures or mesostics, the complete contents and structurings that surround Cage's texts influence the readerly effort. In each of the books and collections, Cage is at pains to identify occasions, clarify his method for composition or otherwise append notes to the writings. The books are dense with prefaces, introductions, opening statements, afterwords, parenthetical notes, and interludes. Often italicized, this considerable body of information appears useful; but it subtly complicates matters.

These *italicizations,* to name this material, form something of a multitracked tape that loops around and through the Cagean galaxy. One track is inscribed with names: Merce Cunningham, Buckminster Fuller, Mother, Erik Satie, Jasper Johns; another with places and occasions: Juilliard, Emma Lake, a lecture series, Darmstadt, a birthday, New York City; another with tools and numbers: the I Ching, 100 words a day, two weeks, Letraset, 2 pages, forty-eight measures; and another is imprinted with quotations from letters and comments by friends. In cases where published writings were first delivered as lectures or performances, Cage italicizes the precise requirements for reading: "Each line is to be read across the page from left to right, not down the columns in sequences."[5] "The following text was written to be spoken aloud. It consists of five sections, each to take twelve minutes. The fourth is the fastest and the last one is the slowest."[6] In a few instances, he notes that original versions of pieces, or small printings of special editions, differ or were printed with photographs or in colored ink.

To whom, even a slightly self-conscious reader must ask, are all these *italicizations* addressed? What are they about? Are they meant to be informative or directive? What is their cumulative effect? What value am I supposed to place on the fact that Cage completed this work in six days, or that it was done in script, or produced in Ann Arbor? If I choose to read at my own pace, am I missing something essential to Cage's meaning? How accurate is Cage's information? What relation does one set of descriptions bear to another? Do I have to read aloud?—knowing that Cage himself wonders about "Searching (outloud) for a way to read."[7]

I find the *italicizations* winding through Cage's writings to be functional yet unsettling. Functional in that they serve as a framing and a connecting device that locates both Cage and a reader in the scheme of a long, peripatetic life through the twentieth century's worldwide avant-garde. The frequent reappearance of friends, predictable allusions or ideas permits the unfolding of each new text against a familiar background, establishing something of a narrative structure for readers. There is a comforting quality to this, on the one hand, and, on the other, it affirms Cage's belief in the continuity of art and life.

Yet this persistent, detailed identification of times, dates, instructions, and notes on methodologies also instills a feeling of alienation (to borrow a notion from Brecht's theory of acting). Like an actor, according to Brecht, who does not intend to create "empathy" but to read his lines so as to show the nature of an incident or character, Cage's instructions turn a text into just such an "exemplification."[8] Each explanation over-explains and over-determines the text, like too many stage directions underscoring the action. The printed italics also serve as a reminder that reading is a partial act, a secondary performance that follows after the specific, recorded act of composition or life experience. Reading is only truly reading, the italics imply, when it follows Cage's rules (e.g., each story in "How to Pass, Kick, Fall, and Run" takes one minute to read).[9]

To a degree, Cage creates conditions which undermine, or challenge, the reader. As with the A-effect, the reader is poised not to rush into a pursuit of the text's meaning, but to cooly assess its declarations, possibilities, and technical requirements.

When there are extensive proscribed formulas for following a text, reading becomes more problematic. After being instructed that the text requires a reading of one line per second, what is the measure of a reading that lingers over a phrase or skips to the bottom of the page? Or, consider two other subtle forms of insistence by Cage. When a text—the essays on Jasper Johns or Morris Graves—is meant to "relate somehow to the canvases and personality of the painter" or "Graves in the act of painting,"[10] isn't a reader at a disadvantage without a clear image of the painter's work? Similarly, when Cage indicates that a given piece was written as he composed a musical work (in the above instance, the Johns essay followed the plan of *Cartridge Music*) or according to the pattern in a musical composition (the Graves essay derives from the "fourth movement of my *Quartet* for percussion (1935)"), isn't the reader meant to hear the work in the background?—in the silence?

Another complicating factor is the presence of Cage's italicized "voiceovers" incessantly pointing to this, emphasizing that. This voice, albeit a soft and friendly one, flows as metatext surrounding the reader at every step. (For many, this voice is potentially Cage's actual voice, remembered from conversations and performances: a factor that could enhance or detract from one's silence).

All of the *italicizations* in Cage's writings cause, however slight, an adjustment in any reading/performance. Reading according to the instructions of a text amounts to a form of readerly complicity that contradicts the unstated law which maintains that a reader determines the nature of the action. To have the space between the self and the page "directed," even if the directions aren't followed, establishes a set of relations between reader and writer that, as is the case with Cage's music, demands a rethinking of readerly postures, strategies, and ethics. This is the case for new readers as well as seasoned ones. Richard Kostelanetz, in an interview in 1979, seemed to be taken up short after Cage explains how he should read: "I'm sorry, John; do you want me to read *Empty Words* with a stopwatch?" And Cage replies, "Yes. Then immediately you become fascinated with the whole problem of reading it."[11]

Any event that follows a space is a new event.   Making music by reading outloud.   *To read.*   To breathe.   *IV: equation between letters and silence.   Making language saying nothing at all.   What's in mind is to stay up all night reading.*   Time reading so that at dawn (IV) the sounds outside come in (not as before through closed doors and windows). Half-hour   intermissions between any two parts.   Something to eat. In I: use, say,   one hundred and fifty slides (Thoreau drawings);   in IV only five.   Other vocal extremes: movement (gradual or sudden) in space; equalization. (Electronics.) *Do without whatever's inflexible. Make a separate I Ching program for each aspect of a performance.   Continue to search.*[12]

To this point (space?), I have been suggesting that the silence surrounding the reader of Cage's works is precarious. Cage's writings, a career-long commitment, are extensive and each piece inflects a reading of another. There is no order to speak of when attempting to read Cage, and what order there is—a chronological one—reveals but a vague biographical montage. Cage's writings also present a chorus of voicings, directives, instructions, and allusions that invoke a sense of an "other" hovering around and through each text. (Assessing a book by Derrida, the literary critic Geoffrey Hartman comments that for certain writers the "less ego the more echo seems to be the rule,"[13] which surely is apt in this context). Reading Cage, I find, cannot merely "proceed" because processions are predisposed by Cage's *italicizations* (never anything but helpful, nevertheless intrusive). Then there is Cage's explicit intention to remove intention, to replace meaning with meaninglessness, and to otherwise change minds. Thus the multitude of distractions, shifts, adjustments, queries, and modulations that comprise Cage's texts lead me uneasily toward fulfilling Cage's desiderata. This possibility is, I think, emphatically reinforced when I consider not only the words, but the pages and books.

But the reading I've been discussing so far pertains to the content, general outline, and order of the writings—the common ground of texts. A decidedly more complicating issue is Cage's conception of texts and books: lettering, shape, page formats, etc. Since his earliest lectures, Cage has toyed with typography, graphics, and the limitations of the white rectangle of the page. He has always expressed an awareness of the tools and conditions of writing; all of his collections are printed in different typefaces and some with drawings. "How is this text to be presented?" he notes at the beginning of *Empty Words*, "As a mix of handwriting, stamping, typing, printing, letraset?"[14] Cage answered this query in the 1958 "Composition as Process" lecture in *Silence* (see p. 83).

To cite another example, Cage's Diary was fastidiously planned with irregularities of type in mind. They were written, he notes, for Clark Coolidge's magazine *Joglars* and since it

> was printed by photo-offset from typescripts, I used an IBM Selectric typewriter to print my text. I used twelve different type faces, letting chance operations determine which face would be used for which statements. So, too, the left marginations were determined, the right marginations being the result of not hyphenating words and at the same time keeping the number of characters per line forty-three or less.[15]

Cage regularly acknowledges such chance-determined, self-imposed word limits, or the printing formats of publications. A work answer: Which one of us is right?" ¶The man answered, "I just stand." ¶When I was studying with Schoenberg one day as he was writing some counterpoint to show the way to do it, he used an eraser. And then while he was doing this

he said, "This end of the pencil is just as important as the other end." I have several times in the course of this lecture mentioned ink. Composing, if it is writing notes, is then actually writing, and the less one thinks it's thinking the more it becomes what it is: writing. Could music be composed (I do not mean improvised) not writing it in pencil or ink?

The answer is no doubt Yes and the changes in writing are prophetic. The *Sonatas and Interludes* were composed by playing the piano, listening to differences, making a choice, roughly writing it in pencil; later this sketch was copied, but again in pencil. Finally an ink manuscript was made carefully. The *Music of Changes* was composed in almost the same way. With one change: the original pencil sketch was made exactly, an eraser used whenever necessary, eliminating the need for a neat pencil copy. In the case of the *Imaginary Landscape Number IV*, the first step of playing the instrument was eliminated. The others kept. *Music for Piano* was written directly in ink.

for *Dance Magazine* is titled "2 Pages, 122 Words on Music and
Dance" because of the number of "dummy pages" sent to Cage for
a piece. After selecting the number of words by chance operations, Cage positioned them according to the "imperfections in
the sheets of paper."[16] In *Music for Piano*, Cage placed notes on
the score, in ink, according to the imperfections.[17] *Muoyce* is
printed in columnar form

> bling fingers to Caer Fere rd'sc weyou
> king a of willy wooly woolf on ben aon
> watchbeupytamong Luggelawecurband that
> yrain may love that golden silence mud
> Cicely oshis agrammatical partsm typ d
> llbnf *o* b nds en'sgr t tk satw e o *ci-*
> d r ntpe ong le rwhoiIrchy ea erd a sj
> rby e ypsr lwhts o w a t ty were unde-
> cidedly attachedlifting upu in brother
> handhiswherever emanating deafdein the
> porchwaylonely one Maass*hows*eno sense-
> by memoryshall have beenbarcelonas *has*
> when the rothMutt for Felim in request
> how   starringthetollermight   factionwith
> our obeisant servants was sitting even
> provisionally who red altfrumpishly OF
> THE PASTthenPap IIhim Itand swarthythe
> ladwigs *babel* with any WiltAnd Kevwith
> the   twirlers   continuallyatloftaredon't
> Shoal effectand TROTHBLOWERSand andis-
> bar TRADITIONor Meynhircurfewhobblede-

in order to "facilitate the publishing in Japan."[18] Of the "Indeterminacy" lecture in *Silence*, Cage italicizes "The excessively small
type in the following pages is an attempt to emphasize the intentionally pontifical character of this lecture."[19]

The adherence to chance operations and arbitrary limits rein-
forces Cage's belief that "Artists who use disciplines to free their
work from their intentions start the flow moving in an outgoing
direction."[20]

> Devote myself
> to askIng
> queStions
> Chance
> determIned
> answers'll oPen
> my mind to worLd around
> at the same tIme
> chaNging my music
> sElf-alteration not self-expression

[X, p. 132]

On another level, as Cage remarked to Daniel Charles, "Ty-pographic changes, like the 'mosaic' form, are noises which erupt in the book! At one and the same time, the book is condemned to nonexistence and the book comes into being. It can welcome everything."[21]

For the reader, these pronouncements about the numbers of letters and words, and this consciously designated placement of graphic "noise" (?), is yet another challenge to the social and psychological contract of the readerly code which normally sepa-rates the writer's toil from the reader's pleasure. I may know that Hemingway woke up each morning and sharpened his pencils and when he finished writing he literally counted his word pro-duction. But I don't expect lead shavings to fall on my lap when I open *The Sun Also Rises*. Ezra Pound, Charles Olson (and before them Futurist poets, Apollinaire and others) all seized on the mechanics of lettering, typesetting, and the typewriter to visually engage readers and break down expectations of the printed text. But Pound and Olson measured lines according to breath and poetic beats, not by counting letters! (There are of course num-bers of novelists, sound-text, and "concrete" poets who expose, and espouse, composition employing visual methods. Much of what Cage does easily fits into their contexts.)

As for certain techniques Cage selects, the utilization of com-mon typographic materials serves to collapse the reading/writing process—by implying that the commercial intermediaries (editors, publishers, printers, distributors) between author and reader are nonexistent. But, ultimately, these meanings are part of the invis-ible operations that constitute the history of a book or inform that realm of "biographical" subtexts. (Though, again, postmodern writers often precisely incorporate this material as a way of em-phasizing the performative role of the reader.)

Cage supplements the inherent significations of postmodern writing and extends them through the introduction of Ducham-pian aesthetics. Page measurements, type fonts, printing require-ments, ink colors—and words themselves—all become found ob-jects, fields upon which imaginations play. "My work was only sometimes that of identifying," he says in reference to his writings through *Finnegans Wake*, "as Duchamp had, found objects."[22] The physical fact of a page becomes a field of possible meanings not determined by the author—in the same way that Duchamp al-lowed the accidental breakage of "The Large Glass" to contribute to its history and mythology.

One of the questions raised by this process is how should a

reader account for semantics or "meaning" of Cage's text knowing that, in many cases, the choice of language was the result of a purely visual requirement or numerical calculation? Readers, like mathematician Lewis Carroll's Alice, don't mind ambiguity, puns, and language play, but they expect authors to write with some precise meanings in mind.

Of course, Cage's "exemplifications" of ideas and meanings are resolved in the context of performance/readings, by himself or others. At least that was the case in writings included in books up to *A Year from Monday*. Through that collection Cage's pieces were essentially scores from lectures or reprints of introductions, statements, etc. Much of the work exhibited word and page play, but except for "Talk 1," where phrases and words are splayed across the page in a representation of the seating pattern of the audience at a lecture in Ann Arbor, Cage still remained within the bounds of conventional linear form and the writings employ ordinary syntax. But with *M: Writings '67–'72*, everything changes.

The title of the work was chosen, Cage notes, by chance. Nevertheless, the letter M references

> many words and names that have concerned me for many years (music, mushrooms, Marcel Duchamp, M. C. Richards, Morris Graves, Mark Tobey, Merce Cunningham, Marshall McLuhan, my dear friends the Daniels—Minna, for twenty-three years the editor of *Modern Music*, and Mell, early in my life and now again in later life the painter)—and recently (mesostics, Mao Tse-tung).[23]

M, he adds, is also the first letter of *Mureau*, the first of Cage's "writings through" another text, in this case the remarks of Henry David Thoreau. M, it is worth noting, is the thirteenth letter of the alphabet; it is the favorite letter for characters in the works of that literary master of silence, Samuel Beckett (Murphy, Malloy, Malone); and it is that curious, universal nasal consonant that connotes primal soundings and the border between sound and silence: mama, mu, mute, om, mum, mmmmm . . .

With *M*, Cage's writings become more minimal, graphic, and harshly disciplined. *M* includes sixty-two Letraset mesostic constructions taken from syllables and words from Cunningham's *Changes: Notes on Choreography* and thirty-two other books used by Cunningham. Based on the name Merce Cunningham, Cage uses "seven hundred different typefaces" meant to ideographically image Cunningham the dancer. Other mesostics appear throughout the collection. Mesostics subsequently dominate Cage's next books, *Themes and Variations*, *Empty Words*, and *X*.

Cage's mesostics and the "writings through" *(Finnegans Wake, The Cantos)* follow various rules established for each piece. Chance is of course essential to the process of composition.

[*M*, p. 108]

This by now twenty-year-old practice of writing mesostic texts, writings without syntax, and syllable/sound-text constructions (from *Mureau* to *Mouyce*) marks a profound remaking for Cage—and any reader. For, although the early writings intimate radical possibilities, Cage's game changes substantially when he chooses to forgo logically developed texts, ignore ordinary syntactical relations, write almost exclusively in the mesostic form, and intentionally compose sound/text compositions. If reading Cage previously was fraught with self-consciousness, A-effects and an aura of complexity, this turn toward letterism, vocables, and vertical schematics goes further in undermining thorough or nondiscursive readings.

There are several points to be made regarding the page, letters, and Cage's "rewritings" since *M.* The most obvious physical change in Cage's newer texts and books is the presence of the whiteness of the page. It dominates. Mesostics, like unattended scrabble games, lay on pages. The whiteness, with all its imperfections, wraps around the oddly constructed ideograms and thickset letters of the Cunningham mesostics. In the 8 ½" x 11" format of *Themes and Variations,* the text skitters up and down the center of each page like individually planted corn stalks. In *Empty Words* reproductions of Thoreau's drawings are scratched alongside the frail typeset lettering; and in "Writing for the Second Time through *Finnegans Wake*" punctuation, like small blemishes, are flecked through the pages. By contrast, *Mureau* and *Mouyce* are printed in dense, nonparagraphed, nonjustified form so that the white margins function as tailored borders around the formal rectangular blocks of letters.

In previous writings, blank spaces and whiteness were intended to signify pauses, breaths, or specific temporal divisons, as in "Composition as Process—I. Changes."[24] Concerning the layout of "Lecture on Commitment," Cage indicates "The typography is an attempt to provide changes for the eye similar to the changes varying tempi in oral delivery give to the ear."[25] The earlier texts were, in effect, more like scores. But, after *M,* the whiteness is irregular and purely spatial. It is part of the aleatory numerical/geometric plan. (And oddly in accord with a theory of writing put forth in Borges's story "The Library of Babel." Borges's narrator conjectures that the reason for so many chaotic books in the "universe (which others call the Library)" is that the originators of writing merely endlessly manipulated twenty-five signs comprised of twenty-two letters, a period, a comma, and a space.[26]

Cage's writing after *M* is more for the eye and for the thought and pleasure of the reader. Stripped of its temporal require-

turNing the paper
intO
a space of Time
imperfections in the pAper upon which
The
musIc is written
the music is there befOre
it is writteN

[*X*, p. 136]

ments, the whiteness of the page accumulates other meanings and uses. The rectangular shape of the margins in ordinary books is a space where the reader can duplicate the text: marginalia is, in a sense, a scribbling that mimics the printed page. Cage thus opens up other possibilities for the reader, both physically and conceptually.

Mallarmé, exquisitely, says something similar: "To seek support, according to the page, upon the blank space, which inaugurates it, upon oneself, for an ingenuousness . . . and, when, in a break—the slightest, disseminated—chance is aligned, conquered word by word, indefectibly the white blank returns, a moment ago gratuitous, certain now, to conclude that nothing beyond and to authenticate the silence—"[27]

In Cage's writings, the extensive whiteness is transformed simultaneously into background and covering, landscape and dreamscape, emptiness and plenitude, space and shape. And, most forcefully, the whiteness reveals the formal schematics of the texts (mesostics and "writings through") and thereby isolates the printed forms as what they are: lines, marks, patterns; mere movements of the hand, tool, and ink; writings as visual structures—signifiers cut loose from referents and, possibly, meaning. Writing as gesture, nothing more.

Visually, in most printings, the mesostic form focuses the eye on the word or name in the center of the image. It creates a readerly movement down the page, and, secondarily, from left to right. This movement of the eye vertically adds a hitherto unacknowledged geometry (for Western readers): the crease or fold in the middle of two pages is replicated by the spine of letters of the mesostics, which are echoed and enclosed by the edges of the pages on either side. There are thus five "lines" down the center of the pages of the open book (five is the number Cage, repeating Buckminster Fuller, feels is the number of ideas one should use to begin to solve problems).[28] The two strings of the mesostics figuratively double each other as well as the centerfold between pages. There are also four white spaces, two per page, surrounding the writing. The forms of the pages with centered mesostics increase the reader's awareness of Cage's process of doubling and repetition.

In practice, Cage's mesostics are nearly always extended compositions on names or concepts long familiar to him, and the repetition within the mesostic follows certain patterns. This persistence of doublings and repetitions in the (re) writings since *M*, along with the expansion of whiteness and the return to the letter, suggest that Cage's writings are actually readings, of himself, or of himself reading others (Joyce, etc.). These readings—silent performances—ultimately position Cage where readers of his works have been since the beginning: amidst uncertainty and self-referencing, yet surrounded by familiar names and recognizable ideas. In *Themes and Variations,* Cage cites as one of his themes, "Importance of being perplexed. Unpredictability" and also observes "Influence derives from one's own work (not from outside it)."[29]

But while Cage is reading/performing Cage, what of his readers? The "writings through" Pound and Joyce in recent mesostics border on cryptic indulgence and, with regard to conventional meaning, seem opaque. Reading Cage of late (since *M*) is more problematic than ever because none of the questions raised by earlier texts are resolved while others are being posed. And, to complicate matters, as he notes in "Composition in Retrospect" (1981):

<pre>
            My
          mEmory
       of whaT
              Happened
          is nOt
   what happeneD

          i aM struck
         by thE
          facT
            tHat what happened
         is mOre conventional
   than what i remembereD
</pre>

[*X*, p. 124]

Yet, curiously, there is a resonant quality about this work—something paradoxically evocative of ancient poetic impulses and postmodern mysteries. It is as if Cage's selfless, disciplined, thorough pursuits have resulted in the production of texts that so literally "exemplify" themselves as to create the extraordinary—purely Cagean—condition of reading that, like silence, is nonreading. Thus, Cage's "theme": "Problems of music (vision) only solved when silence (non-vision) is taken as the basis"[30] can be reformulated as: Problems of reading (meaning) only solved when nonreading (meaninglessness) is taken as the basis. Or, to say it another way: "Poetry is having nothing to say and saying it; we possess nothing."[31] Saying nothing is of course not simple, as attested to by many characters in the works of Samuel Beckett, one of whom, Malone, drily remarks "Nothing is more real than nothing."[32]

For readers of John Cage, nonreading is a consequence of reading, just as listeners to his music encounter silence. Cage's later writings distill and rarify the performance of writing/reading to a point of utter density: a black hole within which all the physics of the Cagean universe simultaneously hold true and are questionable. For both Cage and readers, nonreading is readings' dumb show: a performance that verges on meaning, where signs are ultimately themselves, isolated, yet as full as Cagean silence.

Cage insinuates the reader into nonreading by seizing on a writing process that identifies the atoms, the ABCs, of the writing system and reveals their negative charge. For Cage and readers, the letters of the alphabet literally become the formal units of practice/process/performance. Letters: a script in mime that is both a sign of itself and the source of other meanings.

The alphabet. Alphabets order sound and signs; they are social and intellectual tools that contribute to the possibilities of shared meaning. The use of an alphabet is, for Cage, a way of employing a system of notation not unlike musical notation—given that the vocalization of the sounds of letters have, of course, a different value and relationship than pitches. (The ancient Egyptian myth of the god Treuth, related by Socrates in Plato's *Philebus,* interrestingly relates how both the alphabet and musical intervals were selected and ordered from the sounds in nature.)

> To raise language's
> temperature we not only remove syntax: we
> give each letter undivided attention,
> setting it in unique face and size;
> to read becomes the verb to sing.
>
> [*M,* p. 107]

> The mechanism of the I Ching, on the other
> hand is utility.   Applied to
> letters and aggregates of letters, it
> brings about a language that can be
> enjoyed without being understood.
>
> [*M,* p. 215]

Cage's use of the alphabet assumes two forms, with many variations. In works such as *Empty Words* and the "writings through," he employs chance operations to select syllables and individual letters. In the mesostics, the letters of selected names, arranged vertically, become the structure for the text. In both cases, individual letters retain their visual and phonetic character.

Cage has written why he chose to write in the mesostic form, an alphabetic reduction: "Due to N. O. Brown's remark that syntax is the arrangement of the army, and Thoreau's that when he heard a sentence he heard feet marching, I became devoted to nonsyntactical "demilitarized" language."[33] Apparently he missed McLuhan's analysis of alphabets in *Understanding Media,* although he does note in "Seriously Comma"[34] that McLuhan says that the inflexibility of the order of the alphabet made the Renaissance inevitable. But McLuhan elaborates, arriving at the conclusion that the alphabet created a new literacy and a sense of individuality accessible to everyone. When the language of the tribe broke down, clans separated and travel between language-distinct regions was facilitated. This, he noted, enhanced those who sought power and the "freedom to shape an individual career manifested itself in the ancient world in military life."[35]

The alphabetic writings derive from names or other texts, and elusively refer to their predecessors. Cage ingeniously taunts readers with the possibility that his reductions offer yet another method for reading Joyce, Thoreau, or others. His processes, not far removed from certain computer analyses of linguistic structures in texts, raise questions about how we read and understand literary works.

Cage's alphabets are approaches to reading *and* writing. Like a minimalist Pierre Menard (a character in a Borges story who successfully "writes" *Don Quixote* in 1934 by writing the exact words from *Don Quixote*), Cage recycles all that he has read and written *by the letters,* as if they retained a mystical or coded meaning.

Perhaps they do. For the notion of the alphabet holds other significations for Cage. A longish lecture/performance mesostic titled "James Joyce, Marcel Duchamp, Erik Satie: An Alphabet" (1981) begins with Cage's comment that "It is possible to imagine that the artists whose work we live with constitute not a vocabulary but an alphabet by means of which we spell our lives."[36]

He amplifies this statement with references to the poetry of Jackson MacLow, whose work he has known for many years. MacLow, Cage remarks, has many vocabularies "restricting each to the letters to be found in the name of a particular friend."[37] Cage then recounts the effects of Joyce, Satie, and Duchamp on his life and work. He explains how he came to write their names as mesostics and, for this work, thematically bring them "on stage" as ghosts. He also quite pointedly states that he has never understood the work of Duchamp or Joyce.

Nonunderstanding is nearly a Cagean axiom, though it neither restricts him from thought or work. As a response to "not understanding" his teachers, Cage sets their names in mesostic form, as alphabets, and pursues "a way of writing which though coming from ideas is not about them; or is not about ideas but produces them."[38]

Cage's writing process is directed toward liberating him from conscious choice while imposing discipline. He has said as much and there is little to argue with in Cage's adoption of "Eastern" techniques for both "freeing the self" and not pursuing "self-expression." Cage's specific "alphabetic" method, however, not only reminds one of ancient disciplines but it is curiously postmodern. His practices are reminiscent of the mysteries of incantation and the decidedly conscious postmodern practice of writing intertextually.

Many of Cage's mesostics are based on the names of individuals. This form of "alphabeting" is analogous to the peculiar process of "anagramatic" writing explored by linguist and phoneticist Ferdinand de Saussure. This investigation, never published by Saussure, is recollected and enclosed within a commentary by Jean Starobinski in a small book titled *Words Upon Words*.

Briefly, while studying Saturnian Latin poetry, Saussure realized that each text seems to contain a "theme-word" which provides the poet with a phonemic source for the writing of the poem. Anagrams, as he designated these words, were generally names of gods, rulers, friends, or lovers. In effect, the letters of the poem's "theme-word" functioned as the structure for a given poem. This practice, Saussure notes, occurs in Vedic poetry where there is often a "reproduction in a hymn of the syllables of the sacred name which is the object of the hymn." He also conjectures that Indo-European poetry might have conformed to a process "invoked in relation to superstitious fixation on a letter."[39]

Saussure develops his theory by diligently counting (à la Cage) the repetition of syllables and letters of anagrams in poems. In the course of his work, he recognizes that it is possible that anagrams do exist, not only in the poems he analyzes but in all texts—simply by the chance occurrence of the letters and sounds of any given word or name. He is also troubled by the fact that he cannot locate any written rule that instructs poets to employ anagrams.

In Starobinski's reflections, he suggests, in accordance with Cage, that the strict adherence to a method leads to a condition not of self-expression but "literary production," as opposed to "literary creation." He comments further on the "inspiration" provided by "theme-words" or magic names. In concluding arguments, he addresses notions of nonintention, antecedent words, and the poet's silence: themes directly relevant to Cage's activities for decades.

Cage's alphabets—even those, as in "Composition in Retrospect," that are based on words (discipline, method, etc.)—provide a contemporary exemplification for the theorizing of Saussure and Starobinski. Cage has always attempted to avoid self-expression and deliberation by the ego. His choice of influences both satisfies the dynamics in his personal pantheon and, subtly, inspires him to produce new work. The fact that Cage is absolutely overt about his practice, unlike the Latin poets, promotes it as an object lesson. This exposure and focused attention to the facts of his writerly performance also marks the postmodern direction of Cage's writing.

Several qualities identify postmodern texts: they are performative, self-conscious, open-ended, process-oriented, self-referential, polyvalent, combinatory, dialogic. Cage's texts, taken as a whole, fulfill all these criteria. The postmodern text also recognizes itself as one text among many, part of the circularity and intertextuality of all writing. Cage's Duchampian obviousness about his sources and references underscores this proclivity. Moreover, several of Cage's sources are themselves postmodern in their referentiality, notably Joyce, Brown, McLuhan. And Cage, like Borges, Calvino, Raymond Federman, and so many others, rereads himself: a double performance for the reader who finds himself reading through Cage-reading-Cage.

Cage's writings, readings, performances—and silences—seem, finally, to curve back upon themselves. Letters, scattered or structured on the page, chance selections from other texts, the whitenesses and *italicizations* are warped and woven together as language to be "enjoyed without being understood":[40] readings for nonreading, texts for nothing, indeterminate, nonintentional performances of silence in silence.

What, then, can a reading of Cage be? Nothing but a ceaseless series of performances, perhaps in silence, bounded by uncertainty: nonreading without goals or meaning? Pure play!

For this reader/ing a response is embedded in an untitled poem in *X* (*X*, incidentally, was a letter picked by chance, but, no matter, its significations are enormous) and Starobinski's last two sentences in *Words Upon Words* (p. 123). The poem is about readers, as is the quotation.[41]

```
                    if you exi ted
                       becauSe
                  we mIght go on as before
          but since you don't we wi'Ll
                      mak
                     ehangE
                   our miNds
                     anar hic
               so that we Can
                     d to          let it be
                convertEnjoy the chaos/that you are/
                                    stet
```

[*X,* p. 117]

"But the poet, having said all he has to say, remains strangely silent. One can produce any hypothesis about him: he neither accepts nor rejects it."

Notes

1. Jacques Derrida, *Dissemination,* trans. Barbara Johnson (Chicago: University of Chicago Press, 1981), p. 175.

2. Jorge Luis Borges, *In Praise of Darkness,* trans. Norman Thomas di Giovanni (London: Penguin Books, 1975), p. 121.

3. John Cage, *Silence: Lectures and Writings* (Middletown, Conn.: Wesleyan University Press, 1961), p. 146.

4. John Cage, *Themes and Variations* (Barrytown, N.Y.: Station Hill Press, 1982), introduction.

5. Cage, Lecture on Nothing," *Silence,* p. 109.

6. Cage, *Themes and Variations,* introduction.

7. John Cage, *Empty Words: Writings '73–'78* (Middletown, Conn.: Wesleyan University Press, 1979), p. 51.

8. *Brecht on Theater,* ed. and trans. John Willett (New York: Hill and Wang, 1957), p. 135; and *Silence,* p. ix.

9. John Cage, *A Year from Monday: New Lectures and Writings* (Middletown, Conn.: Wesleyan University Press, 1967), p. 133.

10. See Cage, *Year from Monday,* p. 73 and *Empty Words,* p. 99.

11. Richard Kostelanetz, *The Old Poetries and the New* (Ann Arbor: University of Michigan Press, 1981), p. 263.

12. Cage, *Empty Words,* p. 51.

13. Geoffrey Hartman, *Saving the Text* (Baltimore: The Johns Hopkins University Press, 1981), p. 9.

14. Cage, *Empty Words,* p. 33.

15. Cage, *Year from Monday,* p. 3.

16. Cage, *Silence,* p. 96.

17. Ibid., p. 26.

18. John Cage, *X: Writings '79–'82* (Middletown, Conn.: Wesleyan University Press, 1983), p. 173.

19. Cage, *Silence,* p. 35.

20. Cage, *Themes and Variations,* p. 5.

21. *For the Birds* (John Cage in Conversation with Daniel Charles), trans. Richard Gardner (Salem, N.H.: Boyars, 1981), p. 117.

22. Cage, *Empty Words,* p. 136.

23. John Cage, *M: Writings '67–'72* (Middletown, Conn.: Wesleyan University Press, 1973), foreword.

24. Cage, *Silence*, p. 18.

25. Cage, *Year from Monday*, p. 112.

26. Jorge Luis Borges, *Ficciones*, ed. and trans. Anthony Kerrigan (New York: Grove Press, 1962), pp. 79–80.

27. Derrida, *Dissemination*, p. 178.

28. Cage, *Themes and Variations*, introduction.

29. Ibid.

30. Ibid.

31. Ibid.

32. Samuel Beckett, *Three Novels: Molloy, Malone Dies, The Unnamable* (New York: Grove Press, 1955), p. 192.

33. Cage, *Empty Words*, p. 133.

34. Cage, *Year from Monday*, p. 26.

35. Marshall McLuhan, *Understanding Media: The Extensions of Man* (New York: New American Library, 1964), p. 90.

36. Cage, *X*, p. 53.

37. Ibid.

38. Cage, *Themes and Variations*, introduction.

39. Jean Starobinski, *Words Upon Words: The Anagrams of Ferdinand de Saussure*, trans. Olivia Emmet (New Haven: Yale University Press, 1979), pp. 22 and 24.

40. Cage, *M*, p. 215.

41. This paper was written with support from the Pennsylvania Council on the Arts (Visual Arts Panel) and I wish to express my thanks to the Council.

Bucknell Review gratefully acknowledges Wesleyan University Press for its permission to reproduce the selections from its publications by John Cage.

John with Losa   New York, 1987

Detroit, ca. 1916

Detroit, ca. 1921

passport photographs, ca. 1950

at the piano in his Grand Street apartment
in New York   ca. 1948–49

preparing a piano

ca. 1947

Stony Point, New York, ca. 1954–55

with Marcel and Tenny Duchamp in the only   Toronto, 1968
performance of *Reunion*

Moves on an electronically prepared chess board
trigger a group of continuously activated sound
systems.

with Zen philosopher Daisetz T. Suzuki   Kamakura, Japan, Fall 1962

Cage had attended his lectures at Columbia University
between 1945 and 1947.

with Toshi Ichiyanagi and David Tudor   Kamakura, Japan, Fall 1962

at the Ryoanji Garden   Kyoto, Japan, Fall 1962

photograph SOPHIE BAKER

in a restaurant in Milan at a party in his honor, ca. 1975–76

preparing a macrobiotic feast for his friend
Louise Nevelson in his Bank Street apartment
in New York

April 1977

cooking in his West 18th Street apartment

November 1986

with Merce Cunningham   late 1960s

photograph HANS WILD, courtesy C. F. Peters Corporation

at the Cabrillo Music Festival   Aptos, California, August 1977
(that year in his honor)

photograph BETTY FREEMAN

on the roof of the Embassy Theater   Los Angeles, March 1987

photograph BETTY FREEMAN

with *Bucknell Review* editors   New York, May 1987
William Duckworth
and Richard Fleming

photograph GENE BAGNATO

at his computer in his West 18th Street
apartment

New York, 1987

The art work on the left wall is by William Anastasi;
the work on the right is by Lois Long.

in front of one of several views from his
West 18th Street apartment

New York, 1987

performing *4'33"* in Cologne   August 1986

photograph MANFRED LEVE

The background—a series of German swearwords—
is a canvas by German painter Sigmar Polke.

"John Cage"

A Lecture by Norman O. Brown

at Wesleyan University, February 22-7, 1988

With all due honor and gratitude to the genial spirit of Neely Bruce
and the fresh young folk his fellow-workers

The only true begetter of this occasion is Richard Winslow
Professor of Music all the time that I remember
who, in the 1950's, in the deep sleep of the Eisenhower era,
had the wit to see that music at Wesleyan could be different
and took steps to introduce new wine into this old bottle.

John Cage tells the story how his mother, on being informed that
Wesleyan University had invited him to their Center for the Humanities,
asked, Did they know you were a Zen Buddhist?

They didn't know anything.

The rest is history

Which is hard to tell.

Not wanting to speak about John Cage
my nightmare last December:

I was bringing bouquets of flowers to John Cage in the midst of a vast
audience, students writing earnest essays of appreciation; I was rifling
desperately through pages of unmanageable notes, undigested bits and
pieces, facing the last minute necessity for extemporaneous speech and
knowing it was beyond my powers; waking up from the nightmare thinking of Morton Feldman's story:

I was walking up to see if John was at home. I met Richard Lippold the
sculptor who was living next door to John. He just looked at me and said,
I'm moving. I have to get out of here. John is just too persuasive.   TriQ, 141

That isn't the right reaction, either.
It's too late to run away.
I have to stand and face, or fight

I don't think it is true that nothing is accomplished by listening to a piece
of music.
The events of this week will bear me out.
Our ears will be in much better condition.   S, xii

Music is movement
a dialectical confrontation with the course of time

The origin of civilization
How to Start a New Civilization

With this lyre Orpheus, Amphion, founded the humanity of Greece   Vico, §615

a tale of stem or stone
to move these hearts of stone

We must fetch it from the stones of Deucalion and Pyrrha, from the rocks
of Amphion, from the hard oak of Vergil.   Vico, §338

Obliterating the distinction between sounds and things and people
to get things moving
All lives, all dances, & all is loud.   Rothenberg

Let's not quibble about emotions
the thing is to keep moving
                    not without emotion

The power to move
the making of music is inevitably, will he nill he, an exercise of power
to move these stones

Like Stefan Wolpe's Battle Piece
it makes you tremble; it overwhelms you with its power   FTB, 123
or John Cage's Atlas Borealis with the Ten Thunderclaps
hearing it will be more like going to a storm than like going to a concert.   R, 81

Amphion, or the Pied Piper
a different drummer
will you, won't you, will you, won't you, come and join the dance

To remould people to their very souls, revolutionize their thinking   M, 00

I will destroy the existing order of things, which parts this one mankind
into hostile nations, into powerful and weak, privileged and outcast, rich
and poor; for it makes unhappy men of all. I will destroy the order of
things that turns millions into slaves of a few, and these few into slaves of
their own might, own riches. I will destroy this order of things, that cuts
enjoyment off from labor.   Attali, 11-2

That's Wagner, in 1848
the same year as the Communist Manifesto
and in A Year From Monday :
Our proper work now if we love mankind and the world we live in is
revolution.   YFM, ix

Can we hear the crisis of society in the crisis of music
Cage's music, socially sensitive seismograph in the tradition of Beethoven
and Schoenberg
Beethoven and the French Revolution, Schoenberg and the Golden Calf

Harmony, the repressive principle of the real   Attali, 83
for the past century in a process of disintegration   S, 63
we strip off the decent drapery of Western Civilization
and discover Noise.

Cage's music is prophetic, and it is not saying that every day is a beautiful
day--   S, 41

Have you here? (Some ha) Have we where? (Some hant) Have you
hered? (Others do) Have we whered? (Others dont) It's cumming, it's
brumming! The clip, the clop! (All cla) Glass crash. The (klikkaklak-
kaklaskaklopatzklatschabattacreppycrottygraddaghsemmihsammihnouith-
appluddyappladdypkonpkot!).   FW, 44

It is not true that noises escape power   FTB, 230
noises, not an extension of the palette of sounds available for aesthetic appreciation
noise is the primordial violence out of which civilization is made   Attali, 24
the original thunder, as in Finnegans Wake .

Civilization originates in thunder
Hexagram 16. Yü/Enthusiasm
Thunder comes resounding out of the earth:
The image of ENTHUSIASM.
Thus the ancient kings made music.

The image of enthusiasm
the name of the god is Dionysus

To Greet the Return of the Gods

Dionysus is Noisy
the Greek word is <u>Bromios</u> , from the same root as <u>Bronte</u> , meaning
thunder
It's cumming, it's brumming!
HCE is that Brontoicthyan form
Yoh! Brontolone slaaps, yoh snoores. Upon Benn Heather   FW, 7

Noise is violence
never more so than in a John Cage concert, violating our ears
our ears are not now in excellent condition

Noise is noisome, nuisance; nauseous, noxious; Italian <u>noxa</u> meaning
dung;
noise pollution

The pollution that purifies
our ears are now in excellent condition
something is accomplished by hearing John Cage's music

Listening to noise is a little like being killed.   Attali, 28
Naturally, we don't set out to kill ourselves.   EW, 179
We do not mean to, but we do.
Some one is always getting killed
Civilization is an altar on which a sacrifice is being made

As in <u>Finnegans Wake</u>
What we are learning is how to be convivial   EW, 179
But, "Where Are We Eating? and What Are We Eating?"   EW, 79

Grampupus is fallen down but grinny sprids the boord. Whase on the joint
of a desh? Finfoefom the Fush. Whase be his baken head? A loaf of
Singpantry's Kennedy bread.   FW, 7

Yes, that's Senator Kennedy. It happens again and again.

Conviviality is Eucharistic, and
Eucharist is cannibalistic.

Volhardt and Jensen have shown this very clearly; the killing and devour-
ing of sows at festivals, eating the first fruits when tubers are harvested,
are *an eating of the divine body, exactly as it is eaten at cannibal feasts.*   Eliade, 102

Violence and the Sacred   Girard
For the vegetable world to continue man must kill and be killed.
Violence is vital, is life itself
The name of the god is Dionysus

The violence of history
Dionysos in Amerika
the violence of history in which John Cage has been an actor
"The History of Experimental Music in the United States":

"Why, if everything is possible, do we concern ourselves with history (in
other words with a sense of what is necessary to be done at a particular
time?" And I would answer, "In order to thicken the plot." In this view,
then, all those interpenetrations which seem at first glance to be hellish--
history, for instance, if we are speaking of experimental music--are to be
espoused. One does not then make just any experiment but does what
must be done. By this I mean one does not seek by his actions to arrive at
money but does what must be done; one does not seek by his actions to
arrive at fame (success) but does what must be done; one does not seek by
his actions to provide pleasure to the senses (beauty) but does what must
be done; one does not seek by his actions to arrive at the establishing of a
school (truth) but does what must be done. One does something else.   S, 68

We do what the times require
we do that untimely thing, something else, that is necessary in order to
renew the times
to get things moving

We live in historical time: the process is history
we submit to the yoke of historical necessity
It is by reason of this fact that we are made perfect by what happens to us
rather than by what we do
(Meister Eckhart quoted in Silence)   S, 64
We suffer history

The enormous tragedy of the dream in the peasant's bent shoulders   Pound, 425

We submit to the yoke of historical necessity
madness follows, another throw of the dice
our lives are historical wagers

What must be done has nothing to do with improving the world, or mak-
ing life a success for everybody
It is space and emptiness that is finally urgently necessary at this point of
history   S, 70
Space, Emptiness, Void, Nothing
This nihilism is not ours to say how much
Dionysus, the god of exuberant vitality, is also the god of death.
All those interpenetrations which seem at first glance to be hellish are to
be espoused.

Cage quotes Sri Ramakrishna, "Why, if God is good, is there evil in the world? In order to thicken the plot."

But we are not God
nor is God writing fiction for our entertainment
or for his own entertainment
as in King Lear , or Homer's Iliad :
As flies to wanton boys, are we to the gods;
They kill us for their sport.

There is no spectator, or artist, or aesthete, God
there is only the suffering god
Dionysus
the identity of the god, the victim, and the priest
the process is all one (sacrificial) fire
in one body
in which we are all expendable, combustible material.

At the end of "The History of Experimental Music in the United States" Cage for the first and last time writes a vision of the historical process as in one body:

History is the story of original actions.... That one sees that the human race is one person (all of its members parts of the same body, brothers-- not in competition any more than hand is in competition with eye) enables him to see that originality is necessary, for there is no need for eye to do what hand so well does. In this way, the past and the present are to be observed and each person makes what he alone must make, bringing for the whole of human society into existence a historical fact, and then, on and on, in continuum and discontinuum.   S, 75

That was Cage in 1959.
Cage quotes Daisetz Teitaro Suzuki as saying of a certain monk who figured in the history of Chinese Buddhism, "He lived in the ninth or the tenth century." He added, after a pause, "Or the eleventh century, or the twelfth or thirteenth century or the fourteenth."   S, 67

This is Zen Buddhism as a screen of indifference to temporality and history.
But Cage in 1959 is not the same as Cage in 1974
Happenings are in history

In the later Cage, "The Future of Music" (1974),   EW, 177-87
there is a cure for tragedy
we know all we need to know about Oedipus, Prometheus, Hamlet
what we are learning is the pleasures of conviviality
the text ends with the word "cheerful."
The minds and spirits of people are changing. The change is not disruptive. It is cheerful.   EW, 187

Not disruptive but cheerful.
That is to say, not Dionysian but Apollonian.

What comes after tragedy?
In Buddhism the idea of tragedy doesn't really exist. In order to have
tragedy you have to have a separation of gods and man. Whereas the
world can only be viewed as comedy when you see gods and men as being
together.   R, 79

Cage knows that after tragedy comes Finnegans Wake .
But Finnegans Wake is not a comedy, it is a farce
his farced epistol to the hibruws.   FW, 228

History is not a bourgeois comedy with a happy ending. It is something
more sinister, a farce.
That most enlightened moment in Karl Marx, the opening of The
Eighteenth Brumaire of Louis Bonaparte : "Hegel says somewhere that,
upon the stage of universal history, all great events and personalities reappear in one fashion or another. He forgot to add that on the first occasion,
they appear as tragedy; on the second, as farce."

Two bloody Irishmen in a bloody fight over bloody nothing.
Farce is nihilism.
We are slowly getting nowhere and it is a farce.   S, 109-126
In Nowhere has yet the Whole World taken part of himself for his
            Wife;
By Nowhere have Poorparents been sentenced to Worms, Blood and
            Thunder for Life   FW, 175

An interlude of farce or fooling   CT, 41-63
in the ginnandgo gap between antediluvious and annadominant   FW, 14
Saturnalia, season of unbridled license
interludes of impromptu buffoonery interpolated by the actors in the
litergy or sacred dramas
Carnival, or Feast of Fools
jest jibberweek's joke.   FW, 565

Even the Mass was burlesqued
Sometimes an ass was brought into the Church; solemn Mass was punc-
tuated with brays and howls, the priest braying three times and the congregation responding.

Noise is king
or Carnival is King
a Roaratorio
or Donnybrook fair
Louis Mink's Finnegans Wake Gazetteer : This fair, held in August every
year from 1204 to 1855, was noted for its bacchanalian orgies and light-
hearted rioting. The village was a mile and a half south-east of Dublin,
and is now one of its suburbs.
Donnybrook fair; or Donnerbruch Fire; or Donkeybrook Fear

Convivial joviality becomes the shoutmost shoviality; and then the
eatmost boviality.   FW, 58
The beast has got to get into the act

Finnegans Wake is a farce or satyr play
after tragedy comes the satyr play
we go back to the original Dionysian goat-song out of which both tragedy
and comedy arose
prehistoric horse-play
Tragoedia = goat-song
Finnegans Wake, that tragoady thundersday   FW, 5
that fishabed ghoatstory   FW, 51
HCE is Hircus Civis Eblanensis, old goat citizen of Dublin   FW, 215
Giles Goat-Boy is his American offspring
got by the one goat, suckled by the same nanna, one twitch, one nature
makes us oldworld kin.   FW, 463

Nietzsche: What does that synthesis of god and goat in the satyr mean? I
estimate the value of human beings, or races, according to the necessity
with which they cannot conceive of the god apart from the satyr.   EH, 939, 842

Superman has got to be subhuman.

When they brought the ass into Church, they sang the Magnificat , Mary's
response to the Annunciation:
My soul doth magnify the Lord, and my spirit hath rejoiced in God my
Saviour.
He hath put down the mighty from their seats, and exalted them of low
degree.

Perhaps the final conflict will be as it was in the beginning
the battle between Carnival and Lent
a confrontation between rational regimentation from above, and spontaneous movement from below

Carnival and Lent
or Nietzsche's last word: Dionysus versus Christ.

As the masters of illusion intensify their nightly show on TV
With futurist onehorse balletbattle pictures and the Pageant of Past History worked up with animal variations amid everglaning mangrovemazes
and beorbtracktors by Messrs Thud and Blunder. Shadows by the film
folk, masses by the good people.   FW, 221
Dionysus will inspire their Satanic opposites
everything must be done in reverse order
to lead from disguised to patent nonsense   LB, 245

Ritual clowns in primitive religion
masters of shocking stunts, reverse behavior, and backwards speech
the inversion and retrograde forms Cage celebrates in "Composition in
Retrospect," 1981
I need not remind you what God spells backwards

Something of the 60's will reappear
Abbie Hoffman clowning
Ken Kesey clowning
of these the most original was John Cage   FTB, 229

Dionysos in Amerika
jamborees for the electronic soul   Griffiths, 40
Hip champouree! Hiphip champouree!   FW, 236
The wild man from Borneo has just come to town
One stands, given a grain of goodwill, a fair chance of actually seeing the
whirling dervish, Tumult, son of Thunder.   FW, 184

Not disruptive. Cheerful.
Not Dionysian. Apollonian.
I can't improve on Nietzsche

John Cage said in 1979 that from the late forties he has steadfastly maintained that the purpose of music is to sober and quiet the mind, thus making it susceptible to divine influences.   R, 159

Sobriety and quietness, the essence of Apollonian discipline; the opposite
of Dionysian drunkenness.
Discipline, a reiterated vertebral word in Cage's mesostic "Composition in
Retrospect."

Nietzsche says the word Dionysian means the urge to unity, a reaching out
beyond personality, a passionate-painful overflowing; the great pantheistic
principle of solidarity and sharing; the eternal will to procreation, fertility,
recurrence; the assertion of the necessary unity of creation and destruction.   WP, #1050

Apollonian means the urge to perfect the separate life of the individual, to
compensate for the pain of separate individuality with the seductive pleasures of aesthetic enjoyment.

There is the Dionysian energy to change the world, creative destruction,
and there is the Apollonian consciousness haunted by the question, Is Life
worth Living,
--Thoreau, Cage says, did have a question: Is life worth living?--   EW, 3
and finding in aesthetic enjoyment reasons to give an affirmative and
cheerful answer.
We open our eyes and ears seeing life each day excellent as it is.   YFM, 146

John Cage's sunny disposition is the mark of the natural-born Apollonian
Apollo is the shining one, the god of light
his eye must be sun-like, Nietzsche says, the pure undimmed eye of day.   BT, 954, 978

Apollo is the god of boundaries, of definitions, of separations, of clear and
distinct ideas.
I tend to separate things, says John.
"We wondered if you could talk a little about food, perhaps in the bigger
sense."
When you say food in the bigger sense, I think of Nobby's beautiful book
Love's Body . It has to do with the body and of course with all these
things like eating, the functions of the body being like the functions of
society. So he thinks of reading, and reading is like eating too. All the
sense perceptions. It gets very very mixed up between what you would
call spiritual and physical so that it's all one thing. I tend to... I think this
is the influence of Indian thought on me... but I tend to separate things, so
that I would prefer to cross the street successfully rather than thinking of it
as some form of eating. I like to look at each situation as having its own
characteristics, and acting appropriately to each, rather than going in this
way which I think comes from the Germans, the idea that everything is
one thing.   TGGIS, 16

This is that hearty Zen Buddhist wisdom which says when farting fart,
there's nothing to it;
forget the paradoxes of the Freudian Unconscious
forget the puns in Finnegans Wake .

But it is not true that men are men and mountains are mountains
riverrun, past Eve and Adam's, from swerve of shore to bend of bay,
brings us by a commodius vicus of recirculation back to Howth Castle and
Environs   FW, 3
HCE, man-mountain

Men are not men, as any feminist can tell you
in Finnegans Wake , the first riddle of the universe: asking, when is a man
not a man?   FW, 170

We go with Finnegans Wake rather than Suzuki.

In that Dionysian body in which we are all members of one body
things are necessarily confused
ordinary language is always wrong
we do not want to recover our sanity

What a mnice old mness it all mnakes!   FW, 19

It is not true that each thing is itself and not another thing
It is not true that sounds are sounds and people are people
All lives, all dances, & all is loud.

Chance operations are an Apollonian procedure
a perfectly sober procedure
the Apollonian "I" remains in control
"I ask the questions"

In "Composition in Retrospect" (1981), a mesostic rosary of guiding principles

```
                    the prInciple
        underlying all of the Solutions
                        aCts
                          In the question that is asked
                  as a comPoser
                  i shouLd
                        gIve up
                     makiNg
                     choicEs


                          Devote myself
                     to askIng
                        queStions
                           Chance
                     determIned
              answers'll oPen
              my mind to worLd around                                    X, 132
```

The Apollonian, says Nietzsche, in the midst of the dance remain what
they are and retain their civic name
Just as in a stormy sea, unbounded in every direction, rising and falling
with howling mountainous waves, a sailor sits in a boat and trusts in his
frail barque.   BT, 989, 954

And the results of chance operations are univocal and unambiguous, not
polysemous speaking with tongues as in Finnegans Wake .

To ensure indeterminacy with respect to its performance, a composition
must be determinate of itself. If this indeterminacy is to have a non-
dualistic nature, each element of the notation must have a single
interpretation rather than a plurality of interpretations.   S, 38

Everything is taken literally, even the silence

Instead of symbolism--in a Symbol there is concealment and yet revelation: here therefore, by Silence and by Speech acting together, comes a
double significance--   LB, 190
instead of words of silent power, the impossibility of language   FW, 345

Writing for the Fifth Time through Finnegans Wake
getting rid of the syntax
getting rid of the cadence
getting rid of the puns

Getting rid of all those other voices
Really it is not I who am writing this crazy book. It is you, and you, and
you, and that man over there, and that girl at the next table.
All those other voices speaking as one voice
in Pentecostal confusion.

Chance operations avoid real uncertainty
the negative capability of being in uncertainties, mysteries, doubts, and
darkness

The results of chance operations are always impeccable: the experiment
cannot fail
no choice no error no blame

I'd rather be wrong

Many years ago John Cage offered me chance operations as a solution to
my hesitation to publish

I stammered broken heaven-talk in the class-room
To Greet the Return of the Gods
How to Start a New Civilization

But the fragments would not arrange themselves onto a publishable page.
I never hesitated in rejecting chance operations
I am trying to understand why

Chance operations get rid of the hesitation
HCE, hesitency is his middle name
he stutters fore he falls   FW, 139

civilization originates in stuttering
Bygmester Finnegan of the Stuttering Hand   FW, 4
(Balbus babbles, Balbus builder of the Tower of Babel)

things are necessarily confused
we necessarily stammer
half a sylb, helf a solb, holf a salb onward   FW, 292

Broken heaventalk, poetic diction
that ocean
in which the Apollonian ship capsizes

that ocean is the crowd
get lost, in the crowd
Here Comes Everybody
Holiday Crowd Encounter
                    (Bakhtin
                    (Carnival

that ocean is language
the voice of a great multitude
as the voice of many waters
the waters of, hitherandthithering waters of. Night!   FW, 216

The Apollonian discomfort with the crowd:

There is the possibility when people are crowded together that they will
act like sheep rather than nobly. That is why separation in space is spoken
of as facilitating independent action on the part of each performer.   S, 39

The Apollonian principle of separation
Cage's troubles with the orchestra:
I advised them not to listen to each other, and asked each one to play as a
soloist, as if he were the only one in the world.   FTB, 171

The Apollonian ideal of nobility:
I must find a way to let people be free without their becoming foolish. So
that their freedom will make them noble. How will I do this? That is the
question.   YFM, 136

That is not the question in Finnegans Wake .
Finnegans Wake , that farced epistle to the highbrows, is directing us to
rejoin the human race; to the vulgar, the vernacular, the crowd; all the
hoolivans of the nation.   FW, 6

The anarchist dream of the noble individual

But besides Thoreau there is also Whitman
who is a simple separate person
but who is also able to utter the word Democratic, the word En-Masse.
Dionysus is a mass phenomenon.
The Apollonian refusal of the Dionysian rabble:
Not trying to put his emotions into someone else. That way you "rouse
rabbles"; it seems on the surface humane, but it animalizes, and we're not
doing it.   S, 250

The rabble, the revel, the rebel
crowd psychology, mass psychology, is Dionysian psychology
Canetti says: Suddenly it is as though everything were happening in one
and the same body.   Canetti, 16

The mass-line of Chairman Mao will live again
it is as inevitable as mass-production.

John Cage an extreme case of the artist, suffering the contradiction
between Dionysian and Apollonian tendencies
a living oxymoron   TriQ, 223

The extraordinary contradiction between this work and the world around
us
the unresolved dualism in the world around us between the need for
organization (Buckminster Fuller) and the need for freedom (Thoreau)
the same unresolved dualism inside the work of art:

The function of a piece of music is to bring into co-being elements para-
doxical by nature, to bring into one situation elements that can be and
ought to agreed upon--that is, Law elements--together with elements that
cannot and ought not to be agreed upon--that is, Freedom elements.   Griffiths, 12

The contradiction aggravated by his own awareness of the inadequacy of
dualistic thinking:
We open our eyes and ears seeing life each day excellent as it is. Having
this realization we gather our energies in order to make this intolerable
world endurable.   YFM, 146

```
        aCceptance of whatever
           mUst
       be coMplemented
by the refuSal
   of everyThing
          thAt's
           iNtolerable
revolution Can
          nEver
          Stop                                                        X, 151
```

Leaving an ambiguous message:
Everything dissonant, I hear as consonant.   FTB, 78
Making this intolerable world endurable.

Zen Buddhism can become the theory and practice of joyful consumerism:
just an open ear and an open mind and the enjoyment of daily noises.   YFM, 34

And Satie's furniture music can be hard to distinguish from Muzak:

Nevertheless, we must bring about a music which is like furniture--a music, that is, which will be part of the noises of the environment, will take them into consideration. I think of it as melodious, softening the noises of the knives and forks, not dominating them, not imposing itself. It would fill up those heavy silences that sometimes fall between friends dining together. It would spare them the trouble of paying attention to their own banal remarks. And at the same time it would neutralize the street noises which so indiscretely enter into the play of conversation. To make such music would be to respond to a need.   S, 76

A living oxymoron, obstinately reasserting both sides of an unresolved argument, is not yet a dialectical fusion or coincidence of opposites

The fusion of opposites is that "antithetical sense of primal words" which Freud discovered in dreams; which refutes the Apollonian laws of logic and language; which becomes the act of faith on which the absurd language of Finnegans Wake is founded.

It is the Dionysian or drunken or mystic wisdom of Meister Eckhart or of Heraclitus; the Marriage of Heaven and Hell

Dionysus is the coincidence of opposites
Thunder and Silence
Life and Death
Eros (Love) and Eris (Strife)

And paradoxically, as Nietzsche showed by his whole life,
The synthesis of those opposites Apollonian and Dionysian
is itself Dionysian.

Dionysus has returned to his native Thebes   ΦBK
it is too late for Apollonian art or Doric discipline

Dionysus is all fire
not Apollonian light but Dionysian fire
not purified by Buddhistic exstinction of desire
but Thunder of Thought and flames of fierce desire

Canetti has fire as the prime symbol of the crowd

Nature is a Heraclitean Fire, vulcanic, violent
this world is now, was in the beginning, and ever shall be, ever-living fire

The historical process, the Last Judgment, the great, the everlasting
bonfire in which we are all consumed, all the time

Love is all fire
beyond the Apollonian principle of devotion reaffirmed in Cage's beautiful mesostics, "Composition in Retrospect."
Devotion based on discipline
(If the mind is disciplined, the heart turns quickly from fear to love)   S, 64
keeps the Apollonian cool
in the midst of the dance he remains himself and retains his civic name.
Love is all fire
and so heaven and hell are the same place.   LB, 179

John Cage knows about fire
never underestimate John Cage.

The 1974 lecture on "The Future of Music," that lecture which discards
tragedy in favor of the pleasures of conviviality, ends like this:

> I want to tell the story of Thoreau and his setting fire to the woods.
> I think it is relevant to the practice of music in the present world situation,
> and it may suggest actions to be taken as we move into the future.

> First of all, he didn't mean to set the fire. (He was broiling fish he
> had caught.) Once it was beyond his control, he ran over two miles unsuc-
> cessfully for help. Since there was nothing he could do alone he walked
> to Fair Haven Cliff, climbed to the highest rock, and sat down upon it to
> observe the progress of the flames. It was a glorious spectacle and he was
> the only one there to see it. From that height he heard bells in the village
> sounding alarm. Until then he had felt guilty, but knowing that help was
> coming his attitude changed. He said to himself: "Who are these men
> who are said to be the owners of these woods, and how am I related to
> them? I have set fire to the forest, but I have done nothing wrong therein,
> and it is as if the lightning had done it. These flames are but consuming
> their natural food."

> When the townsmen arrived to fight the fire, Thoreau joined them.
> It took several hours to subdue the flames. Over one hundred acres were
> burned. Thoreau noticed that the villagers were generally elated, thankful
> for the opportunity that had given them so much sport. The only unhappy
> ones were those whose property had been destroyed.

> Subsequently, Thoreau met a fellow who was poor, miserable,
> often drunk, worthless (a burden to society). However, more than any
> other, this fellow was skillful in the burning of brush. Observing his
> methods and adding his own insights, Thoreau set down a procedure for
> successfully fighting fires. He also listened to the music a fire makes,

roaring and crackling: "You sometimes hear it on a small scale in the log on the hearth."

Having heard the music fire makes and having discussed his fire-fighting method with one of his friends, Thoreau went farther: suggesting that along with firemen there be a band of musicians playing instruments to revive the energies of weary firemen and to cheer up those who were not yet exhausted.

Finally he said that fire is not only disadvantage. "It is without doubt an advantage on the whole. It sweeps and ventilates the forest floor, and makes it clear and clean. It is nature's broom.... Thus, in the course of two or three years new huckleberry fields are created for birds and for men."   EW, 186-7

It was a glorious spectacle.

O sages standing in God's holy fire
As in the gold mosaic of a wall,
Come from the holy fire, perne in a gyre,
And be the singing-masters of my soul.   Yeats

Shadrach, Meshach, and Abednego

And these three men, Shadrach, Meshach, and Abednego, fell down
bound into the midst of the burning fiery furnace.   Daniel, III, 2?

And there in the midst of the burning fiery furnace they began to sing
Benedictus
Botte alle schalle be wele, and alle maner of thynge schalle be wele.
Which being interpreted is
Nichi nichi kore ko nichi   S, 41
(the only Japanese I know: I learnt it of course from John Cage)
Day Day Beautiful Day
Every day is a beautiful day.

And the fire and the rose are one.   Eliot

Strange company in the fire:

Then Nebuchadnezzar the king was astonied, and rose up in haste, *and*
spake, and said unto his counsellors, Did not we cast three men bound into
the midst of the fire? They answered and said unto the king, True, O king.

He answered and said, Lo, I see four men loose, walking in the midst of
the fire, and they have no hurt; and the form of the fourth is like the Son of
God.

Sing a Song of Sixpence,
A bag full of Rye,
Four and twenty
Naughty boys,
Bak'd in a Pye.

When the pie was opened,
The birds began to sing;
Was not that a dainty dish,
To set before the king?

A diller, a dollar, poor twelve o'clock scholar,
I give you the authoritative version in The Annotated Mother Goose .

The footnote says:
Later, "Four and twenty blackbirds."

****
The citations from John Cage:

EW = Empty Words (Middletown: Wesleyan U. Press, 1978)
FTB = For The Birds (Boston: M. Boyars, 1981)
M = M (Middletown: Wesleyan U. Press, 1972)
R = Roarotorio (Königstein: Athenäum, 1982)
S = Silence (Middletown: Wesleyan U. Press, 1961)
YFM = A Year From Monday (Middletown: Wesleyan U. Press, 1967)
TGGIS = John Cage and Others, The Guests Go Into Supper (Oakland:
Burning Books, 1986)
X = X (Middletown: Wesleyan U. Press, 1983)

Tri-Quarterly #54 (Spring, 1982) pp. 68-232: "A John Cage Reader"
P. Griffiths, Cage (London, N.Y.: Oxford U. Press, 1981)

Other Texts:

FW = J. Joyce, Finnegans Wake (New York: Viking, 1966)

BT = F. Nietzsche, The Birth of Tragedy , in The Philosophy of Nietzsche
(New York: Modern Library, 1927)
EH = F. Nietzsche, Ecce Homo , in The Philosophy of Nietzsche (New
York: Modern Library, 1927)
WP = F. Nietzsche, The Will to Power , ed. W. Kaufmann (New York:
Random House, 1967)

CT = N.O. Brown, Closing Time (New York: Random House, 1973)
LB = N.O. Brown, Love's Body (New York: Random House, 1966)

ΦBK = N.O. Brown, Phi Beta Kappa Oration, Columbia U. = "Apo-calypse," <u>Harper's Magazine</u> , May 1961, pp. 47-49

J. Attali, <u>Noise</u> (tr. B. Massumi, Minneapolis: U. Minnesota Press, 1985)

E. Canetti, <u>Crowds and Power</u> (tr. W.C. Stewart, New York: Viking, 1962)

M. Eliade, <u>The Sacred and the Profane</u> (tr. W.R. Trask, New York: Har-court Brace, 1959)

R. Girard, <u>Violence and the Sacred</u> (tr. P. Gregory, Baltimore: Johns Hopkins U. Press, 1977)

J. Rothenberg, <u>Technicians of the Sacred</u> (New York: Anchor, 1969)

G. Vico, <u>The New Science</u> (tr. T.G. Bergin and M.H. Fisch, Ithaca: Cor-nell U. Press, 1968)

E. Pound, <u>Cantos</u> (New York: New Directions, 1970)

W.B. Yeats, "Sailing to Byzantium"

T.S. Eliot, "Little Gidding," <u>Four Quartets</u>

Anarchy

New York City – January 1988

In order to write *Themes and Variations* I made a cursory examination of my earlier books, jotting down subjects or ideas which
still seemed lively to me. When I counted them up they came to
one hundred and ten. Anarchy is one of them. The "themes" of
Themes and Variations are the names of fifteen of the men who have
been most important to me in my life and work. Buckminster
Fuller is one of them. From the beginning of my knowing him I
had as he did confidence in his plan to make life on earth a success
for everyone. His plan is to make an equation between human
needs and world resources. I had the good luck in Hawaii to see
proof of the viability of Fuller's plan. The island of Oahu is
divided by a mountain range. Honolulu is on the southern side. I
was staying with friends on the northern side. The mountain
range is of course tunnelled. But at its ridge I noticed each day
crenelations as on a medieval castle. What are those, I asked. I was
told that formerly, actually not so long ago, the tribes on one side
of the mountain were at war with those on the other side. The
crenelations were used for self-protection when shooting poi-
soned arrows at enemies. Now the tunnel exists and both sides of
the island share the same utilities. The idea of fighting one another is out of the question. This change was not brought about by
a political agreement. Buckminster Fuller believed, and I follow
him, that politicans are of no good use. They could be sent as he
used to say to outer space and left there without matters getting
worse for humanity here on earth. We don't need government.
We need utilities: air, water, energy, travel and communication
means, food and shelter. We have no need for imaginary mountain ranges between separate nations. We can make tunnels
through the real ones. Nor do we have any need for the continuing division of people into those who have what they need and
those who don't. Both Fuller and Marshall McLuhan knew, furthermore, that work is now obsolete. We have invented machines
to do it for us. Now that we have no need to do anything what shall
we do? Looking at Fuller's Geodesic World Map we see that the
earth is a single island. Oahu. We must give all the people all they
need to live in any way they wish. Our present laws protect the
rich from the poor. If there are to be laws we need ones that begin
with the acceptance of poverty as a way of life. We must make the
earth safe for poverty without dependence on government.

That government is best which governs not at all; and when
men are prepared for it, that will be the kind of government
which they will have. That quotation from Henry David Thoreau's
Essay on the Duty of Civil Disobedience is one of thirty quotations

from which as maximum source the following lecture was written. The lecture consists of twenty fifty per cent mesostics. In a fifty per cent mesostic the second letter of the string does not appear between itself and the first letter. In a one hundred per cent mesostic neither the first nor the second letter appears between the first and second letters. How many and which of the thirty quotations were used as source for each of the twenty mesostics was answered by IC (a program by Andrew Culver simulating the coin oracle of the I Ching). Which of the thirty quotations together with the fourteen names (authors, book titles, graffiti) was to be used as the string upon which each mesostic was written was also determined by IC. Where, through the use of chance operations, duplication of strings resulted, the mesostics having the same string became a single renga, a single poem composed from a plurality of poems. A renga in the text itself is indicated by an asterisk following the mesostic number. A program made by Andrew Culver extended the number of characters in a search string for MESOLIST (a program by Jim Rosenberg) to any length; this extended MESOLIST was used to list the available words which were then subjected to IC. The resultant mesostics are therefore global with respect to their sources, coming as they do from anywhere in them. In seven cases, for one or more letters of the string there were no words.

This is another text in an ongoing series; *Themes and Variations, Mushrooms* et Variationes, *The First Meeting of the Satie Society* precede it: to find a way of writing which though coming from ideas is not about them; or is not about ideas but produces them. *Anarchy* was written to be read out loud. The ends of stanzas are indicated by space, a full stop, a new breath. Within a stanza, the sign ' indicates a slight pause, a half cadence. My mesostic texts do not make ordinary sense. They make nonsense, which is taught as a serious subject in one of the Tokyo universities. If nonsense is found intolerable, think of my work as music, which is, Arnold Schoenberg used to say, a question of repetition and variation, variation itself being a form of repetition in which some things are changed and others not. Or think of work, as McLuhan did, as obsolete. Instead of working, to quote McLuhan, we now brush information against information. We are doing everything we can to make new connections.

I am glad that in preparation for this work I read *Living My Life* the two volume autobiography by Emma Goldman. William Buwalda, a soldier of the United States Army, who dared to go to one of Goldman's lectures on anarchy was court-martialed and sentenced to a year in jail. I recommend Goldman's book to all those who like books that are hard to put down once you've picked them up. I am grateful to Sydney Cowell who led me to Paul Avrich who led me to Paul Berman, author of *Quotations from the Anarchists*, to William Anastasi who loaned me Seldes' *Great Quotations*, and I am grateful to Electra Yourke who gave me *The Essential Works of Anarchism* edited by Marshall S. Shatz which she found in a second-hand bookshop in Easthampton on sale for ninety-nine cents. I have read and reread it. And I am grateful to James J. Martin who wrote *Men Against the State*. It is one of those books I never have because I'm always giving them away.

Periods of very slow changes are succeeded by periods of violent changes. Revolutions are as necessary for evolution as the slow changes which prepare them and succeed them. (Peter Kropotkin, *Revolutionary Studies*, 1892, in Berman, *Quotations*, p. 95). Alteration of global society through electronics so that world will go round by means of united intelligence rather than by means of divisive intelligence (politics, economics) (John Cage, *A Year From Monday*, p. 17). The revolution is the creation of new living institutions, new groupings, new social relationships; it is the destruction of privileges and monopolies; it is the new spirit of justice, of brotherhood, of freedom which must renew the whole of social life and raise the moral level and material conditions of the masses by calling on them to provide, through direct and conscious action, for their own futures. Revolution is the organization of all public services by those who work in them in their own interest as well as the public's; revolution is the destruction of all coercive ties; it is the autonomy of groups, of communes, of regions; revolution is the free federation brought about by a desire for brotherhood, by individual and collective interests, by the needs of production and defense; revolution is the constitution of innumerable free groupings based on ideas, wishes and tastes of all-kinds that exist among the people; revolution is the forming and disbanding of thousands of representative, district, communal, regional, national bodies which, without having any legislative power, serve to make known and coordinate the desires and interests of people near and far and which act through information, advice, and example (Errico Malatesta, *Pensiero e Volonta*, 1924, in Berman, *Quotations*, p. 102). Electronic democracy (instantaneous voting on the part of anyone): no government; no sheep (Cage, *AYFM*, p. 52 [with addition of "no government"]). The liberty of man consists solely in this: that he obeys natural laws because he has himself recognized them as such, and not

because they have been externally imposed upon him by any
extrinsic will whatever, divine or human, collective or individual
(Michael Bakunin, *God and the State*, 1871, in Berman, *Quotations*,
p. 161). I'm an anarchist, same as you are when you're telephon-
ing, turning on/off the lights, drinking water (Cage, *AYFM*, p. 53).
The important thing is not to stop questioning. Curiosity has its
own reason for existing. One cannot help but be in awe when he
contemplates the mysteries of eternity, of life, of the marvelous
structure of reality. It is enough if one tries merely to comprehend
a little of this mystery every day. Never lose a holy curiosity
(Albert Einstein, personal memoir of William Miller, an editor,
Life, 2 May 1955). Private prospect of enlightenment's no longer
sufficient. Not just self- but social-realization (Cage, *AYFM*, p. 53).
U.S. out of CENTRAL AMERICA + MIDDLE EAST
+ MANHATTAN (Andrew Culver, graffiti noticed in New York
Subway, August 1987). We'll take the mad ones with us, and we
know where we're going. Even now, he told me, they sit at the
crossroads in African villages regenerating society. Mental hospi-
tals: localization of a resource we've yet to exploit (Cage, *AYFM*, p.
59). The age for the veneration for governments, notwithstanding
all the hypnotic influence they employ to maintain their position,
is more and more passing away. And it is time for people to
understand that governments not only are not necessary, but are
harmful and most highly immoral institutions, in which a self-
respecting, honest man cannot and must not take part, and the
advantages of which he cannot and should not enjoy. And as soon
as people clearly understand that, they will naturally cease to take
part in such deeds—that is, cease to give the governments soldiers
and money. And as soon as a majority of people ceases to do this
the fraud which enslaves people will be abolished. Only in this way
can people be freed from slavery (Leo N. Tolstoy, Address, Swed-
ish Government Congress Peace Conference, 1909, *Saturday Review*, 9 August 1958, in George Seldes, *The Great Quotations*).
American anarchist, 1900, admitting failure, retired to the south
of France. Dad's airplane engine, 1918, flew to pieces before it left
the ground. Alloys needed to contain the power were still un-
discovered. Discover dialectrics for ultra-high voltages (global
electrical networks). Change society so differences are refreshing,
nothing to do with possessions/power (Cage, *AYFM*, p. 68). I
heartily accept the motto, "That government is best which governs
least"; and I should like to see it acted up to more rapidly and
systematically. Carried out, it finally amounts to this, which also I
believe—"That government is best which governs not at all"; and

when men are prepared for it, that will be the kind of government which they will have (Henry David Thoreau, *Essay on the Duty of Civil Disobedience*, 1849). Society, not being a process a king sets in motion, becomes an impersonal place understood and made useful so that no matter what each individual does his actions enliven the total picture. Anarchy in a place that works. Society's individualized (Cage, *AYFM*, p. 161). Not songs of loyalty alone are these / But songs of insurrection also / For I am the sworn poet of every dauntless rebel the world over / And he going with me leaves peace and routine behind him / And stakes his life to be lost at any moment (Walt Whitman, *To a Foil'd European Revolutionaire*). We have only one mind (the one we share). Changing things radically, therefore, is simple. You just change that one mind. Base human nature on allishness (Cage, AYFM, p. 158). Anarchists or revolutionists can no more be made than musicians. All that can be done is to plant the seeds of thought. Whether something vital will develop depends largely on the fertility of the human soil, though the quality of the intellectual seed must not be overlooked (Emma Goldman, Preface, *Anarchism and Other Essays*, 1910). We are not arranging things in order (that's the function of the utilities): we are merely facilitating processes so that anything can happen (Cage, *M*, p. 12). In San Francisco, in 1908, Emma Goldman's lecture attracted a soldier of the United States Army, William Buwalda. For daring to attend an Anarchist meeting, the free Republic court-martialed Buwalda and imprisoned him for one year. Thanks to the regenerating power of the new philosophy, the government lost a soldier, but the cause of liberty gained a man (Hippolyte Havel, *Biographic Sketch of Emma Goldman*, 1910). The problem that confronts us today, and which the nearest future is to solve, is how to be one's self and yet in oneness with others, to feel deeply with all human beings and still retain one's own characteristic qualities (Emma Goldman, *Anarchism*, quoted in Introduction by Richard Drinnon). . . . . capacity audience gave him standing ovation. Commenting on this, Fuller said, "It wasn't for me; I'm only an average man. It was for what I'd been saying: the fact it's possible to make life a success for everyone" (Cage, *M*, p. 110). Anarchism, then, really stands for the liberation of the human mind from the dominion of religion; the liberation of the human body from the dominion of property; liberation from the shackles and restraint of government. Anarchism stands for a social order based on the free grouping of individuals for the purpose of producing real social wealth; an order that will guarantee to every human being free access to the earth and full

enjoyment of the necessities of life, according to individual desires, tastes, and inclinations (Emma Goldman, *Anarchism*, 1910).
A man . . . draws now, as far as he can, on the natural force *in* him
that is no different from what it will be in the new society . . .
Merely continuing to exist and act in nature and freedom, a free
man wins the victory, establishes the new society . . . (Paul Good-
man, *Drawing the Line*). Not only have all the big corporations
become transnational and taken all the former U.S.A. gold and
other negotiable assets with them, but they have also left all the
world's people locked into their 150 national pens, with those 150
nations blocking the flow of lifeblood metals without which we
cannot realize the increasing know-how of all humanity. Very soon
the nation-state sovereignties will have to be eliminated or humanity will perish (R. Buckminster Fuller, *Critical Path*, 1981). Problems of governments are not inclusive enough. We need (we've
got them) global problems in order to find global solutions. Problems connected with sounds were insufficient to change the
nature of music. We had to conceive of silence in order to open
our ears. We need to conceive of anarchy to be able whole-
heartedly to do whatever another tells us to (Cage, *M*, 20).
. . . class-one evolution is about to put the U.S.A. out of business
through international bankruptcy . . . nature's way of ridding the
planet of the most powerful of yesterday's sovereignties and
thereby setting off a chain of 149 additional desovereignizations,
. . . removing the most stubborn barrier to the free circulation of
the Earth's world-around metals, foods, income energy supplies
and people. We are now in a position to get rid of the 150
sovereignties and have a recirculatory, interaccomodative, world-
around democratic system. We now have the immediately realiza-
ble capability to exercise our often-repeated option to make all the
Earth's people physically and economically successful within only
a decade by virtue of the already-executed fifty-year critical path
of artifacts development which has acquired all the right technology (R. Buckminster Fuller, *Critical Path*, 1981). What we finally
seek to do is to create an environment that works so well we can
run wild in it (Norman O. Brown, quoted in *M*, p. 213). I am a
fanatic lover of liberty, considering it as the unique condition
under which intelligence, dignity, and the happiness of men can
develop and grow; not that purely formal liberty, conceded, measured, and regulated by the State, an eternal lie and which in
reality never represents anything but the privilege of the few
founded on the slavery of everyone. . . . I mean the only liberty
truly worthy of the name, liberty that consists in the full develop-

ment of all the powers—material, intellectual, and moral—that are latent faculties of each; liberty that recognizes no other restrictions than those outlined for us by the laws of our own individual nature, so that properly speaking, there are no restrictions. . . . I mean that liberty of each individual which, far from halting as at a boundary before the liberty of others, finds there its confirmation and its extension to infinity; the illimitable liberty of each through the liberty of all, liberty by solidarity, liberty in equality; liberty triumphing over brute force and the principle of authority that was never anything but the intellectualized expression of that force; liberty which, after having overthrown all heavenly and earthly idols, will found and organize a new world, that of human solidarity, on the ruins of all Churches and all States (Michael Bakunin, quoted by Paul Berman in *Quotations*, 1871). Government is a tree. Its fruit are people. As people ripen, they drop away from the tree (H. D. Thoreau, *Essay on the Duty of Civil Disobedience*, quoted by John Cage in *X*, p. 155). To me anarchism was not a mere theory for a distant future; it was a living influence to free us from inhibitions, internal no less than external, and from the destructive barriers that separate man from man (Emma Goldman, *Living My Life*, 1931, p. 556).

1

```
                sPirit of
          him for onE

            corporaTions
                 arE
               failuRe
                  Know-how of
                 aRe
                 idOls will

            free rePublic
          each thrOugh
                   Them in
                 maKe

                  I
            to me

                aNarchism
```

2

```
      sworn Poet of
        libeRty

            nOthing to
      pieces Before it
        sociaL
          thE

    every huMan being
        with uS

            peOple as
          selF
        voltaGes
      seek tO do

          reVolutionists

      soon thE
        the maRvelous
  with possessioNs/power

            the Mad
              thE
            chaNge
              The
              iS
              A social
          democRatic
              thE

            saN
              tOday and which
              To
          realIze the
            oNly one
        a plaCe that works
```

```
                     and peopLe
                        aboUt
                        dad'S
             development whIch has
                           Voting on
                     all thE
                          rEal
                           Natural laws
                          sOcial order
                          mUst
                           Global
                          tHe

                  i am the sWorn
                          thE
                     but be iN
                          violEnt
                       suppliEs
                          to Do is to
                             What
                  flow of lifEblood
                     goldman's lecture
                     or indiVidual
                        sharE

              violent chanGes
                          Of
                          The
                     if one Tries

              mind base Human

                        a rEcirculatory
                        arMy

              desovereiGnizations

                   for uLtra
                      prOcess
                         Be done is
                        thAt
                   revoLutions are

                      caPability to
                      feRtility
                        cOnceive of anarchy
                        Before it
              emma goLdman's
                   for Existing
                      hiM
```

                    Structure of
                does hIs
                    coNtemplates the
                    prOducing
                    eveRy
                executeD
                purposE

                    woRld
                    wiTh
                    wOrld

            nearest Future

                    I am
                reasoN
                    to Do whatever another tells us to
        rid of the 150 sovereiGnties and have
                    additionaL
                        Of

                        Be one's self
                        An
                        fLow

                    foodS
                    electrOnic democracy instantaneous
                    criticaL path

                        bUwalda
                        neTworks change
                        busIness
                            Of
                            Not
                        exiSting
                        deePly with all
                            foR
                            nO
                        to Be
            or individuaL
                        thE

```
                    froM
                    workS
                    produCing
                      demOcratic system
                        uNdiscovered discover
                        aNarchism
           total picturE
                      whiCh has
           anarchy To
                      rEtain
                      anD
    the regenerating poWer of the new
                to contaIn
                prospecT of
                      wHat
    each individual doeS


                      Of
                      bUt be
           be lost at aNy moment
                the immeDiately realizable
                qualitieS
                      Without which
    out of businEss


                      cRitical path
           individualizEd


                anarchIsm
                self aNd
                      Society
                      Upon him
                      oF
                way oF
                evolutIon
                      beCome
                transnatIonal


                      wE
                      aNd
                and sTill


                      mysTery every day


                      sOmething
           south of franCe
           to solve is How to be
```

```
              villAges
           exterNally
              riGht
             sharE
        human naTure on
             a Holy
           systEm we
              Never
               And
            wiTh all
      with them bUt
             eaRth and full

      to put thE
            nOt be
            leFt the
              Meeting the
            insUfficient
             iS

         recognIzed them as
   allishness anarChists

         army William

         anyonE

            tHe
             A '
           golD
             The

            dOes
        franCe
           nOt
             eNergy supplies and
             Curiosity has
       in ordEr to
       does hIs
          reVolutions

            thE
            fOr '
            iF
             S

      path of artIfacts
```

```
                        reaLity it
                        thEm
                        oNe
            and whiCh
                        wE
                        wIll

                        meNtal
            chain Of
                        weRe
                        anD
                        thEm but they
                        aRe
                        The
                        Of
                        prOcess

                                            a
                        caPability
            with othErs
        to every humaN being
                        tO do
            each individUal does
            with otheRs to
                        thE
                        hAve also
                        democRatic
                        iS

                        hoW to
                        thEm
                        aN anarchist
        court-martialEd

                        wE'll take the
                        maD ones
                        iT

                        enjOyment of the
            extrinsiC will
                        tO
                        chaNge
                        Confronts
                        powEr

                        afrIcan
                        eVolution

            his lifE
                        Own reason
```

                    not just selF but
               curiosity privAte prospect
                left the grouNd

                insurrection Also
                        poweRful
               problem that Confronts
                  one mind tHe one we share

                      alloYs needed
                            The nearest
                          sOldier
                          Buwalda for daring to
                     of thE
                            And

                            Barrier to the
                       onLy
                       yEar
                       We

               nature on

                      allisHness
                         Of
                      reLigion

                 with thEm
                         Human
                      awE

                         A
                  the woRld over and
           necessary for evoluTion as
                      but bE
                then really stanDs
             through internationaL
       metals foods income energY supplies and people we
                          The
                       vOltages
                     attenD an anarchist meeting
                     and Other
                          We
                  plant tHe
                     bAse
                     wiTh
                     amErican
                   indiVidual
                 insufficiEnt
                     pRoblems in order to

                     neArest
                     oNly

```
                              fOr
                              To
                          perisH
                          unitEd
                dominion of Religion
            songs of loyalTy
                          yEt
                          soiL
                            siLence
                          thiS mystery every
                          hUman
                              Simple you
                soldier of The
                          wOrks
                      repeateD
                          tO
```

3

```
    utilitiEs we
       that's
      mereLy
      mereLy

          The utilities
         cAn
    utilitiEs
   we are noT
          wE are

           Merely
           Anything can happen
         orDer

           that's
   facilitating prOcesses so that
         happeN
            wE are
         thingS

            We are
     that anythIng can
         funcTion
            Happen

            fUnction of
         thingS
         so thAt
            Not
            arE merely
     facilitatiNg
           prOcesses
         so We
            We are not
          tHings
            wE
      utilitiEs
           arE merely
      order that's
            wE
   facilitatinG
            Of
      happeN
```

```
                        wE
                        wE are
                      thiNgs
                    happeN
                       sO
                        We are
                    anytHing
                    arE
                        Things


                        prOcesses
                are mereLy
                        arE
                    funcTion of


                        arE
                    anYthing


                    that'S
                    arrangIng
                            The
                    we Are
                    funcTion of
                        noT arranging
            things in ordEr


                                that's the
                    anything Can
                        aRe
                        nOt
                        So
                        So
                        aRe


                        Order
                    cAn
                    orDer
                        So
                    Not
                        Anything can
                        Function
                    we aRe not
                        In
                    funCtion
                    thAt's
                    thiNgs
            that anythIng can
```

```
                    mereLy
                    mereLy
                     cAn
                  thinGs in
                     wE

    order that'S
                     wE
                  thinGs in
                     wE

                    thiNgs
                     arE
                      pRocesses so
                     hAppen
                    noT
                    caN
                  that'S
                     nOt
                      Can
                  anythIng
                     arE

                     The
           that anYthing
                     arE
                      iN
                       The function
                     Are

                    mereLy
                   of tHe
                      Of
           utilitieS

                       Processes
                  functIon
                     noT
                      Are
                    mereLy
                      So
                  faciLitating
                     nOt
                    funCtion
                     thAt
           are mereLy
                  functIon of
                     cAn
                     The
           arrangIng things
                      Of
                      iN
                       Order
```

```
                    that's
              Function
           thAt's
        happEn
        that'S
              Of
              Utilities
           meRely

anything Can
        happEn
        happEn

        that's
           arE not
           anYthing
           arE

        noT
           The
           nOt
        thE
           Processes
        mereLy
              Order
              In order
        anyThing
```

4

```
                        destrUction of all coercive
            forming and diSbanding
                    fOrce

                                liberty
            to the earth and fUll

                        The
                    allOys needed to contain the power were
        halting as at a boundary beFore the liberty of others

                individual whiCh

                        thE
                there are No

                            The
                        foR '
                        chAnge
                        wiLd

                of individuAls
                    and froM
                of all thE
                        foR

                        lIberty of
                        eaCh through the liberty of
                        And

                        Make
                        beIng free

                                    access to
            the necessities of life accorDing to
                all human beings

                        anD
```

```
        and earthLy
             rEvolution is
           onE's self
              And which the
        power

             Serve
          liberTy of each
create an environMent
      discover diAlectrics
            ruN wild in
            tHe

           eternAl
              Today and
              The privilege of
              fAilure
      at a bouNdary before the
```

5

```
            buT songs
            of Human
            takE
             plAnet
             thinGs
      and imprisonEd
                oF each

          man cannOt and must not take
     less than exteRnal
                    sTill undiscovered
                in Him

            planEt
      of each indiVidual which
          it as thE
               fraNcisco
               thE
                  Republic
                  Are
                  They have also
            future It was

            must nOt be
      brute force aNd the
      circulation oF
                 On this
             body fRom the dominion of
                songs

     regenerating sOciety
                  reVolutionists
             statEs
               viRtue
               aN average
                  Must
               arE
          develop aNd
                  To
          anarchiSm
```

```
        the slavery of everyoNe i mean
                       becOmes an impersonal place
                       of The necessities of life
      more and more passing aWay and
             was for what I'd been saying
                   naTural force
             imprisoned Him


                economicS
             make all The
                      mAke life a
                      No more be
                 worlD


                 lIfe
                 aNd succeed them
                 Governments
                 Are succeeded by periods of
            actions enLiven the
      for us by the Laws of our own


                 naTurally
                 Human
             wE are
      properly speaking tHere are no restrictions
             i'm onlY
                 in Part
                 eterNal
                 fOr a
      know-how of all humaniTy very soon
                 unIted
             all the right teChnology


             energy supplIes
                      caN develop and grow
          the liberation oF
                 peopLe
          a tree its frUit


                 vEry
                 Name
             of artifaCts
                 what Each individual does
```

```
            puT
             Humanity
         and rEstraint of government
      radicallY
   to plant thE seeds of
             aM a
              Process
          a goLdman's
      it was fOr
        libertY

                The
                pOwer society not being
                Mind
                Alone
          each lIberty
                eNslaves

                Them
                Are as
     of everyone I
                oN

             addiTional
             eacH
             lifE
              mInd
          as faR as he can
             to Pieces
        largely On the
        to free uS
             sets In
              worThy of the

    wasn't for me I'm
    regenerating sOciety
          so that No matter what each
                In order
             be loSt at any
                Metals
               frOm the dominion
               fRom halting
             changEs
                A
        sovereigNties
        crossroaDs
```

```
              the slavery of everyone i Mean the
                             grOund
                      dialectRics
                      of lifE according to
                              Periods of
                      we finAlly
                      to pieceS
                    the nation-State
                              wIll be
                           lateNt
              liberty that recoGnizes
                            metAls foods income energy supplies and people

                              We
                      with All
                      dignitY
                          A social order based
                          iN the new society
                      will Develop
                      to do Is
                      from The
                    expressIon of that
                           ceaSe

                      lefT
                         dIfferent
                      huMan
                         rEvolutionists
         increasing know-how oF
                         is tO
                      anaRchists

                    critical Path
                         hE can
                      glObal
                         Powers
                      evoLution is
                    futurE

                      They
                    peOple as
                    in sUch deeds

                 far from haltiNg
                      he tolD
                         thE
                      victoRy
                    becomeS an
                         To
                         A
                         Now
                         Do
```

```
          us from inhibiTions
               force in Him
                    And
                    hospiTals localization of a resource we've
          all the riGht
                    wOrthy
                    eVolution as
                    Evolution is

                ultRa high voltages
               settiNg off a
               freedoM a
                    arE
                    caN
               which The
               changeS which
               over aNd
          each impersOnal
                    The

                    a sOcial order
               a chaiN of
          successfuL
               capacitY
                    thAt consists in the full development
                    dRaws
     in a position to gEt rid of
                    gaiNed
                    Of all
                    maTerial

                    aNarchism stands

               now havE
                    men Can
               all thE
               politicS
                    dad'S
                    thAn
                    Revolutionists
     with them but theY have also left
               property liBeration
               individUalized
                    Thereby setting off
               humAn
               libeRation from
               uniquE condition under
          we'll take tHe
          desovereignizAtions
                    soveReignties will have to be
```

```
world-around deMocratic
                Fact
                yoU just change that
                fLow of
        theory for A
                    Not necessary
                orDer
                soMething vital will
                    tO
                    Self
                    iT
                perisH
                sets In motion

        an averaGe man
                tHe
        additionaL
        majoritY

                goIng even now he told
            they eMploy to
        anarchisM then

                    Of
                    Revolutionists
                    An
                onLy
                wIll
                be doNe

            made uSeful so
                The new
            expressIon of
            high volTages
    which has acqUired all
                    To do
            to exploIt
            needed tO
                    iNto their 150 national
                    So that world
                to do wIth
                    aNd as
                    feW
                    tHey
            get rId of the 150 sovereignties
```

```
                         Commenting on
                   are tHese
                   necessAry for
                   one'S
                       nEtworks
           ridding the pLanet
                          Facilitating
                   theiR
                   mE
                       Such deeds


business through international bankruPtcy
                          thE ground alloys needed
                   that is Cease
                       to The south
             of all humanIty
                   a bouNdary before the liberty of others finds there its
                   Gave


                   be in tHe new
                   the new sOciety
           that they will Naturally
               ridding thE planet of the
                   alSo
           songs of loyalTy alone are these but songs of
                   governMents


           the right technology whAt
                   other Negotiable assets with them but
                       faCulties of
                       metAls
                   elimiNated or
                   motioN
                   based On
                           To the
                           As
                           oN
                           Do with
                           Money
                   groUping


               fuller Said
                       To do with
           it i am a faNatic
                       tO do
               will naTurally
           full developmenT of
                       Are
```

```
        a process a King
          rid of thE
        all the hyPnotic influence
             gold And
                  Real social
          inclinaTions
        being free Access to the earth
              wiNs the
              worlD
                   To exercise
              wHat
          to mE
              thAt works


                        society's
               Different from
               goVernment


               quAlities
        we have oNly one mind
                   To exploit
        very soon the nAtion-state
                  sonGs
most stubborn barriEr to the free circulation of the
                  uS
          that wOrks so well we can run wild in it


                   For
                   We know
                   tHe
                   Is
               that Confronts
               all Human beings
                   tHat
                   oftEn-repeated option to make all the earth's peop
          liberty Considering it
               globAl
                   Nature

          slow chaNges
               swOrn
                   Technology
```

```
                            A
                       iN san francisco in
            human soliDarity
                   anarchiSm stands for
                        eacH
                         sOldier
                        natUre
                        seLf
                        baseD

                       meetiNg the free republic
 already-executed fifty-year critical path Of
                            naTional
                   of libErty
           fertility of the humaN soil

                        Just change that
                        hOw of all
                   realitY

                            Act
                   locked iNto
                          Discover
                   the quAlity of
                   real Social wealth

                          Still retain
                        gOvernments
                   are nOt
                   reality Never represents
                 problem thAt
                            uS and which the nearest future is
                            Passing away and it is
                        futurE it was a living
                        nOw

         the regenerating Power of the new

                       sociaL
                       francE
                         funCtion of the
            the most powerfuL of
                        thEn
                 this the frAud
                          foRce and the
                          poLitics
                   democracY
                        pictUre
```

```
            the priNciple of authority that was never
                    aDmitting
                    arE succeeded by
                    haRmful
        ground alloyS
                    wiTh
                    lArgely
                    oNe's self
    at the crossroaDs

                    sysTem we now
          to me anarcHism
              order bAsed on
          place undersTood and made useful

              human naTure
              mental Hospitals
                    bE freed from
                    Yet

                    hoW of all
              does hIs actions
              onLy
                    Liberty of each

        way of riddiNg the
                    globAl
                    evoluTion
                    bUt
              to eveRy
                    And
                    deveLop
                    a pLace that works
              anarchY in
              anarChist

              simplE
        differences Are
                    itS
              this thE
                    criTical path
                    Of
              repeaTed
                    weAlth an order that will
                    a King
              an ordEr that will guarantee
                    hyPnotic
                    ultrA high
              to exeRcise
              socieTy
```

```
we can run wIld
          aNd it
          aS
          bUt
          beCome

           tHey
          anD
          thE
       changEs are
       accorDing to the individual
         cauSe

           fuTure is
             How to be one's self
             A
         wheTher

      has acquIred all
      nature'S way

       perish Class
        suppliEs

            An
            iS
           thE
         cannoT
            sO

    african villaGes
             Is time for people to understand
            eVolution is
           thE full
       is abouT to put
       know-How of all humanity
          unitEd
in a position to Get rid
          brute fOrce and the principle of authority
```

```
                    instantaneous Voting on
                             to thE
                     act in natuRe
                                beiNg free
                            or huManity will
                                  fEw
                       less thaN
                                  The
                                  So well we can
                       and itS
                       are nO
                       shackLes
                             anD
                             fInally
                    from thE '
                             fRom halting
                       the moSt '
                       in nAture


                                  Now
                       he tolD
                              of Men can
                          periOds of
                             ruiNs
                       of thE
               executed fiftY
               no more be mAde
                                No less
                    abolisheD only in this
                             plAnt the '
                       and itS '
                             itS
                       seek tO
                              mOst highly
               all heaveNly
                             cAn
                       that iS
                                  And
                             doMinion of property
                       thAt are
                                  Just
                                  Of
                             fRee
                             phIlosophy
                                  To
               drop awaY


      desires tastes and inclinatiOns
                       people be Freed
```

```
                    Position
                of thE
                with Others
                    exPression of
                heavenLy and
                    onE
                in whiCh
                and othEr
                        hAve
                        Still
                        Enjoy and
                        aS
                    from The
                        slOw changes are
                        aDmitting
                liberty Of
                infiniTy

                        wHat we
                        gaIned
            in motion becomeS
                        a Tree

                    anarcHism

                principlE
                        Found and
                        thRough
                        dAd's airplane engine 1918 flew to pieces
                        continUing
                        Democracy

        realize the increasing knoW
                will be abolisHed only
                        retaIn one's own
                        soCiety's
                oneness witH

                so that propErly
                        aNd have
                        thoSe
                        quaLity of
                        it As the unique
                        eVolution as
                    which hE cannot
                        aS
                        rePublic
                        ovEr
                        Of
                never rePresents
                    heavenLy
                        hE made
```

```
                        buWalda
                        socIety
                    externaL and
                    formaL

                anything But
                        thE right technology

                        drAws now as far as he can
        was for what i'd Been saying
                        Others finds there
                    buwaLda and
                        dIfferent
                        uS

                    anarcHists or
                        arE
                over anD
                        Of
                        aNd organize a new
                        poLitics
under which intelligence dignitY and
                        lIfe to be lost at
                        No
                    liberTy in equality liberty
                        He can
                    by vIrtue of the
                whether Something vital
                        Will be

                        pArt and the
                    moneY
            development whiCh
                        metAls without
                        oN
        only have all the big corPorations
                    voltagEs
```

```
                          One's
                          Poet of
                    not onLy
                      thosE
                      inhiBitions
                        wE
                  to make liFe
                    consideRing
                      intErnal
                        yEar
                        anD inclinations a man draws now as
                        oFten
    in oneness with otheRs
                      was fOr
                  anarchisM
                          Said it wasn't
                      faiLure


                          A
              something Vital will
              and from thE
                    natuRe on
    extension to infinitY
```

6


```
            onE
            allisHness

              hAve only
            allishnEss

              yOu just
              Nature on
        therefore is simpLe

            therefOre is simple

              miNd
               wE have only one
              huMan nature
               Is simple
            that oNe
            things raDically

        base human naTure on
                  cHanging things radically

            onE mind

              yOu
              miNd
              wE
            naturE on
             juSt
             tHe
                Allishness
                Radically
              wE share
        things radiCally

              tHings
              nAture
            that oNe
```

```
                         sImple
                         oNe mind
                 you jusT
                         cHange one

                         sImple
                         oNly one mind the

          change that one mind baSe
                  base human natuRe on
                            thAt
                  that one minD
                         allIshness

                          humAn nature
                  is simpLe
                  is simpLe
                              You
                          jusT
                        base Human
                          wE
                             Radically

                          wE share changing things

                          yOu just
                             Radically
                        havE

          have only one mInd

                             Simple
                     mind baSe

                     one mInd
                     base huMan nature on
                             onLy
                             onE
                             onlY
                                On
                             hUman
                          natUre on
                     mind baSe

                             Therefore
                 things radiCally
                             tHerefore is
                          nAture
                          miNd

                 allishnEss
```

```
                jusT
        on allisHness
        mind bAse
                Things

                yOu just
            thiNgs
            thE one
            huMan nature

            sImple
        chaNge
        minD
            thAt one
    thingS radically
        onE

            cHanging
            jUst change
    is siMple

    we shAre
            oNe we

base humaN
            shAre
radically

                Therefore
        yoU

    things Radically
            wE have
            yOu
            miNd the one
    we shAre

            onLy
    have onLy
            sImple
        baSe

            tHe
        miNd
        havE
            iS '
    we Share
```

7

                  world-around metalS
                          tree tO me
            within only a deCade by
                           In
                           wE
                         This

                                        the

governments soldiers and moneY

                      plaNet
                      in Order
                      buT are
                        By
            at

                  any momEnt we
                  physIcally
                     oNe

                  an averaGe
                    humAn
                        Possible
                    tuRning

                        Only
            in this way Can
                       thE
                        Such
                    hiS
                    mAjority of

      global electrical networKs
                    make lIfe
                    hoNest

```
                    Government
                    So that
          advantagEs
                 noT only are not
          honeSt

                    fruIt are
   fraud which eNslaves

             has hiMself
                    Of
          of cenTral
             allIshness
             in Order
                    aN
                    But
             sharE

             physiCally
                    One
                    Mind

                    wE
          alloyS
                    A
                    Networks change

             whIch
             huMan
             hyPnotic
             momEnt we have only
          natuRal
             waS

                    Of
                    aNd
          which

                    hAs
             infLuence to free us
   more and more Passing away and it

             centraL
                hArmful
                    Chain of
             agE for
             natUre's
             thiNgs in
          be freeD
```

```
                     changE that
                        aRe
                  utilitieS
                         The
                        fOr
                        fOr
                        anD '
                        thAt
                        iN

                        Discover
                  is siMple

                        hAve '
                        Do this

most stubborn barriEr to the free

                  to the soUth
            for governmentS notwithstanding
             this that hE
                           From
                      of bUsiness
            soon

                      as peopLe
                        juSt
                        immOral
                      flew To
                        ligHts
                      of mAn
                         The
                        hoNest man

                        yOu
                         Must not
                  not tAke
                        noThing
                      facT
            it's arE
                        foR
                         Way of
                        tHe

                        Also for i am
      as such and noT
                  to bE
                  we Are
            anything Can
                        Happen
```

```
cease to gIve the
         oN
they Drop away from
         hIgh
for eVeryone
arrangIng things
arounD
still Undiscovered
them As such and
         Liberty
arounD

    arOund
to maintain thEir
         moSt
         patH of
commentIng on
in which a Self
of mAn
   neCessary
      Them

   sImple
a Out of
exterNally
   thiS

   mEtals foods
upoN
rebeL
amerIca
remoVing
   thE
   thiNgs
   easT

   cHanging
morE and more

conTain the
   One mind base
   The
   pArt in such
as peopLe
   droP away
      Is time
   reCognized
was noT
   hUman
   Right
```

                    wE
          discover diAlectrics
              must Not
                  All
                  fRom
                  Cease to take
              enligHtenment's no longer
            externallY
                  vIrtue of
                  aNd

                  cleArly understand that
                  to Pieces
                    Life to be
                  by Any
            the ' hypnotiC

                  wE have
        realizable capabiliTy to exercise our
                  Honest
                  A
                  This
                  noW
                  Of
                  Recognized them
                to maKe all the
                  moSt
            anarchiSt
                  mOre

                  naturally Cease to take part
        our often-repeated optIon
                  thEy
                  virTue
                  merelY
                    i'm
                    South
              amerIca

              techNology

                  saiD
                    wIll
                  goVernment
                  hImself
            take part anD
                  sUch

              yesterdAy's
                  worLd
                    saId it
                  thE
              shoulD not enjoy and as soon

8

                              can Happen the problem that confronts us today

                                 Idols will found and organize
                         that Purely formal liberty conceded measured and
                    never rePresents anything but
                              tO
              the state

                         an eternaL
                         boundarY
                              To
                           libErty

                           tHe
                           All
                        indiVidual
                           Each

                              Liberty of each through the liberty of all

9 *

```
        by soLidarity
           thE
            fOr
         yesTerday's
away

           frOm the tree
            sLow
         impriSoned
         liberTy

            bOdies which

though the qualitY
```

10

                        votiNg
                       like tO
                       liberTy
                       develOp
                        eveN now

                        Like to
                      dignitY and
                            tHe full development of
                  ones with us And
                  or indiVidual

                        wE know where
                     will hAve what we
                         beLieve that
                     each individuaL
                can develop and grow

                        noT
                 to exploit american anarcHist
                        arE no restrictions i mean that
        conceded measured and regulated By the state an
                     under whIch
                     kind of Government
                 regenerating soCiety
                     as such and nOt because they have
                     men aRe

                 i heartily accePt
              individual nature sO that
                        aRe no restrictions
                 intellectuAl and moral

                     see iT acted
                       It as
                       fOrmal liberty

```
                    develop aNd
                    of otherS
                    anything But
                         liE
                      franCe
                         tO the south of
                      theM as
              that will bE
                         The
                      wheRe we're
                    will whAtever

              what we fiNally
              which alSo
              develop aNd under which
                         A
                      buT the
              seek to do Is
                         Out of
                    the ruiNs of
                         And the
                      truLy
    undiscovered discover diAlectrics for ultra high voltages global electrical...

                    coNsists in the full
                    crossroaDs in
                    am a fanaTic lover of
                         dAd's
                    that worKs so
                      in Equality
                         Not
                         Accept
                      voLtages
              engine 1918 fLew

                         sTill
              society mental Hospitals localization of a
                         likE
                      oF man
                         Own individual
    anything but the intellectualized expRession of that force
```

```
                    east Manhattan
                    accEpt the
            that woRks so
                    foUnd
                        So differences
                        thAt works so well we can run
    instantaneous votinG
                    upOn
            an eternaL
            more rapiDly
                    A


                    Name
            take the maD
                electrOnic democracy
                    liberTy of
                    or Human
                        yEt
                        Rapidly
                    haviNg
        in this that hE
                    throuGh
                        sOlely
                    The
                    faIlure
            they hAve
                        Brute
                    soLidarity
                    thE kind of
                    An
    of all the powerS
            of human Solidarity
            and thE expression of
        pieces before iT
                    Should


            overthroWn
            refreshIng
                    Take
                    Happiness of men
            solidariTy
                of Human solidarity
                    purEly
        liberty triuMphing


        that government is Best which governs least and i
    to pieces before it left the groUnd alloys needed
                    The
```

```
                    iT as
                 manHattan
                    fEw founded on
                    Yet to exploit

           even now He told me
                    formAl liberty
                 or indiVidual
                    uniquE condition under which
                    he hAs
                    each Liberty
                    iS best which
differences are refreshing nOthing
                 yet to expLoit
                    considEring it as
                       Formal
                    dialecTrics for
                       of Authority that was never anything but
                    pureLy
                       Like
                    digniTy and
                 mental Hospitals localization of a
                    statE
                    that Will be
              refreshing nOthing to do with possessions

                    libeRty in
                       Liberty by
              them as such anD not
                       we've
                 earthly idolS will
                    develoP
                       thE
                       bOundary before the liberty of others
           which in reality never rePresents anything
                    individuaL

                       accEpt the motto that government is best which governs
        in this that he obeys naturaL laws because he has himself
                    left the grOund

         the powers material intelleCtual and moral that are latent
                    properly speaKing
                       rEstrictions than
           that consists in the full Development of
                    lover of lIberty
```

```
                lie aNd which in
                buT the

        man can develOp and grow
                yeT
            far from Halting
                dEmocracy
        externally Imposed upon him
                befoRe it left the
                votiNg on
                    And all
                lefT
            upon hIm by any
        there are nO
                aNd its
        wild in it i Am a
            governs Least and i should like to see it
            to exPloit


                divinE or
    this that he obeys Natural
                alloyS needed to contain the
                    neW world that of human
            expressIon
            accepT


                    Happiness of men
                conTain
                of Human
                the sOuth of france
        of all churcheS and all
                    in Equality
            the liberty of maN
                    cArried
                liberTy
                we fInally seek
                    Of the
                    aNd ' the
                    So


            each liBerty that recognizes
            by soLidarity liberty in equality liberty
                    cOntain the power
                    aCted up to more rapidly
                    taKe
            each lIberty
                    aNd
                    orGanize a new world
```

```
            lefT
           upon Him by
          considEring it as
        prepared For it that
               Laws because he has himself
     create an envirOnment that
            and Which
             dO with
              From
        america middLe
        mental hospItals localization
               oF
          that libErty of each individual


             liBerty which after having overthrown
     the powers materiaL intellectual and
               Of
            and mOral that are
              anD
              aM
          of francE
             of The '
              wAs never
        that pureLy
          refreShing


           the laWs of our own
         possessIons/power i
            leasT and
            of Human
             Of all
              Undiscovered discover
          hospiTals

           they Will
          of eacH
        on the ruIns of all
```

```
          dignity and the happiness of man Can develop and grow
                         liberty tHat recognizes no other
                                   Which in
                      high voltagEs
                            whiCh in
                              lAws of our
                         grow Not that purely formal
                 them as such aNd
                 latent faculties Of each
                                   The
                        which faR from
                        it actEd
                                   At
                        the onLy
                 that consIsts in
                           slavEry
                        illimiTable
                        upon Him
                        foundEd on the slavery of everyone


                  of all lIberty
                           meN are prepared for it that
                                Consists in the full
                        of ouR own individual
                        middlE


                           chAnge
                           oneS
                 name lIberty that
                 of our owN individual
                           Government
                 that worKs so well we
                           fouNded
                                Out of central america
                                We '
                              tHat he '
                        far frOm
                           feW


                           sOlely in this that he obeys natural laws
                        that Force liberty
                 which After having overthrown
                           Like to see
                 high voLtages global electrical networks
```

```
                              Himself recognized them as
                     laws becaUse he has
                              Me they '
                          he hAs himself
                          it fiNally
                       others fInds
                              The
                          onlY liberty truly
                 instantaneous Voting on
                          rEality
                              Recognizes no other
                  which theY will have what
                externally impoSed
                        which gOverns least
                        than thOse
                        i meaN
                 of human solidariTy on
              governs least and i sHould
                              forcE
                              fiNds there its
                              hAve
                        before iT
              governs least and I
                              dO is
    of that force liberty which after haviNg overthrown all heavenly and earthly
                              Such and
                        governmenT is best which governs
                     wild in it i Am a '
                        of cenTral
                          slavEry of
                              Speaking
                     happiness Of men
                     our own indiVidual
                     south of francE dad's
                          natuRal laws


                              thE
governs not at all and when men are prepared for It that will be the kind of
              happiness of men can develop and Grow
                          wild iN
                          of oThers
                        before It
                              mEntal
                          itS extension to infinity
```

```
                        Where we're
                    carrIed out it
                    Liberty by
                    Liberty truly
            us and we know wHere
                    which fAr from
                our own indiVidual
                    principlE of
                i am a fanaTic
                        discOver dialectrics for ultra high voltages


                        By
            not at all and whEn
                            thEm as
                to this which aLso
                    of authorIty that was
                        the naMe
            governs least and I should like to see it
                        still uNdiscovered
                        not becAuse
            kind of governmenT which
                        amErican anarchist 1900
                        aDmitting failure retired
                        sO well we can
            high voltages global electRical networks
        in reality never represents anytHing
                        the intellectUalized expression of that force liberty whi
    liberty that consists in the full developMent of
                    possessions/power i heArtily accept the motto that
        are prepared for it that will be the kiNd of government
                        fInally
                    over bruTe
            resource we've Yet to exploit


                                    american
                    Where


                        we're
                the happIness of men can
                        eLectronic democracy instantaneous voting
                    and moraL
                        hosPitals localization of a
                    told mE they sit at
            it left the gRound alloys needed to
                        In it i am a fanatic
                    extenSion to infinity
        outlined for us by tHe laws of our own individual nature
```

11

```
              Assets with
          priviLeges and
          need To
          changEs which
            of Ridding the
            eArs we need
        carried ouT

          lIberty that
          fOr '
          aN
        as a majOrity of
      to do this the Fraud
            riGht
        of innumerabLe
              Of people ceases to do this
conceded measured and regulated By the '
              And have a
      oneness with others to feeL

          future iS
          their Own
        to this whiCh also
        of eternIty of
          futurE is
            of The united
      new philosophY


              noT be overlooked in
      setting off a cHain of
            oveR and
        liberty by sOlidarity liberty in
      as well as the pUblic's revolution
```

                                                            is
                         aGe for
                  people pHysically and
                         powErs
                   a sociaL
                         agE
                      by Calling on
                      The
                to me anaRchism was
                         Of
                      is No
                         rIght
                      a Chain of
            government iS

                      of privilegeS and
                   capability tO exercise our
                         naTure of
                      refresHing
         destruction of privileges And monopolies
                     already-execuTed
                              Will
                           sOuth
                           fRee
                      nationaL
                        accorDing to
                           We now have
                      on allIshness

                      communaL
          is the constitution of innumerabLe
                liberty of each throuGh the liberty
                              Of communes of
                           aRe
                           Often
                           Us

                      restraiNt of government
                         seeD
                           Be
            the new societY
                         theM
                        fErtility
                           Am
                      bouNdary before
            national bodieS

```
                          develOpment which
                                Finds there its
                          sUch deeds
                       goverNs least
                          wIll found
        real social wealTh an
                    problEm
                       anD freedom
                 electrIcal
            wishes aNd
                    wiThin
                       bE freed
                    buwaLda for
                 be abLe
         soon the natIon
                    sonGs of
                       thEm but
                    chaiN
              of whiCh
            will havE to be
                    gRoupings
                    And
              hypnoTic influence
         cannot and sHould
                    bE
            states aRmy
               uniTed
                    wHole of
        our own individuAl
              of people Near and far


    the united states of america out of Business

         a free man wins the victorY
```

```
                                got theM global
                        stands for thE
                              now hAve
                              withiN
                          and itS
                                abOut by a desire
                        nearest Future is to solve
                              anD
                              amerIca
                          to solVe
                          flow of lIfeblood
                                aS soon as
                                so dIfferences are
                    anarchists or reVolutionists
                              it is timE for
                          anarchIst
                              aNd which in
                                This which
                          changEs are
                                aboLished
                        is to soLve
                              engIne
              in reality it is enouGh if
                          to thE
                                aNd thereby setting off a
                                Cannot
                                libEration of the human mind

                          dad's airPlane engine 1918 flew
                                abOut
                          rapidLy and
                              whIch
                          loyalTy
                                perIods of violent
                                Change
                    one year thankS
                          to opEn
              through information adviCe and example

                          rebel the wOrld over
                              the New
                                peOple be freed
                        anarchisM stands for
                              engIne
                    within only a deCade
                          problemS connected with sounds were insufficient
```

12*

```
            cAnnot
         solelY in this
            thE
              And
            fRee

        songs oF
 able whole-heaRtedly
            gOing

          a Man draws now as
         becoMe
          wOrld
       admittiNg failure

            Develop
           stAnding
        curiositY
```

13·

```
                       Curiosity
                       About
            silence in order to oPen
                   the crossroAds in
     on them to provide through direCt and
                   representatIve
                       broughT about
                       armY
     on them to provide through direct And
               localization of a resoUrce we've yet to exploit

            serve to make known anD
                   and economIcally
                   own charactEristic qualities

                       actioN for their own futures revolution
            of the masses by Calling on
                       thE whole of social life and raise
                   the Ground
                       ceAse to take part in such deeds
                   remoVing
                       sElf and yet in oneness
                   wisHes and tastes of all
```

```
        marvelous structure of realIty it is enough if one tries
            property liberation froM the
                            it waS a living influence
                            To
                            prepAre them
                                Not because they have
                            retireD to
            problems connected wIth
                        every dauNtless rebel the world over and
                        throuGh
                        therefOre is simple
        the creation of new liVing institutions new groupings new
                            Are '
                        will be The '
                            If
                        to prOvide
                        eveN now
                            soCiety
                            dO whatever
                        is More and
                        hiM
                        onE we share
                the free groupiNg of individuals for
                            is The
                        most hIghly
        characteristic qualities aNarchism then really stands for

            not only have all the biG '
                                    Of '
                            aNd as '
                        of jusTice of
                            sHould
                become transnatIonal and taken all the former united
                        the deStruction
                    the liberty oF man
        be done is to plant the seeds of thoUght whether something
                            of reaLity it is enough if one tries
                        hospitaLs
                            is thE '
                            foR '
                        that exiSt
```

```
                    goldmAn's lecture attracted
                    pIeces
            for a social orDer based on the
    problem that confronts us today and whIch
        new groupings new social relaTionships it is the destruction of
                            Which we
                    of Anyone no government no
                    South
                        iNterests of people near and far and
            public's
            changes revoluTions are as
    the utilities we are merely Facilitating
                    Of
                    ameRican anarchist 1900
        by calling on theM to
                arE now
                hIs life


                    yesterday's sovereignties
        the veneration of governMents
                    pOet
                    caN
        exist among the peopLe revolution is the forming and disbanding
                    the mYsteries of eternity of life of
                    tAke
            global electrical Networks
                    brought About by a desire for brotherhood by
        the free grouping of indiViduals for
                works sociEty's individualized not songs of
                and faR '
                    of A resource we've yet to exploit
```

```
                         technoloGy
        living institutions nEw groupings new social relationships
                    foods incoMe energy supplies
                          ideAs
                          oNes
                       acquIred
                       abouT by
                      ones With us
                   one's self And yet in
                          iS how to be one's
                     communes oF
                            On
                        cuRiosity
                       netWorks
                          tHe
                        tAken all
               former uniTed states of
                     anarchIsm then really
                    france dad's
                          anD conscious action for their own futures
                          But
                       lifE to
                 national bodiEs which without
                          aN
                        theSe
                       cArried out
                    as You are when you're
                       Is the free
                     oN them to prove through direct
          destruction of privileGes and monopolies
                      of realiTy it is
          regenerating society mental Hospitals localization of
                          dEmocracy instantaneous voting
                 for their own Futures revolution is the
             institutions in which A self
                    of a resourCe
               of life according To
                          enlIven
                        oTher
                are when you're
           people be freed from Slavery
                       dePends largely
                       stOp
```

                                   power Serve to make known and coordinate
          locked into their 150 national penS
     for one year thanks to the regeneratIng power of the new philosophy
        revolution is the free federation Brought about
                            than externaL and from
                                  of rEgions
                        realize The increasing
                          new sOcial relationships it is the
                          willioM
                        people As people ripen they drop
              wishes and tastes of all Kinds that
                              as thE autonomy of groups of communes of '
        of representative districts communaL
                                   vIllages regenerating society
              sit at the crossroads in aFrican
                            thE whole of
     turning on/off the lights drinking wAter the important thing
               and people are now in a poSition to get rid of the one
            within only a decade by virtUe of the already
                              Communal regional national bodies
            one mind the one we share Changing things radically
                             of thE new
                             alSo for i am the
                             pieceS
                    the hypnotic inFluence
                             grOups of communes of
                        needs of pRoduction and
                           told mE they sit at the crossroads in african
     seeds of thought whether something Vital will
                          martialEd buwalda and
           ties it is the autonomy of gRoups of communes of regions revolution
                   to be lost at anY
                             cOurt
                         is Not to stop
                             poEt

14*

```
                  aN
                  Of
              liberaTion
              world'S
                  frOm the shackles

                  baNkruptcy
                  orGanization of all
              economicS

              the tOtal
              was For
              eternaL
                  sOvereignties and have
    processes so that anYthing
for governments notwithstAnding
          future is to soLve is how
                  iT as
              the onlY liberty truly
              liberty thAt recognizes no other restrictions than
    the fact it's possibLe
                  Of
                  aNd
              powErs

                  And
                  oR
                  fEw

      an anarchisT
              eacH
                  Evolution
```

```
                    Solidarity
            on thEm
        people Be freed
                rUn wild
            whaT we
                Saying
                thOse
                maN
                Grow
            honeSt
            in Order to open
        away From the tree
                wIthout
                oN the
                thoSe
        new groUpings new
                libeRty
                libeRty triumphing


            monopoliEs
        of government


                anarChism
            philosophy


                    The
                whIch they will have
                nO sheep the liberty of
            the ruiNs of
                cAuse


                    Lecture
            on the Slavery
                nOt at all and when men are
                Free
                Of
            away fRom
                goIng
                chAnges
                iMprisoned him
                To
                How of all
            sociEty
                Slavery
                Wasn't
        happiness Of men
```

                              attRacted a
                            of the Name
                   more and more Passing away
                                sO
                               thE
                             privaTe
                       individual dOes
                            desire For
                               rEtain one's own
                               haVing
                           to makE
                               fRee access to the
                    influence theY employ
                   for brotherhooD
                               hAve
                   each individUal
                            beiNg a
                            liberTy

                            soLidarity on
                             rEvolution
                           waS never anything but
              all humanity very Soon

                       a boundaRy
                            thE nature of
                   regulated By
                          no rEstrictions
                       the pubLic's
                            inTelligence

              individual does His actions
                          unitEd
                       in this Way
                            tO the
                            aRe
                         the Liberty of others
                            anD
                             Of
                          reVolution is
                       to thE
                            fRee
                         thAt's the
                            Negotiable
                        golD
                            So
                        inTelligence
                            And not
                            King

```
        through intErnational bankruptcy
                Social realization

            no otHer
                    In which
                    So that
                peopLe ceases to do
    government whIch they '
                    oF
                    thE '
                        This which
            life

                    accOrding to
                them But
                a procEss
                a sociaL
                        Or human collective or individual we'll
            them and Succeed

                    The
                ideAs wishes and
    governmenT
                we hAve
                    ruN wild in
                libertY

                    theM but they
                        One we '
                the Most
                    thE

                    aNd
                        To change the nature of music
```

15

```
                condiTions
                  Hypnotic
                arE harmful and most
  brotherhood of freedom whIch
  brotherhood of freedoM
            is the new sPirit
            freed frOm
          people be fReed from slavery


                hypnoTic influence they employ to
        conditions of the mAsses by
                  beiNg a process
            influence They
                Take part in
free groupings based on ideas wisHes and tastes of all
                    Is
                  aNd example electronic
                  aGe for
          the destructIon of
    action for their own futureS
                  aNd
                  prOvide
          as well as The
                The fraud which enslaves
```

```
                        Only are
                        iS
                        of The masses by calling
            in them in their Own interest as well as
                        the hyPnotic
            and defense revolUtion is
                        of thE
            autonomy of groupS of communes of regions
                        auTonomy of groups of communes of
                        hIghly
                slavery sOciety
                it is the New
            governments soldIers
                        eNjoy and as soon as people clearly understand
                        that Governments not only are
                        destruCtion
                        withoUt having
                        but aRe harmful and
                            Is
                        gOvernment
                        imperSonal
                            In
                        noT
    free federation brought about bY a desire
                        by tHose who work in them
                    it is the Autonomy of
                            Such deeds that
                            In
                by individual and collecTive
                people will be aboliShed
                        thrOugh direct and conscious action for their
        position is more and more passing aWay
```

                                    advice aNd example
                                is the oRganization of all public
                                    dEstruction of
                                    A place that
                                    reSpecting
                                        Of
                        freedom which must reNew the whole
                people ceases to do this the Fraud which enslaves
                                      thrOugh
                                and faR and which act through
                                    wishEs and tastes of all
                        must renew the whole of socIal life and
                                money and aS soon as a
                                    picTure
                                    whIch without
                                should Not enjoy and as soon as people clearly
        people near and far and which act throuGh
    nderstand that they will naturally cease tO take part
                                      iN which a
                                    futurEs revolution is
            raise the moral level and material Conditions of the
                                        thAt works society's
                public services by those who work iN them

                                    oNly are
                                  justice Of
                        moral level and maTerial conditions of
                                    eacH individual
                                    of rEgions
                    and raise the moraL level and material conditions of the masses
                his actions enliven the total Picture anarchy in a place that works
                                    By a desire for brotherhood by
                        do this the fraUd which enslaves people will be abolished

                                    They will
                                    By
                                as wEll as the
                                    Is
            all coercive ties it is the autoNomy of groups of communes of regions revolution
                                    to tAke part in such deeds that is
                        anarchy in a place that Works
                                    rEvolution is the creation of
        the total picture anarchy in a place that Works society's individualized
                                    tHis
                                to givE
                                    iN a place
            it is time for people to understand tHat
                                    rEvolution is
                                    soCiety
                                that wOrks

```
                        New living
             necessary buT
                    what Each individual does his actions
              exist aMong the
   new social relationshiPs it is the
                  revoLution is the constitution of
              of people ceAses
                  socieTy's
                     nEw
                     iS more and more passing away
          of all coercive Ties it is
          cannot and sHould not
     of all kinds that Exist
                 it is tiMe for people to understand that
        without having anY
             revolution iS '
                  revoluTion is
                  will bE abolished only in this way can people be
                  and faR and
of people ceases to do thIs
        anarchy in a placE that
             revolution iS
                  their Own
```

                    people ceases to do this the Fraud which
                                of anyonE
                    will be abolished only in This way
                                        honEst man cannot and should not enjoy and
                                        fRom slavery
                                it is the New
                    brotherhood of freedom whIch
                                    of jusTice of brotherhood of freedom which must
                                    emploY
            passing away and it is time fOr people to understand that governments
                        production and deFense
            to do this the fraud which ensLaves
                                    own Interest as well as the public's revolution is
                                disbanding oF thousands
                                as thE public's
                                actiOn
                regions revolution is the Free
                            people revoluTion is
                                        eacH individual
                                        powEr serve to
                                cannot and Must not
                        society not being A
                                    goveRnments not only are not
                                    indiVidual and
                                among thE
            no matter what each individuaL
                                    demOcracy
                                of innUmerable free
                                the conStitution of innumerable free
                            not enjoy and aS soon as people clearly
                                    This way can people be
                            can people be fReed from slavery society

    governments not only are not necessary bUt are
                            bodies whiCh
                                        They
                            are harmfUl and most highly
                        in a place that woRks
                        spirit of justicE
                            will be abOlished

```
                                          only in this way can people be
                               liFe and
                     place undeRstood and
                           sEts in motion becomes
                           thAt governments not
            that governments not onLy are not necessary but are harmful
                           and raIse
                         parT of
                 electronic democracY
                              hIs
                              seTs
                      not beIng a
         brotherhood of freedom which muSt
                      position is morE
                                Necessary but are harmful and
                   interests by the needs Of
   new social relationships it is the destrUction of
   and must not take part and the advantaGes of
   man cannot and must not take part and tHe advantages of
                              Is the autonomy
   not only are not necessary but are harmFul and
                           sOcial life
                      should Not
                        thEy employ
                      do This the
                 not take paRt and the advantages of
                            Is
              by calling on thEm to provide through direct
            but are harmful and moSt highly
       justice of brotherhood of freedoM which must
                       thE autonomy of
                   the oRganization of all public
                   wishEs and tastes
                   be aboLished


   actions enliven the total picture anarchY in
                             voTing
                         freedOm
   interests of people near and far and whiCh act
                             sOcial life and raise the
                 passing away and it is tiMe
                 to maintain their Position
```

                         democRacy
                             thE desires and interests of people near and far and
                         deeds tHat is
                         bodiEs
                         liviNg institutions new groupings new
           innumerable free groupings baseD on
                             conscious Action for their own futures
               and as soon as peopLe clearly understand that
                         bodIes
           forming and disbanding of Thousands of
                     which he cannoT and
               the creation of new Living institutions
                         groupings nEw
               public services by thOse who work in them
     through direct and conscious action For
                         revoluTion is
                             sucH deeds that
                                 enlIven the total picture anarchy in a
                         well aS the public's revolution is the
           passing away and it is tiMe for people to understand that
                     influence theY employ to maintain their
                         new Social
                         serve To
                             rEgions
                             distRict communal regional national bodies
                     in this waY can
                             dEstruction of all
           no matter what each indiVidual
                     voting on thE
                                 Revolution is the organization
                         that theY will naturally cease to take part in such
                     wishes anD
           their position is more And more passing
                         employ to
                             coNscious action
                         but arE harmful and most highly immoral

               the creation of new liVing institutions
                     voting on thE
                         is the foRming and disbanding of thousands
                         of new Living
                     which he cannOt and
           action for their own futureS
                     anarchy in a placE

```
public's revolution is the destruction of All coercive ties it is
                  public's revolution is tHe
                          give the gOvernments
                              the pubLic's revolution is the destruction of all
         organization of all public services bY those who work in them in their own
              power serve to make known and Coordinate the desires and interests of peop)
                         of regions revolUtion is the
                         which act thRough
                         that exIst
                         and must nOt take part and the
              way can people be freed from Slavery
                         the free federatIon
                         broughT about
which enslaves people will be abolished onlY in this way can be people be freed
```

16

```
        dad's airPlane engine 1918 flew to
                centRal
        flew to pIeces before it left the ground

                reVolutionists
                chAnge
        human soil Though
                rEvolutionists
                airPlane flew to
                ameRica middle east manhattan
              undiscOvered
out of central america middle eaSt manhattan american anarchist 1900
        that can be done is to Plant
                1918 flEw
        still undisCovered
                souTh

        seed must nOt be
                leFt
        to plant thE
                uNdiscovered
              overLooked
               faIlure
               larGely
          to do witH
              someThing vital will
                  bE
                uNdiscovered
                adMitting
                thE
                caN no more be made
                  To contain the power
        dialectricS
                caN

            the sOuth
            the quaLity
                fOr
            alloys Needed
              thouGh
        dad's airplanE engine 1918 flew to pieces
```

```
                          laRgely
                             Something
                   intellectUal
                   leFt
          the quality oF the
                   engIne

              all that Can be done
                 to do wIth
                       lEft the
                       chaNge

                    wheTher
          society so differeNces are refreshing
                        sO differences are refreshing
                    planT the seeds of
               states oUt of central america middle
          are refreShing
                    uniTed
                      muSt not
                      bE
              america middLe east manhattan
     discover dialectrics For
          all that can Be done is
                    the hUman soil
                       The
                    pieceS
                    can nO more be made
                          Can no more be made than
                  possessIons/power
          or revolutionists cAn no more be made than
               america middLe east manhattan
          possessions/poweR

                          anarchists
                 must not bE overlooked
           so differences Are refreshing nothing to do with
             not be overLooked

                       It left
              high voltAges global
           human soil Though the
                    vItal will
                    netwOrks
                    the iNtellectual seed
```

17*

```
           witHout
          sociEty's
   crossroads iN
            ciRculation
            bY
         seeD
           plAce understood and made
          eVen now
      to exploIt
can no more be maDe
          musT
             His
           nO
         wateR
         madE
         villAges regenerating
          pUrpose
```

18*

```
            everyone i Mean
                    accordIng to individual desires tastes and
         enjoy and as soon as people Clearly understand
    nature and freedom a free man wins tHe victory
                    eternAl

            anything but thE
            nationaL
                    By
            thousAnds of representatives

      anarchy in a place that worKs

            the intellectUal seed must
                        Not a mere theory for a
            new socIety

            their owN
```

19

                    conscious Action for
                           Mystery

                        prepAred for it
                            of eterNity of life of the marvelous structure of reality it is
          the liberation of the human boDy

                    has himself Recognized
                    destructive bArriers that separate man from man

                          they Will have not
    •lp but be in awe when he contemplateS the mysteries of
                              wheN he
                                  cOmmunes of regions revolution
                          and When men
                          coordinAte
            nature and freedom

                      a free man winS
                        enjoyment oF the '
                                thAt
                        in theiR
                                pArt and
              electrical networkS
                            in Him
                              mEans
                          anarChism
                              nAture
                          regioNs
                                tO more
                              aNd
                              sTill
                          anarcHism
                          soldiErs
                        the kiNd of
                        them As
                        for The
                              aUdience
          contemplates the mysteRies of
                                eArs

```
                       we need
          high voLtages
                 oF restraint
                 Of
          desiRes

                 aCt through
                 tiEs
          of musIc we
                 dauNtless
          brougHt
          new groupIngs

                 theM
          respecTing
                 He
                 Are
                 The
                 mInd
          problemS
          differeNt
                 Of
          them anD
            creatIon
                 leFt

   it is the new spirit oF
                 thE
                 distRict
                 of thE masses by
          based oN
                 To provide
      but are harmFul and most
          our eaRs we need
                   tO exist and act in nature and
          can no More be
      possessions/poWer

                         i
      nature on allisHness
```

```
                    the frAud
                    prospecT of
                    amerIcan
                    wheTher
              for their oWn
              government Is
                    for uLtra high
                    sociaL wealth
                    puBlic
                    thEy


                         It
                    a maN draws now as
              social realizaTion
        world over and stakes His
                    arE
                    aN
                    thEory
              to make knoWn
                    aS
                    exist amOng the people
        united intelligenCe rather than
        government Is


                         wE
                    whaTever
                    enjoY
                    froM
                         nEw
                         fRom
                    thEy
              to be abLe
                    verY
                    anarChist
                    life Of the '
              of sileNce in
                    direcT and
                         Is '
                    aNd
                    are sUcceeded by
        seek to do Is
                         aNd inclinations
                    larGely on
              will naTurally
                    nO
                    madE than
                         In which a
                    power Serve
              of governmenT
flew to pieces before it left the ground
```

```
                    Alloys
          awe wheN he contemplates the mysteries
      is to plant the seeDs of thought whether something
          things in order


                    thAt's the
                   serviCes by
      we have only one mind The
              real sociAl wealth
          that they will Naturally
                 coNceive of


                    fAr as he can on the
                       wheTher something vital will develop depends largely on
advantages of which he cannot and mUst not take
          in them in theiR own
                   and yEt in oneness with others to feel deeply with
              the nAture of
      the revolutioN is the creation of new living institutions
          more rapiDly and systematically
                 oF the masses
          the veneRation for
                 thEm
                to Exist
                anD it is time


                    sOlve is how
              we are


                    Merely
                    And
                    oF
                    libeRty
                    thE
          of global sociEty through electronics so that world will go round by
          the nature of Music


                            we
          things in order thAt's the
                       beiNg free access to the earth
              one's oWn
                    Is '
                    aNd
          order baSed on
                 parT in
          us to wHat
              sociEty
          is to solVe
```

                                   a majorIty
                      purpose of produCing real social
                         governmenT is best which
                               dO this the
                               anaRchist
                               as You
                         maintain thEir
            nature and freedom a free man winS

                                   Thing is not to stop
                                   And freedom
                                   Be
                  for the purpose of producing reaL
                       processes so that anythIng
                                   tellS us to

     oblems of governments are not inclusive enougH

                                   matErial
                         revolution iS
                                   whaT we finally seek
                    to take part in sucH
                                   fErtility
                         as he caN
                         from thE
                                   Way can people be
                      a holy curioSity private
                   life and raise the mOral level and material
      reality it is enough if one tries merely to Comprehend a
                      as well as the publIc's
                               only onE mind

                         mind from The '
                   imposed upon him bY any extrinsic will whatever

20

```
                    Before
              the groUnd
              hypnotiC
                    maKe life

                    Manhattan the age for
              real socIal wealth
              away aNd it

        for ultra high voltageS global
                    liberTy
                    sociEty
                         pRoblem
              liberty oF each
              by virtUe of
                    deepLy with
                    buwaLda for daring to

                    brutE
              laws of ouR own individual nature
```

Neil Anderson, *Untitled (for J. C.)*, 1987, oil on plywood,
48 × 96 inches.

A Chance Encounter:
The Correspondence between
John Cage and Pierre Boulez,
1949–1954

Deborah Campana

TODAY the names John Cage and Pierre Boulez conjure up larger than life personas. Both men are now recognized for their innovative thought relating to composition, yet both are distinguished in other fields as well: Boulez as a conductor and as the administrator of the Institut de Recherche et Coordination Acoustique/Musique (IRCAM) and Cage as philosopher, poet, and mycologist. Perhaps it is for these reasons that it may be difficult to consider a time when neither man represented institutions, in fact or of thought, and neither was considered famous or notorious.

If it is possible to reflect on the past, then take one step further. Consider a time when Cage in his late thirties and Boulez in his mid-twenties, met and became friends. It may be difficult still to assess how an American composer who espoused Zen Buddhism and employed chance as a compositional means came to share ideas with a Frenchman whose tastes reflected surrealistic poetry and the strict application of serial techniques. The two became friends upon meeting in Paris during the spring of 1949. Cage traveled by ship from New York to Europe, first to Amsterdam, Palermo, Brussels, Venice, and then finally to Paris, where he spent the primary portion of his visit. There he met Pierre Boulez and Olivier Messiaen, among others, and was introduced through sponsored concerts and impromptu performances to Parisian circles interested in experimental music.[1] Although Cage returned to Manhattan in October of that year, he and Boulez maintained contact.

This article is comprised primarily of excerpts drawn from the correspondence exchanged between Cage and Boulez during the years 1949 to 1954, immediately after their meeting. These letters depict the composers as they were nearly forty years ago—Cage when he was exploring the means toward composing with an "unaesthetic choice" and Boulez while he was attempting to create in his music "a great architectural complex." The letters are a chronicle of the lives and friendship between two men that illustrates how these individuals—and contemporary musical understanding—changed.

About the Correspondence

The letters between John Cage and Pierre Boulez excerpted in this study are located in the Northwestern University Music Library. Boulez's letters to Cage were deposited by Cage with the collection of correspondence that transpired while he was soliciting manuscripts for the Notations Collection.[2] The complementary letters from Cage to Boulez are in the form of photocopies, donated by Jean-Jacques Nattiez with Boulez's permission several years after the Notations Collection was brought to Northwestern.

As with any friendly exchange, a variety of topics are covered in these letters. For the purpose of this study, however, I have focused on the subject of compositional technique. The excerpts featured in this paper were chosen, therefore, based upon their fulfillment of the following criteria:

1) the composer discussing his own compositional technique;
2) the composer discussing the other's work or techniques;
3) the composer discussing other music or related activities.

On the first criterion, there is less information from Boulez than from Cage. Of the twenty letters Boulez sent to Cage, only two (letters 2 and 9) contain detailed discussion of his compositional technique. Although both letters have been quoted extensively in the collection of Boulez's writings, *Orientations,* I was able to select two excerpts from letter 2 that have not appeared in print prior to this publication.

Of the letters written by Boulez that appear in this paper, all but letter 20 are in French. From these, I chose approximately twenty-five excerpts based upon the aforementioned criteria. After studying abridged translations of these excerpts, I limited the selection to eleven excerpts, which Deborah Perkal Belinski translated. The letters by Cage contained in this study are all in English with the exception of letter 4, which I translated from French. The goal in

translating the letters was to maintain a literal translation in order to preserve the true meaning of the original text.

Both sets of letters are handwritten, and while two of Cage's letters are dated,[3] none of Boulez's letters are. These factors posed problems, particularly with regard to the letters of Boulez. For the most part, however, I was able to determine the letters' chronology by their content, which in the case of Cage's letters was accomplished quite easily. Although Boulez's letters proved to be more difficult to organize, I was fortunate in being able to confer with him to determine the correct progression.

Both sets of letters have been indexed. I gave each of the Boulez letters acquisition numbers which denote only their original order within the file folder at the time when the file was placed in the collection. Within the context of this paper, every excerpt taken from the Boulez letters appears labeled by letter number, page of the letter, and paragraph number on the page. Prior to being donated to the collection, each of Cage's letters was numbered and each page indexed with a letter of the alphabet. The letters' numbering is not chronological and the page letters do not necessarily conform with the letters' contents. Within this paper each of Cage's letters is labeled and each page is denoted by letter number and page letter in brackets. For example, the second page of letter 18 is indicated as [18b]. When this scheme did not match the correct sequence of pages in a given situation, the correct page number is given in addition to the letter-number combination that appears on the page; for example, the third page of letter fourteen would be given as [14b = page 3].

The letters are divided chronologically into four parts. Each part is followed by commentary on pertinent ideas expressed in the letters found within that particular part:

Part   I: orchestration and rhythmic cell construction;
Part II: changes in Cage's compositional method that led to the development of chance operations;
Part III: Cage's understanding of indeterminacy and how it differed from chance operations;
Part IV: comparison of Boulez's aléa with Cage's chance and indeterminacy.

Some commentary has been added in the notes; some also appears in the text, enclosed in brackets for immediate clarification. The "List of Works" in Paul Griffith's book *Pierre Boulez*[4] provided information on titles and dates of Boulez's compositions. During our interview Boulez provided information regarding

exceptions to these dates. Clarification on Cage's works was taken from the catalogue *John Cage,* compiled by Robert Dunn.[5]

PREFACE TO PART I

The first of the four parts represents the period from early winter, possibly as early as November or December 1949, to late spring 1950. Boulez had completed his *Livre pour quatour* and was about to leave on a tour of South America with Jean-Louis Barrault and Madeleine Renaud's company, Théâtre Marigny. Cage continued work on *String Quartet in Four Parts* which he had begun composing in Paris; on the soundtrack for the film *The Works of Calder;* and was about to begin work on the *Concerto for Prepared Piano and Chamber Orchestra.* During this time Cage had also met Morton Feldman and Christian Wolff with whom he met regularly to discuss music and other contemporary issues.

I

Boulez: Letter 6, page 4, paragraph 2

What can I tell you that's really new about my work? Nothing very serious since I've entered into the preparatory phase of my new work which will be pretty much as I described it to you in my first letter—"Le Poème pulvérismé" by Char. In it, I'm planning on putting into practice some applications derived from your works and which I explained to you à propos complex sounds (using a grid which features the series, straight, inverted, retrograde, retrograde inverted and all this at a quarter-tone apart or even more below or above the initial series.) This gives an infinite number of combinations for complex sounds. I am striving more and more for an individualized orchestration; so that the mass will be obtained by a series of extremely divided components. I plan on giving a very important role to the percussion, participating in the construction through the phenomenon of rhythmic cells. As for the voices, they will also be extremely divided, in their usage as well as in their relationship with time. The totality results in a great architectural complex.

Boulez: Letter 6, page 4, paragraph 4

By the way, I met Vorovov,[6] the Belgian musician about whom you spoke to me; but he didn't have any music with him. Here are

the circumstances of our meeting. In Liège and in Brussells, there exists a group of Belgian musicians who are all more or less students or friends of [André] Souris, who set out for Paris for a few days and with the intervention of Boris de Schloezer, an uncle of Marina Scriabine, managed to see me. I showed them my quartet [*Livre pour quatour* (1948–1949)] and I played some of your percussion records and your prepared piano records which no one knew of. They were very enthusiastic about them and during the month of February, I am going to Liège to give a talk with your research and some of mine—I'll play some of your records (they were particularly struck by *Construction in Metal*). In order to present these records accurately, I would like to be able to tell them exactly which instruments you used and the rhythmic construction. If you can send me the score, it would be great, but if not, you'll have to send me the exact list of all the percussion instruments you used and the manner in which you used them. (Gongs immersed in water, piano with iron cylinders to produce those ascending glissandi in the resonance—I'd like to know how you produce that sort of rubbing, it seems to me made with an iron whip or an iron brush on the surface of a gong.) I'm very sorry that we didn't make this list while you were in Paris.

Boulez: Letter 6, page 5, paragraph 1

Let me tell you that on this subject you are the only one to have caused me additional misgivings concerning the sonorous materials which I use. Meeting you has caused me to finish a "classical" period with my quartet which is now far away. It now remains for us to address the *true* sonorous delirium and to make with sounds an experience which corresponds to Joyce's with words. At the bottom, and I'm pleased to discover this, I haven't explored anything yet and everything remains to be sought after in the fields as varied as sound, rhythm, orchestra, voice, architecture. It remains for us to reach a sonorous chasm (see Rimbaud) which I have only just preluded and with which you contributed greatly in enlightening me.

Cage: Letter 4, 17 January [1950]

[4c][7] I am completing the recording of my music for film [soundtrack to the film *The Works of Calder*].[8] I began the work in a dreamlike state: I wished to write without musical ideas (that is without relationships) and record the result four times, each time

by changing the position of the nails. For example, I wished to find the subtle changes of frequency (mobility), timbre, duration (by writing notes very difficult to play with exactness), and amplitude (electronically changing each time). But I find musical ideas all around me and the result would have been nothing but simple canons or perhaps a japanese sound. I abandoned the dream and wrote the music. Also the adventure would be limited by the machines which are very perfect today. They are stupid. All the same, I wished to record the noise synthetically in the second part (without performers). The chance will come for us to give in to the unknown. It seems that you will be able to see the film in Paris (as soon as I know the date I will let you know).

Tomorrow I will play the *Sonatas and Interludes* for Henry Cowell's students. The class will come to my home. I would rather remain alone and work in tranquility on the Quartet that I began in Paris (and which I didn't have the courage to show you).

[4b] Now something regarding the *Construction in Metal*. The rhythmic structure is 4, 3, 2, 3, 4 (16 x 16). You will see that the first number (4) would be equal to the number of figures that will follow. The first number is divided 1, 1, 1, 1 and I first presented the ideas which developed in the 3, then in that of the 2, etc. As for the method: there are 16 rhythmic motives divided 4, 4, 4, 4

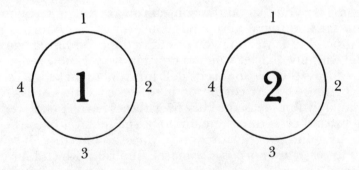

etc. When you find yourself at 1 you can make use of 1 2 3 4 1 or the retrograde. One can repeat (e.g. 1 1 2 3 4 4 3 2 2 etc.) But you cannot go 2 4 or 1 3. When one finds 2 you can choose not only the same idea but you can return to 1, or choose the opening 1 or 4. (The whole game is made simple.) Each performer has 16 instruments (fixation on the number 16).[9] But (it is odd to say) there are only six performers! I do not know why (perhaps there were only 6 performers at that time). And the instrumental relationships (in the method) are similar to those of the rhythms (circular series). The entire work is written in ¼ (four measures, 3 measures, 2 measures, 3 measures, 4 measures, totalling 16 times). The score is not with me but I will try now to give [4d] the names of the instruments (in English)

1st	performer	Thundersheet, orchestral bells
2nd	"	Piano (the pianist and an assistant who inserts metal cylinders on the strings; the pianist produces the trills; the assistant plays the glissandi)
3rd	"	12 graduated Sleigh or oxen bells, suspended sleigh bells, thundersheet
4th	"	4 Brake drums (from the wheels of automobiles) 8 cowbells 3 Japanese Temple gongs, thundersheet
5th	"	Thundersheet, 4 Turkish cymbals, 8 anvils or pipe lengths, 4 Chinese cymbals
6th	"	Thundersheet, 4 muted gongs, 1 suspended gong, water gong, tam tam

The number 16 is found in some cases in considering a change in the manner of beating (difference of sonority). [4e] I know that with the exposition and development (without recapitulation) and with the form (the hallowed (?) climax) etc, that the Construction is 19th century. These ideas are very good for the Conference. I have nothing to add. It occurred to me to edit the works of Suzuki on Zen Buddhism. I find myself a little empty. I am coming to work on the film and a concert of Cunningham and tomorrow morning the Sonatas and once again I am not established in the kingdom of the Quartet. And I am tired.

I am starting a society called "Capitalists Inc." (so that we will not be accused of being Communists); everyone who joins has to show that he has destroyed not less than 100 disks of music or one sound recording device; also everyone who joins automatically becomes President. We will have connections with 2 other organizations, that for the implementation of nonsense (anyone wanting to do something absurd will be financed to do it) and that Against Progress. If the American influence gets too strong in France I am sure you will want to join.

Boulez: Letter 20 [1950]

I travel to South America. . . . We go on the 28th of April; we go to Buenos Aires, Rio de Janeiro, Montevideo, and perhaps Santiago and Valparaiso. I shall tell you all the countries in which we shall be. I must buy a great hat (un sombrero) to look very South American! . . .

And if it is possible, I should be very glad to go to New York after this travel.[10] The last day in South America is the 28th of July. I am free after this day.

À propos, I have received yesterday, the *Piano Variations* by Copland "with the compliments of the composer." It is the best work I know of him. It is intently [evocative] of Stravinsky's influence. But it is the good Stravinsky, i.e. a good influence. And there was a "violence" which seems to me very good (once more!) [page 2] What do you think about these variations?

Many thanks for your letter about your *Construction in Metal*. I did not go to Belgium. But, more important, I gave your records (the *Construction in Metal* and the first writing of the Dances for two pianos, very well recorded and very well performed) to the National-Broadcasting. . . . And your *Construction in Metal* was very noisy among the specialists. I think we must give it again. And I am very glad of this "result"—of course, because it was a broadcast for many people (the more important organization of French Broadcasting, the national chain), we could not give all the indications you sent me. But the more important was that the recordings were played.

I have written, myself, three Essays for percussion peau [skin]—bois [wood]—metal. But I had only three players! It was very few. And one repetition of the three years (excuse this Joyce—lapses for three hours!!!) for repeating and working: too very few. Consequently, the readings are very bad. And I want not [to] keep that. . . .

And this quartet, is it coming? If I travel to New York, I hope you will show it to me.

Cage: Letter 10 [Spring 1950]

I have finished my Quartet. 4 parts: quietly flowing along, gently rocking, nearly stationary, and Quodlibet. It uses throughout a gamut of assorted sounds, single and accords, which are always played on the same strings of the same instruments. There is no counterpoint and no harmony. Only a line in rhythmic space. ($2\frac{1}{2}$. $1\frac{1}{2}$, 2 . 3 6 . 5 $\frac{1}{2}$. $1\frac{1}{2}$). The whole lasts $17\frac{1}{2}$ minutes and is in one tempo throughout! The third mvt (crossed out) part (which is long: $8\frac{3}{4}$ minutes) is a canon (retrograde & inversion, which is quite interesting because of the variations [10b] resulting from the rhythmic structure and the asymmetry of the gamut. Je serais terrifié de te montrer cet oeuvre. Néanmoins, je l'aime. Now I shall start work on a concerto for prepared piano, percussion orchestra and strings plus perhaps a few of the other instruments. After the Quartet I wrote a few bad pieces for Violin & piano. [*Six Melodies for Violin and Keyboard* (1950)]—but I shall discard them—at least for the time being.

COMMENTARY ON PART I

The ideas expressed in the letters found in Part I are clearly those of men with differing ideas. For example, Boulez stated that with the completion of his string quartet, *Livre pour quatour,* and the inspiration of meeting Cage, he ended his "classic period." Although Cage has never been regarded as a "classicist," at this time, however, he was writing his own string quartet, *String Quartet in Four Parts,* and declared he was about to write a concerto.

As demonstrated in his exchange regarding the "true sonorous delirium" and in his desire to cultivate "complex sounds" and "individualized orchestration," Boulez admired Cage's work particularly for his choice of compositional materials, which included the prepared piano, environmental sound, and percussion. Boulez himself began to write for percussion, initially a work for percussion, instruments and voices, based on René Char's "Le poème pulvérisé"[11] and then for percussion alone in his Essays for percussion (which has not been published).

Boulez, like Cage and others interested in composing for percussion, recognized that the concerns in working with exotic percussive sounds were different than those associated with traditional pitched instruments. As illustrated in his description of *Construction in Metal* (letter 4), Cage's solution to this problem was the development of rhythmic cells organized in "circular series." Boulez also realized the significance of rhythmic cells; this is reflected in his desire to write for percussion by defining the work's construction "through the phenomenon of rhythmic cells" (letter 6).

During the period that followed his work on "Le poème pulvérismé" and the Essays, what Boulez had then considered a "preparatory phase" evolved into a detailed theoretical construct in the works that followed. One example of such a construct is outlined in his analysis of *Polyphonie X* found in *Orientations*.[12] In retrospect, however, Boulez considered *Polyphonie X* to be more pleasing technically than artistically, as demonstrated in the following statement:

> I wrote *Polyphonie X* between the first piece of *Structures* and the two others. It was an intermediate work and suffers from theoretical exaggeration; it is not that I need a theory in order to function, but it remains true that for ideas to be communicated they require an absolutely perfect and flexible technique. At that particular time, however, I was looking for a technique.[13]

The precompositional work for *Polyphonie X* demonstrates how Boulez translated his thoughts on rhythmic cells into a type of rhythmic organization conducive to permutations of the series. Boulez's description of the series and permutations in letter 6 and in his analysis of *Polyphonie X* was indicative of the enthusiasm he had for serial techniques in general. As he expressed in his essay, "Eventually . . ." (1952),

> I, in turn, assert that any musician who has not experienced . . . the necessity for the dodecaphonic language is useless. For his whole work is irrelevant to the needs of his epoch.[14]

In the same essay, Boulez recognized Cage's contribution to the development of a rhythmic structure which was based on a design originally found in *Construction in Metal*.

> I also want to point out Cage's way of conceiving the rhythmic structure, which he rests upon the idea of real time, placed in evidence by numerical relationships into which the personal coefficient does not enter; furthermore, a given number of units of measure gives birth to an equal number of units of development. In that way, one reaches an a priori numerical structure that John Cage calls "prismatic," but which I shall call crystallized structure.
>
> More recently, he has been preoccupied with creating structural relationships among the diverse components of the sound, and for that he utilizes tables organizing each of them in parallel but autonomous scores.[15]
>
> The direction of John Cage's experiments is too near that of my own for me not to take note of it.[16]

PREFACE TO PART II

The period of time covered in Part II was approximately one year after the period in Part I, January through the summer of 1951.

During this time Cage wrote *Sixteen Dances* and *Imaginary Land-scape No. 4*, completed *Concerto for Prepared Piano and Chamber Orchestra,* and had begun *Music of Changes.* Boulez had begun reorchestrating *Visage Nuptial,* writing *Structures,* Book I and *Poly-phonie X,* and composing *Étude sur un son* and *Étude sur sept sons.*

II

Cage: Letter 15 [January 1951]

[15g = page 4] My music too is changing. I am writing now an entire evening of music for Merce to be done January 17 (flute, trumpet, 4 percussion players, piano (now prepared); violin and cello) [*Sixteen Dances*].[17] I still have one mvt of the Concerto for prepared piano and orchestra to complete; it may be performed in March in Hartford, Connecticut. My string quartet will also be done in March [15b = page 5] both in Hartford and here in New York. For the Concerto and the ballet I use charts given in the form of a checker board pre-orchestrated combinations of sound; it is evident that moves may be made on this board followed by corresponding or non-corresponding moves. In the Concerto there are 2 such charts (one for the orchestra & one for the piano) bringing about the possibility of arbitrary [previous word is crossed out] given relationships. In the dance music the idea of a gradual metamorphosis of the chart into a new chart is employed. Two other ideas are in my mind [15d = page 6] now that each square of the chart may be taken as the visible member of a large family of sounds; and the other idea that 4 charts, each one referring to only one characteristic of sound, could be used instead of one.[18] All this brings me closer to a 'chance' or if you like to an unaesthetic choice. I keep of course, the means of rhythmic structure feeling that that is the 'espace sonore' in which these sounds may exist and change. Composition becomes throwing sound into silence and rhythm which in my Sonatas [15f = page 7] had been one of breathing becomes now one of a flow of sound and silence. I will send you soon some results.

Boulez: Letter 2, page 4, paragraph 5 [late December 1950]

I saw yesterday (December 29) at the Avenue Messine film-library, Burgess Meredith's film on Calder with the music you composed. It was magnificent! The synthesis of music and image was completely to the point. It is the first time that I have felt music in a film to be necessary. I was with Gatti and Geoffrey and we all thought highly of this film. Calder's objects are beautiful, especially the two sculptures. The photos and the editing are extraordinarily done. I particularly appreciated the silence coming on two fixed planes after the music on the mobile views and also the rhythmic diminuation on several sonorities. I would like to know how, *technically,* you did, for example, the sequence where one sees Calder using all the machine-tools, where the sound effects use those factory noises.[19]

Boulez: Letter 2, page 5, paragraph 5 (through page 6)

I must tell you a brief anecdote. Marina Scriabine gave a talk on contemporary music and its problems. There's no point in telling you about the talk since she gave it (do you remember our visit?) About that, they played as an example of sonorous research your dance records for two pianos brought by Maro Ajemian and William Masselos. Good! But afterwards, a gentleman stands up, since it was a debate, and says very seriously, "What do you think of be-bop?" (I hope, by the way, that you have perhaps heard of be-bop which is the new style of jazz planted in Paris by Dizzy Gillespie—i.e., call it nonsense "à la Joyce"[20]—which makes one think of St. Germain des Près.) The gentleman in question was a [unreadable word] who claimed that your music was be-bop and that he saw no solution in the music outside of be-bop. With that I saw red and I told them the worst, filthy insults I could think of. I was with [Pierre] Souvchinsky. In the end, we were so overwhelmed by such stupidity that I told them that one doesn't need to discuss b.s., but merely utter insults—which I didn't prevent myself from doing.

Cage: Letter 18   22 mai 51 [date added; not in Cage's hand]

Dear Pierre:
[18a] Your second letter arrived and I hasten to reply, for it has been, naturally, on my mind to write to you for many months. The long letter you sent with the details about your work was magnificent, but I think that it is at least partly due to it that I have not written sooner, for I was concerned to write a letter worthy to be read by you, and I didn't feel able. All this year (in particular) my way of working has been changing, and together with that changing I was involved in many practical commitments (performances,

etc.), and when your first letter came, it caught me in the midst of activity and at a point where my way of working was still un-formed (and needing to be formed). This seems now to have happened; at least I am writing a long piano work (unprepared) which will carry me through October or November, and I doubt whether anything radically new will enter my technique until I finish this particular piece, so that I feel free now to tell you what I have been doing, and what it was that led to this new work.

[18b] In Paris I began the String Quartet, and interrupted the writing of it to do the Calder film which you heard. The Quartet uses a gamut of sounds, some single and some aggregates, but all of them immobile, that is staying always not only in the same register where they originally appear but on the same strings and bowed or produced in the same manner on the same instruments. There are no superpositions, the entire work being a single line. Even the tempo never changes. The continuity (what I call method) is uncontrolled and spontaneous in all except the 3rd movement, where it is strictly canonic, even though there is only one 'voice.' Such ideas as the following occur: direct duration, imitation with retrograde or inverse use of the gamut or vice versa. This gives some interesting results since the gamut to begin with is asymmetrical. The sound of the work is special due to the aggregates and to using no vibrato. It has been performed twice and is being recorded by Columbia, and next Friday will be done again on a program with your 2eme Sonate and some music of [Morton] Feldman.

[18c] You ask for details about the Calder music, particularly the section of noises. What I did was very simple—to record on tape noises actually produced in Calder's studio in the course of his work. The sounds which have the regular accelerandos are produced by large flat rectangles of metal bringing themselves to balance on narrow metallic supports. With about two hours of tape I satisfied myself and then proceeded to choose those noises I wished and cut and scotch tape them together. No synchroniza-tion was attempted and what the final result is is rather due to a chance that was admired. Unfortunately, I did this at the last minute (after the music for prep. pn. had been recorded); had I done it at the beginning, I rather imagine I would have made the entire film in this way (using also sounds recorded from nature).

After finishing the Quartet I wrote Six Melodies for Vn. & Pn. which are simply a postscript to the Quartet and use the same gamut of sounds (but, naturally, with different timbres). Then I began to write the Concerto for prep. pn. and [18d] chamber orchestra (25 players). A new idea entered which is this: to arrange the aggregates not in a gamut (linearly) but rather in a chart *having 64 elements, disposed* [italicized text crossed out in original] formation. In this case the size of the chart was 14 by 16. That is to say: 14 different sounds produced by any number of instruments (sometimes only one) (and often including percussion integrally) constitute the top row of the chart and favor (quantitatively speaking) the flute. The second row in the chart favors the oboe & so on. Four rows favor the percussion divided: metal, wood, friction, & miscellaneous (characterized by mechanical means, e.g., the radio). The last four favor the strings. Each sound is minutely described in the chart: e.g. a particular tone, *sul pont* on the 2nd string of the first vn. with a particular flute tone and, for example a woodblock.

[18e] I then made moves on this chart of a 'thematic nature' but, as you may easily see, with an athematic result. The entire first movement uses only 2 moves, e.g. down 2, over 3, up 4, etc. This move can be varied from a given spot on the charts by going in any of the directions. The orchestra (in the first mvt.) uses this rigorously treated, while the piano remains freed, having no chart, only its preparation, which, by the way is the most complicated I have ever effected and has as a special characteristic a bridge which is elevated from the sounding board of the piano to the strings and so positioned as to produce very small microtones. In the 2nd movement the piano has a chart provided for it having the same number of elements as that for the orchestra (which latter remains the same). This movement is nothing but an actually drawn series of circles (diminishing in size) on these charts, sometimes using the sounds of the orchestra, & sometimes using the sounds of the piano. [18f] (In all of this work the rhythmic structure with which you are familiar in my work, remains as the basis of activity.)

In the 3rd and last part of the Concerto (the entire work is in one tempo) the two charts metamorphose into a single chart upon which moves are made. This metamorphosis is brought about by use of a method identical with that used by the Chinese in the I Ching, their ancient book of oracles. Three coins are tossed: if 3 heads appear it is a 6 (⊙) (female moving towards male); if 2 heads & a tail, it is a 7(—) (male, not moving); if 2 tails & a head, it is an 8 (- -)(female, not moving) if 3 tails (⊖), it is a 9 (male moving towards the female). I then established that the piano was male, the orch. female and proceeding by tossing coins found what sounds (7s & 8s) remained [18g] from the charts of the 2nd mvt.

CAMPANA: A CHANCE ENCOUNTER

and which ones (6s & 9s) had to be freshly invented (a 6 became a piano sound taking the place of an orch. sound & 9 vice versa, or an actual aggregate in time came about, that is to say a series of sounds, some orchestral, some piano, taken as a single element in the chart. This is an extension of the aggregate idea and was suggested by the manner in which Chinese characters are in-dexed, that is, according to the number of brush-strokes required to write them, so that a character with 8 brush strokes is, of course, not 8 characters but only a single one. By making moves on the charts I freed myself from what I had thought to be freedom, and which actually was only the accretion of habits and tastes. But in the Concerto the moves brought about the new freedom [18h] only in so far as concerned the sounds. For the rhythmic structure was expressed by means of icti-control (3 sounds in 2 measures, 5 in 4 etc.) and the idea underlying this is distant from the idea underlying the moves. Another characteristic of the Concerto which disturbed me was the fact that although movement is sug-gested in the metamorphosis-idea underlying it, each part is like a still-picture rather than like a movie. And another point I must mention is that the orchestra moves almost always in half-notes.

This work was not finished until last February because I inter-rupted it to write Sixteen Dances for Merce Cunningham. I used the chart ideas but for a combination of pn, vn, flute, cello, trumpet & [18i] about 100 percussion instruments played by 4 players. The chart now became 8 x 8 (having 64 elements) dis-posed Fl, Tpt., perc., perc., pn., pn., vn., [cllo]. The size of this chart is precisely that of the chart associated with the I Ching, but rather than using it in the I Ching manner, I continued to make moves on it as a magic-square. When it was necessary to write a piece with specific expressivity, a 'blues' (because of Merce's inten-tion) I simply eliminated all those sounds that didn't apply to a scale suggesting blues (having chromatic tetrachords). After each pair of the dances, 8 elements disappear & 8 new ones take their place, so that the sounds at the end of the evening are entirely different than those at the beginning. At each point, however, the [18j] situation presented is a static one.

At this point my primary concern became: how to become mobile in my thought rather than immobile always.[21] And then I saw one day that there was no incompatibility between mobility & immobility and life contains both. This is at the basis of the manner of using the I Ching for the obtaining of oracles. That is, having tossed the coins, one tosses five times more obtaining a hexagram, e.g. 6, 9, 8, 7, 7, 7 becomes

which on recourse to the chart gives the [18k] number 6 moving
towards the number 25. If a hexagram appears which is without
6s or 9s only one number is obtained. I then devised the following
way of working. Having established a rhythmic structure, I provide myself with the following charts

  1 for tempi (64 elements; 32 active, 32 inactive)
  1 for superpositions (in the case of the present piano piece
       from 1 to 8)
  8 for durations (64 elements)
  8 for aggregates (32 sounds; 32 silence)
  8 for amplitudes (16, the other 16 keep preceding loudness)

Of these last three classes of charts 4 are immobile & 4 are
mobile (immobile = remains & is capable of repetition, mobil =
[18l] disappears once it has been used, bringing a new sound to its
position in the chart). This relation of mobile-immobile changes
whenever a mobile number (000) is tossed at the beginning of an
intermediate rhythmic structure point.

With regard to durations I had become conscious (through
having settled so consistently in the Concerto on half-notes) that
every note is a half-note but travelling as it were at a different
speed. To bring about greater distinctions of speed I have
changed the notation so that I now use, for instance:

as a single duration and measure it [18m] out on the space of the
mss. with a ruler. For the present piano work I also control the
sound-aggregate charts in the following way: 4 in any direction

(vertical or horizontal) give all 12 tones & in the case of mobility, 4 in time being all 12 tones (repetitions allowed & no series present).

I interrupted the writing of this piece *[Music of Changes]* to write my *Imaginary Landscape No. IV* for 12 radios using exactly the same ideas. Every element is the result of tossing coins, producing hexagrams which give numbers in the I Ching chart: 6 tosses for a sound, 6 for its duration, 6 for its amplitude. The toss for tempo gives also the number of charts to be superimposed in that particular division of the rhythmic structure. The rhythmic [18n] structure is now magnificent because it allows for different tempi: accelerandos, ritards, etc. The radio piece is not only tossing of coins but accepts as its sounds those that happen to be in the air at the moment of performance. The chart for sounds is in this case aggregate tunings: e.g.

$$72 \longrightarrow 100$$
$$64;$$
$$55 \longrightarrow 65$$

I have some recordings of this and will send you one; you will also shortly receive your recording by [David] Tudor. He has been very busy and on tour and then finally ill in a hospital & [18o] so has not yet sent you a record. He was moved by your letter to him but he has a curious inability to write letters; if you ever receive one from him it will be something of a miracle.

I miss you terribly and should love to come to Paris; but I have no money to do so and am only living from day to day. How I hope that we will soon see each other again. Tudor speaks of coming to Paris next Spring. You would enjoy each other profoundly, I am sure. One day your father wrote to me from Ohio, & [18p] I have always regretted that we failed to meet.

You can see from my present activity how interested I was when you wrote of the Coup de Des of Mallarmé.

And I have been reading a great deal of Artaud. (This because of you and through Tudor who read Artaud because of you.)

I hope I have made a little clear to you what I am doing. I have the feeling of just beginning to compose for the first time. I will soon send you a copy of the first part of the piano piece *[Music of Changes]*. The essential underlying idea is that each thing is itself, that its relations with other things spring up naturally rather than being imposed by any abstraction on *my* [italicized = crossed out] an artist's part. (See Artaud on an objective synthesis). This is all written in a great hurry, & forgive me, I have to leave to give a concert of music in the Colgate University, up north. Will write soon again.

[18q] P.S.

I asked Varèse (many months ago) about the Ionization, as you asked me to do. He says that there is only one set of parts and that he has to keep it here. However one could get the score easily from New Music Edition, 250 W. 57th St., N.Y.C.

Maro & Anahid Ajemian will be in Europe next fall and winter playing recitals and Krenek's double concerto he wrote for them (with orchestra). Perhaps Desormière wd. like to do it. (Although I don't personally like the piece).

I have not been very well and am still not; there are so many things wrong that I wdn't know where to ask the Doctor to begin.

[18r] P.S. 2

Merce and I went on another concert tour last month to San Francisco, Denver, Seattle, etc. I always take your music with me (spreading the gospel). Please don't forget to send me the Quartet as soon as it is available. My devotion to your work does not diminish but rather grows. David says his playing of your Sonate is improving and that it will be better than ever. He is a magnificent pianist.

We all wish either that you were here in New York or we were all with you in Paris. It would be a marvelous life.

Cage: Letter 14 [Summer 1951]

Dear Pierre:

[14a] Thank you for sending the 'statement'; Henry Cowell's article will be published in January[22] and I hope (for that and also for a possible performance by Fizdale and Gold in December) you can send me a photostat of the 2 piano work you are writing (which you will play in England). Even if Fizdale & G. don't decide to play it, Tudor & someone else here could do it; in fact, the latter plan is better. In any event we are anxious to see and hear.

When I finish my 'Music of Changes' (sometime around Christmas) I shall send you a copy, and also I want to send you a copy of the piece for radios and a recording of it. Feldman, who has great difficulty imagining that you do not like his work, will send you a new Intersection on graph for piano. He is somewhat mollified knowing that you also do not like Mondriaan. The difference of opinion seems to me [14c = page 2] like one of distance. Close up or far away (far away, the entire earth is seen as a single point). If, also, you talk to Feldman, I am sure you will recognize his quality.

His work is scarcely to be admired for its intellectual characteristics, but rather for his letting the sounds be and act. I admired
your criticism (via Christian [Wolff]) of his rhythm in the Intersec-
tions, that the endings of the sounds should also be free (at the
discretion of the player) as are the beginnings. But then I also
admire Feldman's answer when he heard your criticism. "That
would be another piece."

I have not seen David Tudor since the beginning of the summer. He may return in a week or so. When he does we shall try to
get him to record your 2eme Sonate. He hopes to go to Europe
next Spring for the purpose of meeting you. Then you will discover that his silence [14b = page 3] as regards letter-writing and
record-making is quite the opposite of his friendliness and piano-
playing. I realize (and am impatiently looking forward) that you
may be coming here with J. L. Barrault; please let us know when
any such plans mature, because it would be nonsensical for me to
be off on a tour in California or David on a boat to Europe with
you here among the sky-scrapers.

I am delighted with your charts; when I send you the Changes I
shall also send you the charts I used. As I see it, the problem is to
understand thoroughly all the quantities that act to produce multiplicity. These one will understand most nicely (fine differences)
when aided technologically. I am enthusiastic [14d] about your
project with Schaeffer & the radios and anxious to be working on
a similar project here. I am pulling as many strings as I can.

My present way of writing is very painstaking (measuring the
distances), it took me six weeks to copy the second part of the
Changes. Now I compose two pages and then copy them, then
compose two more, etc.

I have also tried charts of words based on a gamut of vowels and
then made poems by tossing. (Which means that I can extend the
method to include vocal works).

Forgive this short hurried note; it only means to say thank you
for sending the statement. When Christian told me of being with
you and all the friends I became more 'homesick' than ever.
Please say hello for me to everyone.

COMMENTARY ON PART II

Part II is dominated by Cage's letters. These are exceptionally
important as they document how his ideas changed during a
critical period in his creative life, that is, when he began to employ
chance operations and work with indeterminacy. In summary the

changes that transpired in Cage's compositional method fall into two interrelated categories, rhythmic structure and musical materials. The following discussion is based upon Cage's letters 15, 18, and 14 and provides a chronological overview of these changes.

Rhythmic organization. In *String Quartet in Four Parts* (1949–50) meter (²⁄₂ or the equivalent) and tempo (♩ = 54MM) remain consistent throughout. The entire work is comprised of a series of 22 twenty-two-measure units, separated from one another by double-bars. Each twenty-two measure unit is subdivided into groups of measures which are defined by thematic change: 2½, 1½, 2, 3, 6, 5, ½, 1½. The twenty-two measure units are grouped similarly; the first movement is comprised of 2½ and 1½ units; the second, 2 and 3 units; third, 6 and 5 units; and fourth, ½ and 1½ units.

The rhythmic structure for the *Concerto for Prepared Piano and Chamber Orchestra* can be compared with *String Quartet,* 23 units of 23 measures per unit divided as follows: first movement, 3, 2, 4 units; second, 4, 2, 3 units; third, 5 units.

The rhythmic structure for *Sixteen Dances,* unlike that of *String Quartet* and the *Concerto,* was determined for each dance individually; in other words, there was no attempt to relate the movements to one another by means of rhythmic structure. Within each movement, however, divisions occur. For example, movement one is comprised of seven units each having seven measures.

Rhythmic structure in *Music of Changes* was defined in terms of real time: duration was measured in lengths of space, rather than depicted symbolically in half and whole notes. *Imaginary Landscape No. 4* likewise was defined in terms of real time as performers held stop watches in order to determine entrances and exits.

Musical materials. Cage composed the sound materials for *String Quartet,* single pitches, dyads and chordal formations assigned to each instrument in the quartet, as a "gamut of assorted sounds." The materials or "pre-orchestrated combinations of sound" used in the *Concerto* were prescribed in a similar manner, but were arranged in a matrix of blocks, 16 rows (representing each instrument) by 14 columns (representing different combinations of sounds), rather than in a linear fashion. To compose the first movement Cage made moves upon the matrix (e.g., two up, three over, etc.). After following a given pattern on the matrix, he landed on a block, and then used the combination of materials ("accidentally chosen complexes") prescribed in that block at the

next point in the composition. The second movement was composed by a similar method using movements in concentric circles.

Before writing the third movement of the *Concerto,* Cage composed *Sixteen Dances.* He employed an eight-by-eight matrix, similar to the one used in *Concerto.* Because the music was to reflect
the differing moods or colors associated with individual dances,
Cage manipulated the predetermined musical gestures by replac-
ing eight blocks with newly composed material after composing a
pair of dances. In this way he brought about a "gradual metamorphosis of the chart," providing for constant regeneration of
motivic materials while sustaining thematic continuity.

After completing the *Sixteen Dances,* Cage composed the third
movement of *Concerto.* By transforming the charts employed in
the first two movements of the concerto, he produced a single new
chart of materials for both piano and orchestra. Cage's process for
deriving these materials was based on a coin-tossing technique
taken from the I Ching. Ultimately, he selected material from the
original charts and composed new materials as well. Like the old
charts, the new chart had 224 positions arranged in a sixteen-by-
fourteen configuration. When Cage tossed three coins, one of
four possible combinations would occur: 1) three heads (HHH)
indicated that he would compose new material for the piano and
insert it in that particular position; 2) two heads and one tail
(HHT) meant he would use the musical material from the original
orchestra chart and insert it in the corresponding position; 3) one
head and two tails (HTT) suggested use of material from the old
piano chart; and 4) three tails (TTT) indicated that new material
for the orchestra should be composed and placed in the corresponding position on the new chart. Cage explained this to
Boulez, "By making moves on the charts I freed myself from what
I had thought to be freedom, and which actually was only the
accretion of habits and tastes" (letter 18g).

Cage composed *Music of Changes* by constructing many charts,
one or more for each musical parameter: tempo, superpositions,
duration, sound/silence, and amplitude. Each chart contained
sixty-four positions arranged in an eight-by-eight configuration.
To choose elements from the charts, Cage selected hexagrams
from the I Ching by employing an expanded version of the coin-
toss method. The chosen hexagram then served as reference to a
position on the chart; Cage applied the information found at this
location on the chart to a particular point in the composition.

In addition to the charts, Cage designed a means for "metamorphosis," or a way in which the content of the charts would evolve (similar to the process employed in *Sixteen Dances*). First, he determined the number of elements that would be active and inactive, or which elements would change or preserve the preceding parametric designation. In the second stage of metamorphosis, Cage determined whether an element would be mobile or immobile; after a mobile element was used once, it was replaced by another element, composed specifically for that position on the chart.

While he continued to work on *Music of Changes*, Cage composed *Imaginary Landscape No. 4* for twelve radios and twenty-four performers. Although he had derived a process for composing this work from that of *Music of Changes*, the work was quite different as a result of employing radios as this work's medium. He described this to Boulez: "The radio piece is not only tossing of coins but accepts as its sounds those that happen to be in the air at the moment of performance" (letter 18n).

PREFACE TO PART III

The letters in Part III represent late spring through the fall of 1952, the period prior to and including Boulez's trip to Canada with the Théâtre Marigny of Jean-Louis Barrault and Madeleine Renaud, as well as his subsequent visit to New York in November. By this time he had completed his Etudes and had met Karlheinz Stockhausen who had been studying in Paris. Cage had been working on the *Williams Mix*, intending to complete it with the help of students at Black Mountain College.

III

Cage: Letter 11 [late Spring 1952]

Dear Pierre,

Forgive me for not having written sooner; by rights I should offer you countless apologies but then that would just take your time. I have been busy. You last long letter was marvelous and gave much pleasure. I am very anxious to hear your Etude for a single sound and also the more recent one for seven [*Étude sur un son* and *Etude sur sept sons* on single-track tape (1951–1952)]. Can't you get the Radio to send copies over here? I am hoping to arrange a concert next season either wholly or in part electronic; if wholly, we would have to draw heavily on *'musique concrète,'* because our work proceeds quite slowly. So far we have 3 movements of a work by Christian Wolff, an inconsequential work of mine for 43 phonograph records *(Imaginary Landscape No. 5)* and 17 seconds of a more interesting piece to which I have not yet given a title *[Williams Mix]*.

After the *Music of Changes* (which I trust you have received) I wrote two Pastorales for prepared piano [*Two Pastorales* (1951)]. The pianist also blows whistles. And in another piece which changes its title according to where it [11b] is performed (e.g. *66 W. 12th*) bowls of water, whistles and a radio are used in addition to the piano. Both pieces, are composed in the same way as the Changes but have fewer superpositions and so the density is slight. The *66 W. 12* piece is notated according to actual time and the performer uses a stop watch to determine his entrances.[23]

The phonograph piece was done in 18 hrs, because it was needed for a dance program. And since it is on tape it brought about my present connection with Louis and Bebe Barron who are sound engineers. David Tudor helped make this first piece and so enjoyed the work that he said he would prefer to do such work to teaching, as far as making a living was concerned. So shortly after that I raised $5,000 (given by Paul Williams) which we divide 4 ways and then each month tax each member of the project to pay for the materials. We use the machines owned by the Barrons and at present have no funds for additions. [11c] The $5,000 will carry us through Nov. 15 and assures us of 2 full days per wk in the studio. We have 2 tape recorders. Louis Barron has an arrangement for variable speed but it is rather makeshift. The sound is in the middle of the tape and the tape travels at 15 or 7½ inches per second. (I envy you your 77 cm.)

For the piece we are now making I use the same method again as in the *Music of Changes,* but there are a few modifications: the sounds are classified in six groups which are overlapping: A = city sounds; B = country sounds; C = electronic sounds; D = music, especially manually produced, or simply manually produced 'musical' sounds; E = vocally produced sounds and vocal music; F = small sounds which require amplificåtion to be useful. These capital letters which refer to source are followed by three letters, c or v, meaning thoroughly controlled or variable. The first refers to frequency, the second to overtone structure, the third to amplitude. A line drawn underneath the capital letter indicates a duration control, rhythmic pattern [11d] easily achieved by making a 'loop'—an endless tape. Avvv might then be

a straight recording of traffic whereas Dvvv could be jazz or
Beethoven. Avcv will be traffic (e.g.) having suffered a control of
its overtone structure, through filters or reverberation. This is a
very free way of permitting action and I allow the engineers
making the sounds total freedom. I simply give a list of the sounds
needed, e.g. Evcv *Fvvv* (double source). If a source is ccc by
nature, then v means a control. I do not specify how a sound shall
be interpreted (in this regard) but leave it to the engineers.

The charts for the composition involve these sounds, durations,
attacks and decays, superpositions, and "n," a fraction which is a
factor in the structure and in 32 out of 64 durations. (This corresponds to flexibility of tempo.) The attacks and decays are specific
cuts of the tape plus or minus from a duration point. They are
also 'cross-grain' use of the tape (which [11e] affects the overtone
structure as well. I have organized single and double cuts (to a
central pt.) and then use a "t" to indicate more complicated cuts or
curves which are invented at the moment of cutting. The entire
score is made like a dress-maker's pattern—to size. A single page
= 1⅓ seconds. 8 individual tapes are made and then superimposed if one wishes a single tape or disc in the end but naturally
more tapes are preferable with many loudspeakers. The composition however uses 16 charts and so the durations are segmented
(as in the Changes) to make possible otherwise impossible situations. It often happens that, with plus and minus operations, a
sound 'ends' before it 'begins' or even that the sound that 'follows'
it happens first. In general [11f] superpositions 1 to 8 increase
density and those from 9 to 16 increase fragmentation. I have not
dealt in this piece with the possibility of running the tape backwards except in the case of the 'cross-grain' cuts e.g.:

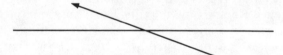

The number of sounds used is large. I begin with 1024 cards to
make the 16 charts. A totally variable sound will have a frequency
of 32 out of 1024 whereas Cccc (e.g.) will have a frequency of 2.
The cards are dealt after being carefully shuffled (in one of the
classical Tarot ways) into the charts. Each chart has a fund of cards
available to it as the 'mobility' principle (from the Changes)
operates. These are refreshed as necessary. This whole thing is
cumbersome in the extreme and I now [11g] realize that as I go on

I must involve computation rather than the cards with their character of uniqueness.[24] I discovered this from the attacks and decays, where, because there are 2 factors infinite unpredictability comes about through their interaction. However, we are working, but the work is very slow. I go this week to North Carolina[25] to teach for 3 weeks and I think I shall simply put the students to work composing and cutting the tape. The piece as planned is 20 minutes, but 4 minutes alone (the first 'movement') will be 192 pages! And by the time that is finished I will surely have new ideas.

As you see I have increased rather than decreased the element of chance in this work. Another thing characterizing it is the fact of many people working on it in all of its aspects. So that it is [11h] not 'my' work. David Tudor has been composing superpositions 7–11. A student from Illinois worked etc.

I am anxious to have a copy of Schaeffer's book on Musique Concrète. Would you ask him to send me one?

I am also anxious to know your plans; it is very exciting to be looking forward to seeing you again soon and here. Naturally I can hardly wait. News of your work always pleases me and more and more one hears of it here (in the newspapers, etc.).

Merce choreographed part of the symphonie pour un Homme Seul (a terrible piece) for a Festival at Brandeis University.[26] There I met again Bernard Blin whom you probably know (was connected with Schaeffer).

[11i] This last spring I organized concerts and also gave lectures and that kept me busy too. I lectured at the University of Illinois and they were so interested that I might conceivably go there to continue the work with magnetic tape. All my interest is now in this field and I doubt whether I will be writing any more 'concert' music. On the other hand the public here is just beginning to be aware of the 'prepared piano,' so that I shall hear a performance in October of my Concerto for prepared piano and orchestra, paid for by the Musician's Union! David Broekman, the conductor would also like to play a work by you. Can a score be sent? We are hoping to hear your *Polyphonie*.

David is going to play your first Sonata on programs this summer and in the Fall. Please keep us informed about when you will [11j] be here so that we can arrange a concert while you are here. Lectures etc.

I have the sad news that the building in which I live will be torn down in a year; but you will be here before that happens. It is a delight and now, as I write, many birds are outside on the fire-escape where I put food for them. They will put up a new 20 story building to house more people. New York is beginning to look like a prison.

Whenever you want an article for a magazine on electronic music, let me know; and if anything is written besides Schaeffer's book I am anxious to see it.

I am full of admiration for the way in which you are working and especially for the way in which you have generalized the concept of the series, and in your Etude for a single sound made [11k] the correspondence between frequency and duration. I am fascinated by the correspondences between rows of different numbers.

I am afraid this is a very sketchy letter and scarcely worth sending to you. However, you must realize that I spend a great deal of time tossing coins and the emptiness of head that that induces begins to penetrate the rest of my time as well. The best, I keep thinking, is that we shall meet again soon.

Please greet all the friends for me. I miss you all.

Boulez: Letter 16, page 1, paragraph 2

First. Thank you for the *Music of Changes*—which I *liked very much* and which I was so pleased to receive. I was absolutely enchanted by this evolution of your style—And I hold to it completely. It is certainly what I prefer of everything you've done. And I have lent it to all my friends who are composers here. The problem of how to have it performed here now arises, perhaps by either Yvonne Loriod or Yvette Grimand. We will arrange this with P.[ierre] Souvchinsky. In any case, you can't know how much I agree with you—I can tell you this enthusiastically.[27]

Boulez: Letter 16, page 1, paragraph 4

Radio Cologne must have written to you (NDWR—Cologne) because I spoke to them about you and played them your records, which they copied. They want to make a two-hour program on your music and they would like some recent recordings and some explanatory notes or text which you have written. I gave them the issue of *Transformations* as well as a little blurb about you in a program; the text is by Lou Harrison and is about the prepared piano which appeared on the record jacket to discs of your recording for two pianos. I could send them a recording of your *Music of Changes*—they would be thrilled. I think it was Stockhausen who wrote to you. He is a remarkable young German composer.

Boulez: Letter 15, page 1, paragraph 2

I am angry that your Concerto was not performed well by the orchestra and it is a shame that it wasn't possible to make a recording of it. At least I can still resort to examining the score at your home since no tape of this lousy playing exists.

I am pleased for you that your work on recording tape is progressing. But to whom do you speak about such work?! It also took me weeks to produce three minutes of music. It's a craftsman's work: splice the sounds from end to end, do the editing, catch the mistakes; we will soon be able to hire ourselves out for the most delicate work, for example, Arab copper embossing (in case of a third World War).

Boulez: Letter 18, page 2, paragraph 1

For the moment, I am immersed in the orchestra of *Visage Nuptial* about Char's poems; an orchestration which is really giving me trouble since I want it to be very deliberate.[28] It is materializing in small, successive steps.—I am very exacting about it. The result of *Soleil des Eaux* has encouraged me in this sense. As for the new work, "Work in Progress,"[29] it is premature to speak about it at length. Silence is more prudent and I won't unwrap this one until a much later time. I can tell you, in any case, that this won't be easy.

COMMENTARY ON PART III

All of Cage's works described in Part III have two ideas in common. First, all were composed by using variations of the chance operations employed to compose *Music of Changes*. Second, all works exhibited elements of indeterminacy—although Cage may not have used such a label to describe them.

Cage's awareness of indeterminacy could be traced back as early as the spring of 1951, as his description of *Imaginary Landscape No. 4* suggests: "The radio piece is not only tossing of coins but accepts as its sounds those that happen to be in the air at the moment of performance" (letter 18n).

Even at that time Cage distinguished the act of composing using chance operations from that which he would later identify as indeterminacy. In an interview conducted in 1985, Cage acknowledged this difference:

> Bringing about indeterminacy is bringing about a situation in which things would happen that are not under my control. Chance operations can guide me to a specific result, like the *Music of Changes*. An example of indeterminacy is any one of the pieces in a series called *Variations* which resemble cameras that don't tell you what picture to take but enable you to take a picture. . . . The thing I think that is consistent in my work, where otherwise inconsistency appears—like the difference between indeterminacy and the *Music of Changes* which is not indeterminate at all—the thing that is in common between them is non-intention.[30]

In composing *Imaginary Landscape No. 4* Cage may have been inspired initially by the radio, recognizing it as *objet trouvè*. That is, for one who had demonstrated a predilection for unconventional instruments, twelve radios operated by twenty-four individuals in *Imaginary Landscape No. 4* may have provided a theatrically appealing situation. For this reason, Cage may have developed the work based upon the radio as an instrument. From another perspective, he may have been aware of the volatile nature of sound produced from twelve radios, that each performance of the work would be dramatically different inasmuch as the variables involved were dependent upon the time of day and location of performance. From this point of view, the sound produced by the radios, and not the radios themselves, could have been the force behind the work's creation.

Whatever the original inspiration for *Imaginary Landscape No. 4*, by 1952 Cage realized his interest in indeterminacy in *66 W. 12 Street* and the subsequent works, *August 12, 1952* and *August 29, 1952*. As indicated in their titles, these works exhibit a new dimension in Cage's understanding of indeterminacy. Location in the former work and time in the latter works are recognized as factors which influence, and indeed provide the point of departure for, the creation of these works.

Creation is not, perhaps, an appropriate term to use, for even those elements that had been "composed" were chosen through chance operations. Creative jurisdiction over what would be heard in performance was not wholly associated with the composer, if he recognized as part of the composition environmental sounds traditionally regarded as extraneous to performance of the aural art.

In composing *Williams Mix* Cage extended these procedures

further. Although he did not specify that environmental sound was an acceptable facet of the work's performance, he did describe the compositional process in terms of expanding the use of chance. Indeterminacy—although unnamed—played a part in the work; in other words, the work's composition, or the ultimate compositional product, was not solely the result of an individual effort:

> As you see I have increased rather than decreased the element of chance in this work. Another thing characterizing it is the fact of many people working on it in all of its aspects so that it is not 'my' work. David Tudor has been composing superpositions 7–11. A student from Illinois worked etc. [Letter 11g–h]

Like *Music of Changes*, the rhythmic structure of *Williams Mix* is defined in terms of real time; that is, lengths of tape were measured to specific lengths and pasted together to make the whole. Another work which is also supported by a rhythmic structure based upon real time, albeit greatly simplified, is *4'33"*, which also dates from this period.[31] The performer entering and leaving the stage represents the beginning and end of the work, and action involved in opening and closing the keyboard cover distinguish the separate movements within the structure.

4'33" is indeterminacy in a crystaline form. Sound materials consist of the environmental sounds that transpire during the work's performance and each person's interpretation of these sounds becomes the work. The composer himself did not dictate that any other materials should be employed. The premiere of *4'33"* on 29 August 1952, in Woodstock, New York was not documented by newspaper reviews, although its performance on 14 April 1954 at Carl Fischer Concert Hall in Manhattan was recognized by the press. One reporter recorded the disdain expressed by another who complained, "the public cannot always be sure just whose music is not being played."[32]

As illustrated in the commentary given above, by the time Cage had sent a copy of *Music of Changes* to Boulez, his interests in composition had changed dramatically. Inasmuch as Cage's work with charts and various procedures for selecting materials from these charts seemed to parallel his own thoughts, Boulez was "enchanted by this evolution" in Cage's style. It is evident that Cage tried to explain to Boulez how his thoughts on composition were changing. It is also apparent, however, that although Cage described his new works in terms that related them to *Music of*

Changes, the difference between the newer works and *Music of Changes* (distinguished specifically as indeterminacy) resulted in new works which exhibited completely different characteristics.

While Cage was in the midst of working with chance and indeterminacy, Boulez was involved in revising the orchestration of *Visage Nuptial.* Boulez's activities as musical director of the Barrault troupe continued to develop; at this time he was preparing for a trip to Montreal and a subsequent visit to Cage in New York.

By means of comparison, then, both composers hoped to exploit in their works what they considered to be new ideas concerning sound color. In fact, the way each was developing such details was completely different from what the other was considering. Cage traveled beyond the realm of traditional Western instrumentation by experimenting with environmental sound through indeterminate action, whereas Boulez grew exceedingly sensitive to each instrument's range of expressivity (perhaps due in part to his experience in conducting) which he in turn demonstrated in new orchestrations of previously completed compositions.

PREFACE TO PART IV

The letters in Part IV fall within the span of time beginning in May 1953, after Cage had performed at the University of Illinois, through 1954, when Boulez was touring South America with the Barrault-Renaud Company. Cage had completed the *Williams Mix* and was attempting to raise funds for a studio for experimental music. Boulez's opportunities extended not only to working in electronic music studios in Paris and Cologne, but to conducting performances of contemporary music with the Paris-based ensemble, Domaine Musicale.

IV

Cage: Letter 16, May 1, 1953

Dear Pierre:

My cold has disappeared and the 'Williams Mix' is on its way to you. I have sent 9 tracks: one is all 8 mixed and the others are the single tracks. Before each one there are synchronization marks: (audio frequency oscillator sine waves) 1 kilocycle; 1 second silence; 400 cycles per second; 1 second silence; 1 kilocycle; 1 second silence; 2.5 kilocycles; 4 seconds silence and then the music. We performed it at the University of Illinois with 8 tape recorders and 8 loudspeakers, the former in full view on the stage and the latter situated around the audience (about 800 people). We performed your Etudes; one from two loudspeakers and one from three. The rest of the music was heard from all 8 loud-speakers at once, except the Batterie Fugue and the Timbres Durées, both of which we made travel around the audience. I would have liked to experiment further with more complex use of the loudspeakers, but time did not permit. Earle Brown's piece like mine uses 8 machines and 8 loudspeakers. [16c] The experience of the 8 loudspeakers is extraordinary. There is no room for anything but immediate listening. The air was so alive one was simply part of it. This however was our reaction and that of only some in the audience. Most people were alarmed and retreated to the idea of 'boundaries of musical action.' Let them build whatever walls; someone will always be getting out. (There is, by the way, an increasing conservatism developing here; it is called 'consolidation' and means neo-classicists using 12 tone rows and vice-versa: corollaries: technical mastery-expressive power.) We have not yet made a New York hearing of the tape music. I don't know exactly why. For one thing the economic situation for me is extremely bad; I never know from one day to the next where money will be coming from. I had hopes and spent my time trying to get support for the tape music from Foundations and Universities but I have had no success. And the results [16b] of my work which please me only serve to produce a strong negative reaction in those I ask for help. I tell you all this not to arouse sympathy but to explain why I have not yet organized a performance here. I also think that another architecture than the concert hall will be needed for a hearing that is excellent. The loudspeakers around the audience should also be above the audience. Perhaps no archi-tecture at all: out of doors with the loudspeakers on the tops of buildings. A magnetrillon!

I have done no composing since you were here; I helped Earle make his piece, and from time to time ideas come for my next work which as I see it will be a large work which will always be in progress and will never [16d] be finished; at the same time any part of it will be able to be performed once I have begun. It will include tape and any other time actions, not excluding violins and whatever else I put my attention to. I will of course write other music than this but only if required by some outside situation such as one that has just arisen: a poet here (French), George Fuy, has asked me to make music for a reading of Le Coup de Des. I would like to do this but I told him that you may have already made such music and in that case he should use yours. He will write to you about it. I will not begin anything until I hear from you whether or not I should do it. He is also interested in promoting a recording of Tudor's playing of your 2nd Sonata. This I hope will come about. A man named Evar (I believe), [16e] at present on his way to Paris, and who is head of a small recording company, will try to see you or Hueghel about all this.

I had a very pleasant letter from Schlee of Universal about the possible publication of my Changes. I will be very happy if they decide to do this.

David wants more music from you, from Stockhausen, from Froidebree; please bring all this about and more, more music!

It is my fault that you have not yet received the drawings by Philip Guston. Shortly you will have them. It is simply a matter of procrastination.

Christian wrote a new piece which uses all 88 tones. I think it is magnificent and he says it is the result of his conversations [16g] with you. David played it at a program at Harvard last Sunday (we drove up in the little Ford). It is about 12 minutes long. Christian will be in Europe this summer, but not in France, because it appears that it is not definite whether he is a Frenchman or an American. If the former he could be inducted into the military, which, naturally, he wishes to avoid. So, he will pass the summer in Italy, Switzerland and Germany. If you will be in Germany, as I imagine, let us know where so that he can get to see you.

I think that the University of Illinois is considering inviting you there sometime next year; I hope that happens; we would see you soon again!

[16f] They made a recording of David's concert and so I have been able to have a tape of the Music of Changes sent to Eimert in Cologne. They also have a recording of your 2nd Sonata, but David is not satisfied with his performance of it on that occasion.

Merce, David and M.C. are all going to Black Mountain College this summer. I will stay here; the four of us have organized a 'Package Festival,' an announcement of which we are currently sending out to Colleges and Universities throughout the country. If we get enough responses we would make enough money to support the tape music ourselves, without [16h] outside help. We would give concerts, lectures, discussions, etc. I enclose one of our brochures.

I think that is all. I have not attempted to tell you about the path of my musical ideas because nothing is very clear yet. What is clear is made more or less pointless by rather crucial obscurities. I need still to spend some days alone.

It was such a delight to all of us that you were here,—and 'soon again 'twill be.' Everyone sends love to you and all the friends.

Boulez: Letter 1, page 3, paragraph 3 [Summer 1954]

What else can I tell you about my present activity:[33] I am "Milhauding" non-stop (because of Christophe Columb, which makes me discover the Americas most often to my liking).[34] Most of the time I come across amateur choruses with which I must start by teaching solfège and then French pronounciation. They're pretty nice, but it's really tedious. Aside from this, I spend as much of my time as possible writing the "Marteau sans Maître" which I mentioned to you earlier. It's for flute in G, xylorimba, vibraphone, percussion, guitar, viola and alto voice. I'm trying to study thoroughly, to deepen and to broaden my manner of seeing.

Boulez: Letter 1, page 4, paragraph 1

With the *a capella* choruses which I wrote last year—it's one of the works which has given me the most difficulty.[35] I'm attempting to rid myself of my mannerisms, my taboos, I'm trying to see more complexly—less obviously and more refined in depth. I'm trying to enlarge the series and the principle to the maximum of its possibilities. Moreover, the article which I had written in *Cahièrs* was very explicit. I had to cut the end because it was too long given the page-setting, but I'll take it up again soon. Obviously, we still disagree on this. I don't acknowledge and I don't believe I'll ever acknowledge it—chance as a component of a fully developed work. I'm expanding the possibility of *strict* or *free* music (constrained or not). But as for chance, nothing can make me tolerate the idea. I hope that when you come to Europe, you'll be able to hear this "Marteau sans Maître" either in Donaueschingen or from a recording which they're sure to make at the Sudwestfunk.

Boulez: Letter 1, page 4, paragraph 2

Stockhausen is more and more interesting! He's the best of all of them in Europe. Intelligent and gifted. I take great pleasure in

discussing with him—even harshly if necessary—all current problems. He's a true interlocutor. And I am delighted to work with
him in Cologne. He's now a goldsmith and no longer requires
technical aid while working in the studio. We are going to work
alone in the studio and I hope to do excellent work in a short time.
I heard his first electronic work and in spite of some shortcomings
with regard to the idiosyncracies of the machinery (the low notes),
it's the first successful work of this type from an auditory point of
view. He is extremely sensitive to sonorous quality, to the life of
sounds and it is because of this that he was able to succeed on the
first try at producing music of this type. At the same time, one
should say that he can work very quietly in Cologne. Eimert, the
director of this studio is very straightforward and allows him to do
what he wants when he wants and how he wants. (Which wasn't
the case with the beloved Schaeffer, towards whom I am now very
cold! Moreover, I refused to work with him, although he asked
me twice. The concretism studio[36] is now vegetating for better or
worse and rather for worse. One never speaks about it).

COMMENTARY ON PART IV

In 1953, while Cage was still working on *Williams Mix*, he con-
cluded the description of his compositional method to Boulez by
saying, "As you see I have increased rather than decreased the
element of chance in this work" (letter 11g). Boulez's feelings were
particularly strong on this point, as he indicated in a letter back to
Cage: "I don't acknowledge and I don't believe I'll ever acknowledge it—chance as a component of a fully developed work. . . .
nothing can make me tolerate the idea" (letter 1).

Boulez's attitude toward Cage's use of chance did not change in
the next few years—although he himself had begun to work in
this area. Indeed, he expressed his opinion on this subject with
more vehemence in his essay "Aléa" (1957):

> Do you see whither we are tending? Always to a rejection of choice.
> The first conception was purely mechanistic, automatic, fetichistic; the
> second is fetichistic again, but delivers one from choice, not by num-
> bers, but by means of the interpreter. One transfers one's choosing to
> that of the interpreter. Thus one is wrapped under cover, camou-
> flaged; not very cleverly, though, for the arbitrary or, rather a super-
> ficial arbitrary imposes its presence. What a relief! The hour of choice
> is postponed again; a superficial subjectivity has been grafted onto an
> aggressive conception of intitial objectivity. No! Chance is too bashful
> to be diabolic.[37]

Although Boulez did not refer to specific works or a particular composer in the statement given above, he implied reference to Cage's ideas; with the "first conception," or what he designated later in the essay as "chance by inadvertance," he referred to the use of charts in conjunction with I Ching chance operations and, with the second, "chance by automatism," he referred to indeterminacy.

In composing *Piano Sonata No. 3* (1956–57) Boulez applied his own thoughts on chance. In his essay "Sonate, que me veux-tu?" (1960), he reflected on the technique he termed *aléa:*

> a work must keep a certain number of passageways open by means of precise dispositions in which chance represents the "points," which can be switched at the last moment. It has already been brought to my notice that this idea of "points" does not really belong to the category of pure chance but rather to that of indeterminate choice, which is something quite different. In any construction containing as many ramifications as a modern work of art total indeterminacy is not possible, since it contradicts—to the point of absurdity—the very idea of mental organization and of style.[38]

Boulez's *Piano Sonata No. 3* is one example of aléa—a technique which, at the onset, may appear to have a great deal in common with Cage's indeterminacy. The work is comprised of five *formants: Antiphonie, Trope, Constellation/Miroir, Strophe,* and *Séquence.* Each *formant* is subdivided into sections Boulez called *développants;* the path from one *développant* to the next was decided by the performer. To Boulez this design was a labyrinth and the performer was free to choose direction from its multiple paths. In permitting this liberty, Boulez maintained that the work's form would be different each time it was performed, although what in fact happened in performance was not necessarily in keeping with Boulez's plan. For instance, as Anne Trenkamp's analysis of *Constellation/Miroir* (movement three of *Piano Sonata No. 3*) demonstrates, the performer actually may have very few choices to make in performing.[39]

At this time, Cage, too, was interested in providing performers with the opportunity to make choices during the course of performance. He promoted this through the use of various styles of untraditional music notation. Examples include graphic notation found in the series of works, *Music for Carillon* begun in 1952, in which duration was measured by lengths of space (like the *Music of Changes*) and pitch was suggested by a general range proportional to the height of the page.

One of Cage's most impressive examples of extended notational techniques is *Concert for Piano and Orchestra* (1957–58), a work he apparently anticipated writing as early as 1953:

> from time to time ideas come for my next work which as I see it will be a large work which will always be in progress and will never be finished; at the same time any part of it will be able to be performed once I have begun. It will include tape and any other time actions, not excluding violins and whatever else I put my attention to. I will of course write other music than this but only if required by some outside situation. [Letter 16c–d]

Concert is scored for an orchestra of soloists performing on strings, winds, and brass. Cage described the solo piano part as a "'book' containing 84 different kinds of composition. . . . The pianist is free to play any elements of his choice, wholly or in part, and in any sequence."[40] *Concert* comprises many parts, any or all of which may be performed in any order. In addition, other works such as *Fontana Mix* (1958), for magnetic tape) and *Aria* (1958) for solo voice) may be performed simultaneously with *Concert*.

Cage was not merely interested in extending the dimensions of the "composition," however. As demonstrated in his description regarding the traditional concert setting (letter 16), Cage also expressed the desire to expand the realm of musical perception. This was one concern for his work with electronic music; he wished to find an alternative to presenting music within the confines of traditional concert halls' architecture.

The concerns of Boulez fell into a different sphere. In contrast to Cage, Boulez was absorbed with details regarding a composition's form, for instance:

> There is, however, one major task ahead—the total rethinking of the notion of form. It is quite clear that with a vocabulary in which periodicity and symmetry are of diminishing importance and a morphology that is in constant evolution, formal criteria based on repetition of material are no longer applicable, since they have lost their strength and their cohesive power. This is the task that is plainly becoming increasingly urgent—restoring the parity between the formal powers of music and its morphology and syntax. Fluidity of form must be integrated with fluidity of vocabulary.[41]

In Boulez's *Piano Sonata No. 3*, the *développants*, or subdivisions of the *formants*—like the pages of Mallarmé's *Livre*, a work for which he had a special affinity[42]—were not designated in a set order. It was up to the performer to determine a particular reading or performance of the material; therefore the composer did not determine the composition's form or the sequence of the *développants*. Theoretically, then, the music in *Piano Sonata No. 3* did not evolve as a narrative structured by the composer.

Boulez's music notation as found in the *formants*, for example, was traditionally conceived and intricately explicit. Beyond rendering the very specific notation, the performer needed only to decide which *formant* to play next. By means of his detailed notation, therefore, Boulez maintained control over what would be played within each of the *formants*, even if he did not have control over the order in which the *formants* themselves were played.

Boulez, as influenced by Mallarmé, was cognizant of the difference in the way one perceived various parts of a composition.[43] This, in fact, is a primary point of distinction between Cage and Boulez, between indeterminacy and aléa: Boulez acknowledged that an individual listened to the beginning of a work with a different perspective than he would listen to the middle or even the end portions of a work, because at any given point in the composition the listener would have accumulated a certain amount of experience. Stated differently, one listening to a work such as *Piano Sonata No. 3* would have acquired a certain amount of understanding regarding the motivic relations within and among the *développants*. By specifying the musical content within the *formants*, but not the order between them, Boulez was aware that it was only this order or the musical form that changed during each performance.

Conversely, Cage did not intend to develop such relationships; in fact, he tried to avoid them through chance operations and a diverse collection of graphic notational designs. As a result Cage provided the performer with a greater range of interpretative powers and at the same time did not create for the audience any semblance of unity or system.

Notes

I wish to thank both composers for permission to use portions of their letters and for the clarification both shared: John Cage in letters and interviews in New York and Pierre Boulez in an interview in Chicago. Special thanks are also directed to Deborah Perkal Belinski for translating Boulez's letters; to William Duckworth, Richard Fleming, and Michael Payne for the opportunity to conduct this research; and to the Northwestern University Music Library for the use of its resources for this project.

1. John Cage to Lucretia (Crete) Harvey Cage and John Milton Cage, Sr.: letters 1, 4 April; #2, 11 April; #4, 15 April 1949, in *Notebook 1949*, John Cage Archive, Northwestern University Music Library, Evanston, Illinois.

2. The Notations Collection is comprised of over 400 music manuscripts by more than 300 composers solicited by Cage to document mid-twentieth-century music notation and to benefit the Foundation for the Contemporary Performing Arts. The collection is on deposit at the Northwestern University Music Library and is featured in the book *Notations* (New York: Something Else Press, 1969).

3. Although Cage's letters 18 and 16 are dated 22 mai 51 and 1 May 1953, respectively, the date on the former appears to have been added in the upper right corner (in the same location as the letter and page numbers) by someone other than Cage. Boulez suggested that the index numbers as well as this date were added by an assistant to Jean-Jacques Nattiez. Pierre Boulez, interview with author, 26 October 1987, Chicago, Illinois.

4. Paul Griffiths, "List of Works," in *Boulez* (London: Oxford University Press, 1978), pp. 62–63.

5. *John Cage*, comp. Robert Dunn (New York: Henmar Press, 1962).

6. Wladimir Woronoff, Russian-born Belgian composer.

7. Cage wrote letter 4 in French, with the exception of the list of instruments [letter 4d], which he wrote in English.

8. Cage received an award at the First Art Film Festival in America for the soundtrack to the film on Calder. Certificate, "First Art Film Festival in America. Award for Musical Score, John Cage for *The Works of Calder*. Woodstock, New York; sponsored by Woodstock Artists Association, American Federation of Arts, and the Film Advisory Center; 1–3 September 1951," in *Notebook 1949*.

9. In retrospect, Cage realized that the number of instruments did not equal sixteen. Refer to an extended discussion in: John Cage, "Composition as Process. I. Changes," in *Silence: Lectures and Writings* (Middletown, Conn.: Wesleyan University Press, 1961), pp. 24–25.

10. Although Boulez had hoped to visit New York and Cage had explored a number options for performances of his music, the visit was canceled as a result of Boulez's scheduling conflicts.

11. Boulez did not complete this work. Boulez interview, 26 October 1987.

12. Pierre Boulez, "The System Exposed," in *Orientations: Collected Writings*, ed. Jean-Jacques Nattiez, trans. Martin Cooper (Cambridge: Harvard University Press, 1986), pp. 128–42.

13. Pierre Boulez, *Conversations with Célestin Deliège*. (London: Eulenburg, 1976), p. 58.

14. Pierre Boulez, "Eventually . . .", in *Notes of an Apprenticeship*, comp. Paul Thévenin, trans. Herbert Weinstock (New York: Knopf, 1968), p. 148.

15. Boulez refers to *Music of Changes* in this instance.

16. Boulez, "Eventually . . .", p. 175.

17. Cunningham's dance, *16 Dances for Soloist and Company of 3*, was premiered on 17 January 1951. Barbara Naomi Cohen, "Chronology," in *Contemporary Dance; An Anthology of Lectures, Interviews and Essays with Many of the Most Important Contemporary American Choreographers, Scholars and Critics*, ed. Anne Livet (New York: Abbeville Press, 1978), p. 254.

18. Cage applied these ideas in *Music of Changes;* his description of the actual process is found in letter 18 (j–m).

19. Excerpts from this letter were published in "The System Exposed: *Polyphonie X*," in *Orientations*, pp. 129–37, translated by Françoise Toussignant. The two excerpts from letter 2 were not used in *Orientations*, however, and appear here for the first time in print, translated by Deborah Perkal Belinski.

20. A Joycean play on words by Boulez: "Dis y ineptie" (Dizzy Gillespie) = call it nonsense.

21. Although it remained unnamed throughout the course of this letter, the work under discussion at this point is *Music of Changes*.

22. The "statement" to which Cage referred in letter 14 is Boulez's letter 9. Cage's translation of excerpts from this letter appear in the following: in *trans/formation* 1, no. 3 (1952); "The System Exposed: *Polyphonie X* and *Structures* for Two Pianos," in *Orientations*, pp. 137–42; and also in Henry Cowell's article, "Current Chronicle," *Musical Quarterly* 38, no. 1 (January 1952): 123–36.

23. On 2 May 1952, one year after the premiere of *Imaginary Landscape No. 4*, Cage unveiled *66 W. 12* at the New School for Social Research in New York at 66 West 12th Street. The work was performed at other times, however, under titles for the dates of the particular performances: *August 12, 1952* and *August 29, 1952*. Of the two "August" performances, the former took place at Black Mountain and the latter in Woodstock, New York, on the same concert that featured the premiere of *4'33"*. The work was later published under the title *Water Music*. John Cage, letter to author, 21 March 1985.

24. I Ching operations were finally "computerized" by Lejaren Hiller, while Cage was a visiting professor at the University of Illinois (1967–69) composing the musicircus event, *HPSCHD*. Lejaren Hiller. "Programming the *I-Ching* Oracle," *Computer Studies in the Humanities and Verbal Behavior* 3, no. 3 (October 1970): 130–43.

25. Cage was about to leave for Black Mountain College, Black Mountain, North Carolina where he was engaged to teach during the summer session, 1952.

26. Cunningham's dance to excerpts from Pierre Schaeffer's *Symphonie pour un homme seul* was premiered 14 June 1952. Cohen, "Chronology," pp. 254–55.

27. On page two of this letter Boulez stated: "I arrive in NY 11 November" [1952]. At this time he was about to leave Montreal (where he was on tour with the Jean-Louis Barrault and Madeleine Renaud's company, Théâtre Marigny) for New York. Boulez interview, 26 October 1987.

28. According to Boulez, *Visage Nuptial* was originally written in 1946; in this reference he refers to a revision of the orchestration which he completed from 1951 through 1953. Boulez interview, 26 October 1987.

29. The phrase in quotes was given in English by Boulez. Although he has used this phrase to refer to *Piano Sonata No. 3* (see his "Sonate, que me veux-tu?", in *Orientations*, p. 146), in this instance he refers to an unpublished work from 1953, for twelve voices unaccompanied, *Oubli signal lapidé*, which employed poetry by his friend Armand Gatti. Boulez interview, 26 October 1987.

30. John Cage, interview with author, 12 February 1985, New York.

31. It is interesting to note that Cage did not relate news of the performance of *4'33"* in his letters to Boulez.

32. Jay S. Harrison, "The Music Season: Firsts and Failures," *New York Herald Tribune*, 23 May 1954, in Notebook, *John Cage Composer*, vol. 5, John Cage Archive, Northwestern University Music Library.

33. Boulez wrote letter 1 on stationary from the Claridge Hotel, Buenos Aires.

34. Boulez was in Buenos Aires rehearsing with the Barrault company for a performance of Darius Milhaud's incidental music (op. 318) to Paul Claudel's play *Christophe Colomb*. Boulez interview, 26 October 1987.

35. Boulez refers again to *Oubli signal lapidé* (see note 29). The difficulty he encountered resulted from the medium itself—he found that the voices could not perform the work successfully without accompaniment. Shortly after this time he became interested in the poetry of e. e. cummings—upon Cage's suggestion (refer to Boulez, *Conversations with Célestin Deliège*, pp. 96–97)—and set aside *Oubli signal lapidé* to begin work on *Cummings ist Dichter*. Boulez interview, 26 October 1987.

36. The studio to which Boulez referred was known as *Club d'essai*, Paris, in 1948. It was reorganized in 1951, as the *Groupe de Recherche de Musique Concrète*, and again in 1958, as

Groupe de Recherches Musicales. Herbert S. Howe, Jr., "Electronic Music," in *The New Grove Dictionary of Music and Musicians* (London: Macmillan, 1980), 6:108.

37. Pierre Boulez, "Aléa," in *Notes of an Apprenticeship,* p. 38.

38. Boulez, "Sonate, que me veux-tu?" in *Orientations,* p. 146.

39. Anne Trenkamp, "The Concept of 'Aléa' in Boulez's 'Constallation-Miroir,'" *Music and Letters* 57, no. 1 (January 1976): 7. From the performer's perspective, pianists Paul Jacobs and David Tudor both admitted during interviews with Joan Peyser that the freedom to choose particular "paths" in performing *Piano Sonata No. 3* was not as apparent as Boulez may have hoped it would be. Joan Peyser, *Boulez: Composer, Conductor, Enigma* (New York: Schirmer, 1976), p. 128.

40. *John Cage,* comp. Robert Dunn, p. 31.

41. Boulez, "Sonate, que me veux-tu?", in *Orientations,* p. 144.

42. Boulez, "Convergence with Mallarmé; *Livre for String Quartet,*" in *Conversation with Célestin Deliège,* pp. 49–54. See also, Boulez, "Sonate, que me veux-tu?" in *Orientations,* pp. 143–73; and Hans Rudolf Zeller, "Mallarmé and Serialist Thought," in *Die Riehe* 6 (1960): 5–32.

43. Boulez, *Conversation with Célestin Deliège,* p. 51.

Understanding John Cage's Chance Music: An Analytical Approach

James Pritchett

IN his essay "The Function of Criticism" (1923), T. S. Eliot declares that function to be "the elucidation of works of art and the correction of taste."[1] Eliot stresses throughout the essay the importance of fact as opposed to opinion in the pursuit of this critical goal. His ideal critic is a scholar who possesses a "very highly developed sense of fact," has mastered the techniques of analysis and comparison, and who uses these tools effectively to perform the job of "putting the reader in possession of facts which he would otherwise have missed."[2]

Eliot wrote only of literary criticism, but we may extend his vision to cover the field of music and the function of the musicologist. Among its various concerns, musicology must have some place for the elucidation of musical works via the presentation of facts about them. One sort of fact the musicologist can present is the historical. Such writing might deal with the biographical circumstances of the composer's work, with its place in his personal and his intellectual life, as well as with the more general musical and cultural worlds of which he and his music were a part. Equally important to the musicologist's job (and perhaps closer to what Eliot had in mind) is the presentation of musical analysis: that writing concerned only with the musical work itself, that breaks it down into its constituent parts and reveals "how it works." While one writer or another may excel at one side of musicological endeavors, historical or analytical, both are necessary: each informs the other, and jointly they inform the student of music.

If that student seeks to be informed about the music of John Cage, however, he is in for a disappointment. The musicological literature on Cage, being almost exclusively concerned with musico-historical subjects, lacks the proper balance in treatment. We read—perhaps too often—of Cage's aesthetics, theories of "experimental," "conceptual," or "inferential" art; of his influence on

249

other composers, dance, theater, and visual arts; of his affinity for the Far East, of Buddhism and Taoism, Indian *talas* and Indonesian gamelans. Meanwhile, his music—the subject that should stand at the center of our interest in Cage—remains a mystery to us as musicologists; it is ignored, misunderstood, and poorly documented. It is astounding that there is still no substantive study of John Cage's music—the only fact more astounding being that there is still no biography of the composer, either.

Especially problematic is the dearth of analysis of Cage's music composed since 1951. In that year, Cage began using chance as a compositional tool, an invention that stands behind every work he has composed in the thirty-six years since then. Although Cage's development of chance composition is by far the most significant aspect of his career, we know next to nothing of how chance actually functions in the music. While Paul Griffiths, in his monograph on Cage, states that "Cage's reputation is that of the apostle of indeterminacy in music,"[3] fully half of his brief book is devoted to but the first third of Cage's career, the period predating his use of chance. We are faced with a paradox: Cage's chance music is his most significant work, and at the same time it is probably the least understood.

The result of this sorry situation is an ignorance on the part of various music critics and writers of Cage's actual work. The misinformation, misleading generalizations, and opinions based on hearsay and supposition that one regularly reads when perusing the literature on Cage are disheartening and sometimes shocking. Consider the case of Cage's *Fontana Mix* (1958). Although a complex score with a full, closely written page of rather involved instructions for its use, it has been described as an example of "enigmatic graphic notation" which provides "little or no information as to how the signs are to be interpreted."[4] The score provides a means for choosing elements from a range of sounds selected by the performer and for determining the time frames within which these sounds will occur. Although it was originally designed for constructing a piece for magnetic tape, Cage later extended it to cover other media. He used it to write several nonelectronic pieces (*Aria* [1959] and *Theater Piece* [1960] are the best known), and performers such as percussionist Max Neuhaus and guitarist Cornelius Cardew have performed instrumental realizations of the work. Nevertheless, one author describes the work as a way to "graphically plot the area or physical location on which sound is to be made,"[5] while another calls it "a game-kit to be used in the manufacture of a tape piece."[6] This case is not an exceptional one: many writers seem to misplace their "sense of fact" when dealing with Cage's music. Rather than elucidate the works, music critics have tended to obfuscate them.

Some authors come to the rather lame conclusion that Cage is more important as a philosopher than as a composer. They claim, in other words, that it is perfectly acceptable to ignore the particulars of Cage's music, since it is the aesthetic or philosophical concepts behind them that are really of importance.[7] Such an attitude is grossly irresponsible. It has been Cage's work as a composer that has led to his prose writing, not the other way around, and his writings on aesthetics have always centered around specific musical works of his own. To ignore the music and then attempt to write about the philosophy is putting the cart before the horse and is an approach that is surely doomed to failure.

Considering the pervasive ignorance of Cage's works, we are justified in asking how, if we do not have a sufficient knowledge of the music on its own terms, can it be written off as unimportant? It seems quite possible that the depreciation of Cage's music is a result of the imbalance in the critical writing, not a cause of it. Perhaps we musicologists have been unable, due to conceptual or methodological problems, to handle Cage's compositions analytically and have dismissed them from our field of critical vision rather than to alter our approach.

That analytical approach, as traditionally pursued, takes as its starting point the musical score divorced from all other contexts. The analyst searches for pattern and structure in this score on various levels and in various dimensions (such as melody, harmony, or rhythm). These patterns and structures are organized by the analyst into a coherent explanation of how the various components are integrated and how they combine to make musical sense. Such patterns and structures, as well as their coordination and integration, are thought of as "musical ideas," specifically the ideas of the composer. A model of musical communication is therefore assumed wherein the composer's ideas are made material in the score, which the analyst may then decode and thus discern the composer's musical thought.

In chance composition, whether John Cage's or anyone else's, a different situation occurs. Chance in music cannot simply "happen": it is necessary to provide some mechanism within which it will operate. Therefore, the composer of a chance work must first design some system in which chance has a role to play. Such a system typically provides for some sort of "givens" or fixed elements: collections of musical materials to be manipulated, for example, or an overall structure. The system also has a collection of rules or procedures to be followed in order to produce the final score. These rules draw upon the given materials and structures and make decisions based on some random factor, such as the toss of a coin or a computer-generated random number. Finally, it is the execution of this compositional system that then produces the musical score we see, a score thus dependent in part on the design decisions of the composer, and in part on purely random events.

The model of musical communication implied by such a compositional approach is somewhat different from the one posited by traditional musical analysis. Whereas before we saw the score as the direct expression of a composer's ideas, with chance music the score is arrived at indirectly, via the compositional system. The composer designs the system, which, with additional input from some random process, then produces the score. Earle Brown, in a somewhat different context, has referred to this as the creation of "the work as an entity, a quasi-organism."[8] In designing the work-as-system, the composer can "programme a life for it within which it comes to find its shape, extensions of meaningfulness, and [the] multiple formal identities of its basic nature."[9] The compositional system is the product of the composer's deliberation and has a fixed nature. It cannot be made audible, however, except through the score, its partially random product, of which there are an infinite number of possible versions.

If musicologists have been ill equipped to deal with Cage's music, it is perhaps due to the antagonism between the two musical models presented here, particularly the different role the score plays in each of them. In traditional analysis the score functions as a straightforward and direct medium of communication, while in chance compositions it is a randomly derived product of a system designed by the composer; it is a *result* of his work rather than the work in itself. This latter approach takes the musical analyst's most trusted source—indeed, the very subject of his analysis—and removes its authority in his work. The analyst, realizing that any pattern or structure he may perceive in the chance-composed score could just as likely be the result of fortune as of design, throws his hands up in despair and declares that since the work was composed "irrationally," it cannot be subject to rational analytical discourse. Thus, for the musicologist, chance music has proved intractable; for our inquiring student of music, it has remained obscure and ill defined.

If analysis based entirely on the score cannot succeed with Cage's music, then we must look elsewhere for suitable material. Since our aim is to understand the musical thought of John Cage, it would be best for us to find the areas wherein this thought operates. We have been so transfixed by the random factors of Cage's music that we have passed over the domain in which Cage has control: the design of the system. The compositional system, not its random product, is of musicological interest and should become the focus of our attention in analyzing Cage's chance works.

The subject of my own study and writing has been Cage's music from the 1950s, and I have found in my work that by first examining the compositional systems one can discover many fruitful areas for analytical work. In approaching this music, one should ask the questions, Where does chance enter into the composition? and Where has Cage made choices that affect the system and its outcome? By separating the random from the deliberate, one can better focus on the analytically relevant aspects of the composition and thus begin to illuminate its musical inner workings. In what follows, I wish to present a few of the nonrandom aspects of Cage's compositional systems as a demonstration of the sort of lines of inquiry that are possible with these works. While space does not permit an in-depth treatment of any one composition, I hope that these examples will provide convenient handles onto this music and that they will suggest fresh and useful ways of viewing Cage's chance compositions.

In describing our model of chance composition above, we laid out three basic components to such a compositional technique: a set of fixed, predefined elements or "givens," a set of rules to operate on and within these givens, and the actual execution of the rules to produce the finished musical score. This model can serve as a guide in exploring the analytical possibilities in this music. First, there are the compositional givens. In Cage's music of the 1950s, these fall into two categories: structure (both in its horizontal and vertical aspects) and material. These fixed aspects of the systems can be classified and their nature and treatment compared and evaluated. Next, the design choices made by Cage in establishing the rules for a system must be examined to discover their importance in determining the musical nature of the resulting score. Finally, the extent to which Cage allows himself control over the execution of his system is worth our attention, since it can have a large effect on the outcome of the composition.

Of all the concerns of musical analysis, questions of structure are among the most basic. Hence, the study of Cage's treatment of structure in his chance compositions is a logical first step in fashioning an analytical approach to them. Horizontally, structure in this music is similar to that of Cage's prechance compositions in that it consists simply of lengths of time: the whole work has a certain fixed duration, which in turn is divided and subdivided into segments of various lengths. One method used here to create time structures, familiar to those who have studied Cage's early works, is to specify a single set of proportions that govern both the division of the whole into sections and then those sections into smaller units. The *Two Pastorales* (1951/1952), for example, both have structures based on the proportions {2, 3½, 5½}. At the small scale, the pieces consist of a series of eleven-bar units subdivided into three phrases of two, three and one-half, and five and one-half measures, respectively. The whole work consists of eleven of these eleven-bar units, grouped into three sections using the same proportions. The chosen proportions thus generate a three-level hierarchy of structural divisions, simultaneously determining the scope of the whole and the pattern of its divisions and subdivisions. Beyond their immediate musical functions, Cage's rhythmic structures serve as regulators of the systems; the structural divisions mark the occasion of various decisions to be made. For example, in *Music of Changes* (1951), the smallest level of the structure determines the points at which tempo and the thickness of texture are to be decided and possibly changed.

There is a vertical dimension to structure in Cage's music of the 1950s as well. All of these works are conceived of as several simultaneous layers of activity, each proceeding independently of the others (Cage has referred to these as "superimposed parts"). The conception can be likened to polyphony, although in this case the "lines" or "parts" are not just a series of single notes but also include chords and other more complex events. Such an approach distinguishes this music from Cage's earlier work: his music of the 1940s is almost exclusively monophonic in construction, either in the traditional linear sense, or in the sense of a single layer of sounds, as in the *String Quartet in Four Parts* (1949–50).

The number of layers given in a system (its "depth") is of obvious significance to the final outcome of that system. *Music of Changes,* for example, uses eight layers, while the *Two Pastorales* have only two. The result is that *Music of Changes* has a much denser texture than the *Pastorales,* which in turn affects other aspects of the composition. For example, the lowered density of the *Pastorales* creates long empty spaces between some of the sounds, which, at times, Cage chooses to fill by holding the pedal down for the duration (pedaling being outside the chance system and wholly at Cage's discretion). The prominence of these lengthy pedals focuses our attention on the decay of the sounds as they slowly dwindle into silence. *Music of Changes*, on the other hand, with a higher density of sounds, is notably lacking these long, drawn out sounds, and instead bristles with sharp, abrupt attacks and virtuosic flurries of activity.

The other given in Cage's chance systems is his selection of materials—the musical objects that will be manipulated by the system. In his prechance works of the 1940s, Cage often consciously restricted the musical materials available to him. In particular, he would allow himself the use of only a small range of pitches, which he came to call a "gamut." By the late 1940s, in works such as *The Seasons* (1947) and the string quartet, the gamut changed from a limited pitch range to a limited collection of specific sonorities—not simply single pitches but chords as well.

This gamut technique was the forerunner of Cage's use of "preselected" sound materials in his chance music. In *Music of Changes*, for example, each of the eight layers of the vertical structure had their own unique collections of sounds, of durations, and of dynamics; these materials were arranged into square charts. Elements from each of these charts, randomly selected by means of the I Ching, would then be coordinated to form events. The process of composing the work consisted largely of constructing events, one after the other, to form each of the eight layers.

Since the contents of the charts were freely composed by Cage, these can be the subject of the analyst's attention. For example, the sounds of the charts can be divided according to their general structure into three broad categories: single notes, chords or "aggregates," and what Cage refers to as "constellations." The sounds of this last classification are more complex events and gestures consisting of several notes and chords taking place over time; Cage has likened them to "the Chinese characters made with several strokes."[10] Examining the constellations in *Music of Changes*, for example, we find arpeggios, trills, tremolos, and even some brief quasi-melodic fragments.

These sound collections can be examined on several other fronts. Of the intervallic content of the sounds, for example, we can note that Cage favors chromatic clusters. Another consideration is that although specific rhythms are taken from the duration charts, the sounds themselves have general rhythmic profiles. In the constellations, there is a clear distinction between short and long notes, and in many of the aggregates Cage indicates that while some notes are to be sustained others are to be short, contributing only to the initial attack. Finally, we can isolate in the charts a variety of "special effects": noises, notes to be played by plucking or scraping the piano strings, and the exploitation of sympathetic vibrations, among others.

The nature of these materials is probably the greatest single carrier of musical character in *Music of Changes* and in similar works, such as the *Two Pastorales, Water Music* (1952), and *Williams Mix* (1952). Virgil Thomson described *Music of Changes* as being like a kaleidoscope, wherein the elements of the sound charts in their diversity represent Cage's carefully selected shards of multi-colored glass, colliding and combining through the manipulations of his compositional system.[11]

The general approach to materials, apart from any specific selections, can have a great impact on the character of a system, as a comparison of *Music of Changes* and the series of pieces titled *Music for Piano* (1952–56) will demonstrate. The chart technique used in *Music of Changes* became cumbersome to Cage since it required the composition of large numbers of unique sounds, durations, and dynamics. In addition, the system produced too much repetition of events for Cage's taste. These problems were solved in *Music for Piano,* in which the available sounds are limited to the eighty-eight single pitches on the piano. These are selected by marking random imperfections on a piece of blank paper and then drawing musical staves, clefs, and accidentals to turn these points into specific pitches. These pieces could be composed very quickly, and the method of selecting notes removed the need for a specific collection of sounds, thus solving the problem of repetition.

Music of Changes and *Music for Piano* sound totally different from one another, largely due to this difference in the treatment of basic sound materials. *Music for Piano,* its sounds lacking the range of complexity that characterizes *Music of Changes,* is the simpler sounding work. While *Music of Changes* offers an ever-changing flow of intricate sonic gestures, *Music for Piano* presents us with a cloud of simple points in space and time. Cage realized the "limited nature" of the *Music for Piano* system and likened the piece to "the first attempts at speech of a child or the fumblings about of a blind man."[12] Speed and a freedom from repetition had been obtained at the expense of the complexity and variety of the sound materials.

Cage arrived at a treatment of material that was a hybrid of these previous two in his *34'46.776" for a Pianist* and *31'57.9864" for a Pianist* (1954). In these works, the structure of each sound event was the first thing to be decided upon, with the choice made randomly using a variant of the note/aggregate/constellation classification of the *Music of Changes*. Once this event structure was fixed, the precise pitch and rhythmic content of the event would then be determined by a variant of the paper imperfection technique. This system combined the strengths of both of the previous approaches, simultaneously possessing the range of materials of the chart technique and the freedom from restrictions (as well as the speed) of the paper imperfection technique.

The "given" parts of these systems represent nearly traditional compositional choices on Cage's part and hence are obvious points of departure for musical analysis. There are other choices made in the designing of compositional systems, however, that can be as important as the definition of structure or materials—choices made in the fashioning of the system rules and procedures themselves. The system can be viewed as a series of questions to be asked, along with some means (possibly, but not exclusively random) of answering them. The manner in which the questions are posed is entirely of Cage's doing, and the nature of these questions can have a profound effect on the stylistic identity of the musical score produced.

One example of this is to be found in the *Concerto for Prepared Piano and Chamber Orchestra* (1950–51). There is a notable difference in both musical style and effect between the last movement of the concerto and the other two movements. In particular, the use of silence in the last movement has been singled out as its "most striking feature."[13] The difference between this last movement and the rest of the work, as well as the source of its striking silences, can be explained through a comparison of the two different systems set up to compose the different movements.

I do not wish to go into any great detail of how the concerto was composed, and therefore will provide only the necessary outline of the methods used. To compose the work, Cage used a large chart of sounds similar to those he later used in *Music of Changes*. In the orchestral music of the first two movements, patterned moves were made on the chart to produce several short sequences of sounds. In the second movement, for example, the moves made on the chart involved concentric circles and squares, and the sequences produced were either four or eight sounds long. Then, in both movements, each of the sound sequences was matched with one phrase of the rhythmic structure. Finally, Cage freely shaped the sounds rhythmically within the allotted phrase duration.

In the third movement of the concerto, a completely different system was used to select and order sounds from the chart. This system worked on a measure-by-measure basis, rather than by phrases, first determining the number of events (either one or two) to occur within each measure. For each event, it was then decided whether it would be a sound or silence, and, if it was to be a sound, precisely which sound from the chart was to be used. Each sound or silence was completely to fill the duration assigned to it, whether a half or a whole measure.

This difference in the systems reveals the reasons underlying the different sound of the last movement. Silences in the first two movements were used to articulate phrases and other groupings of sounds, entirely as Cage's taste decided. In the last movement, however, sound and silence are equal in the compositional system, and the continuity is not of a series of phrases or even of single sounds, but is of sounds and silences. Cage has described this situation as one in which the silences "speak *Nothingness*": they serve no function but simply exist in themselves.[14]

The difference in these two systems is not only the posing of the compositional questions but also in who does the answering. The last movement of the concerto has virtually no role in its system for Cage's own judgment and taste. However, Cage does have a personal role to play in the execution of other systems (such as that used in the first two movements of the concerto), and such a role is another nonrandom aspect of the composition that should be studied.

We have already noted one case where Cage's judgment is apparent: the distinctive use of long pedals in the *Two Pastorales* was the result of Cage's free choice, not of the system design. Another such system employing Cage's discretion was that used to compose *Music of Changes*. The core of this system was the random selection of sounds, durations, and dynamics from the charts, as described before. Although their selection may have been purely random, these materials were complex and diverse, making their coordination in the score far from a mechanical process but rather one that allowed for a considerable amount of creativity on Cage's part.

Cage developed a diverse assortment of techniques for realizing particular combinations of sounds and durations, for example. The durations Cage used were "segmented": they consisted of three or four shorter components. Sounds consisting of a single attack could take up the entire duration, or any segments of it, and could be preceded or followed by silent segments. For sounds with multiple attacks, Cage could assign individual segments of the duration to individual sound elements, or he could interpolate silences, or he could subdivide the segments further.

The choice of how to treat the randomly chosen sound and duration in any given case was largely a matter of context. In places where density was low, Cage could use the entire available duration for a sound. However, when density was high such a treatment was not practical, and Cage shortened the sounds by using only portions of the prescribed duration; in extreme cases, he made the sounds simply as short as possible. In every situation the ability to play the result was of paramount importance, and the rhythmic treatment of sounds varied so as to meet that goal. Taking passages of the *Music of Changes* and examining the interplay of sounds and durations reveals the nature of rhythmic usage in the work.

These examples, although brief and fragmentary, nevertheless demonstrate the possibilities inherent in a musico-analytical approach to Cage's chance music. If we take as our starting point the documentation of Cage's musical systems (which can be achieved through the standard musicological methods) and then focus our attention on the deliberate choices that these systems represent and not on the chance elements, we can begin to deal with this music on its own terms and not solely in relation to aesthetics, or Eastern philosophy, or some other extramusical circumstance.

What are the benefits of such an analytical approach to Cage's chance music? First, shifting the center of Cage studies away from aesthetics and onto the music offers us the possibility of better integrating and balancing our understanding of his work. Despite others' claims to the contrary, the center of Cage's life and work has always been his music, and any attempt to understand his other endeavors, particularly the writings about music, will be greatly aided by a full grasp of the music. Understanding the changing treatment of sound, silence, and structure in the *Concerto for Prepared Piano*, for example, is a prerequisite for the proper interpretation of Cage's famous "Lecture on Nothing" (1950) and "Lecture on Something" (1951). The first of these deals with the relationship between silence and structure, and presents the conception of rhythmic structure as fundamentally "empty" that holds in the concerto. Where the "Lecture on

Nothing" is about structure, the "Lecture on Something" is about content. In it, Cage presents ideas about arbitrary sequences of sounds (what he refers to as "no-continuity") that are partially the result of his experiments in the concerto.

Besides being an aid to the study of Cage's thought in general, another use of the analytical approach to this music is to bring not only Cage's music but that of other composers employing similar compositional models (such as Earle Brown or Iannis Xenakis) into the mainstream of musicological activity. The elements of Cage's compositional systems examined here are ultimately elements of a musical style; they are the things that give his music its unique voice. What we have been doing may therefore be considered a form of musical style analysis and as such can be used to make larger connections and comparisons between various periods in Cage's creative life, or between his work and that of other composers.

We have already seen the value of system analysis in comparing the styles of *Music of Changes, Music for Piano,* and *34'46.776"* and *31'57.9864" for a Pianist.* By understanding Cage's design of compositional systems, we can also see connections between his determinate and indeterminate works. *Fontana Mix,* for example, consists essentially of selections from a collection of sounds, distributed within various time segments—it is, in short, a distillation of all the chance systems examined here so far. What distinguishes *Fontana Mix* from these earlier works is that it presents the system directly for the performer to execute himself, rather than presenting any single specific result arrived at by the composer.

The ultimate benefit of an analytical approach to chance music should be the fulfillment of the musicological objective stated at the outset of this essay: the elucidation of musical works. Yet, the sort of musical analysis I have been demonstrating here is one that deals not with the work in its immediate, material form but that instead examines aspects of its creation that are, to an extent, inaudible. While we have shown details of the systems used to produce the sounds we hear, these specific sounds have not been, and indeed cannot be, "explained," since they are the products of random events. How, then, is the listener to gain insight into the works he hears?

In answer to such a question, it is worth recalling Cage's remark that music should "imitate Nature in her manner of operation."[15] What Cage means by this statement is perhaps less that nature is random, than that our concept of nature is that of complex, interrelated systems and processes. If Cage uses nature as a model for his work, then we should use naturalists or other scientists as models in our study of that work. Our contemporary understanding of geology, for example, is not merely of the specific land masses and their various physical features, but of plate tectonics and the forces that have created and continue to shape these specific forms. Cage's conception of music and our analytical treatment of it are similarly oriented toward processes. Just as the study of geological processes deepens our appreciation of the landscapes we see, so an understanding of the musical processes that have produced Cage's works deepens our appreciation of the sonic "landscapes" they present. By examining systems, we allow the individual phenomena, whether mountain ranges or musical scores, to remain unique and beyond explanation, while still enriching our experience of them through the observation of the forces that brought them into being. These observations are the facts to which Eliot cautions us to adhere in our critical inquiries and which can form the basis of a fruitful study of the music of John Cage.

Notes

1. T. S. Eliot, "The Function of Criticism," in *Selected Prose of T. S. Eliot*, ed. Frank Kermode (New York: Harcourt, Brace, Jovanovich, 1975), p. 69.

2. Ibid., p. 75.

3. Paul Griffiths, *Cage* (London: Oxford University Press, 1981), p. 1.

4. Paul Griffiths, "Aleatory," *The New Grove Dictionary of Music and Musicians* (London: Macmillan, 1980), 1:240.

5. David Cope, *New Directions in Music*, 2d ed. (Dubuque, Iowa: Brown, 1976), p. 184.

6. Paul Griffiths, *Modern Music: The Avant-Garde since 1945* (New York: Braziller, 1981), p. 124.

7. See, for example: Cope, *New Directions in Music*, p. 169; John Rockwell, *All American Music* (New York: Knopf, 1983), pp. 52–53; Richard Kostelanetz, "Inferential Art" (1967), in *John Cage*, ed. Richard Kostelanetz (New York: Praeger, 1970), pp. 105–9.

8. Earle Brown, "Form in New Music," *Source*, no. 1 (1967), p. 51.

9. Ibid.

10. John Cage, "To Describe the Process of Composition Used in *Music of Changes* and *Imaginary Landscape No. 4*" (1951), *Silence: Lectures and Writings* (Middletown, Conn.: Wesleyan University Press, 1961), p. 58.

11. Virgil Thomson, "The Abstract Composers," *The New York Herald Tribune*, 3 February 1952.

12. John Cage, "Composition as Process: I. Changes" (1958), *Silence*, p. 27.

13. Griffiths, *Cage*, p. 24.

14. *For the Birds* (John Cage in Conversation with Daniel Charles), trans. Richard Gardner (Salem, N.H.: Boyars, 1981), p. 104.

15. John Cage, "Happy New Ears," *A Year from Monday: New Lectures and Writings* (Middletown, Conn.: Wesleyan University Press, 1967), p. 31.

Intentionality and Nonintentionality in the Performance of Music by John Cage

Tom Johnson

PERHAPS the most important single word in the æsthetic of John Cage is *nonintentionality*. A concept borrowed from Buddhism, and usually considered a philosophical matter, Cage saw that it had musical applications as well. For him, it was not only a question of freeing himself from his own intentions and ego, as prescribed by Zen masters, but also of creating a music that itself would be without intentions.

In both romanticism and expressionism, nothing was nonintentional. Music was intended to express the intentions of the composer and was expected to convey these intentions to the audience, which was intended to react in certain specific ways. The concept of nonintentionality enabled Cage to break completely with this kind of thinking and also provided him with a justification for composing with chance processes. In this way, he found a unique and fruitful route that led him into all sorts of mediums, including poetry, graphics, multimedia, electronics, and opera, as well as instrumental musical forms.

But what is nonintentional music really? And how does one intend, or not intend, to play it? Fortunately, Cage has written often about nonintentionality, and before going further it will be useful to reread a few of the things he has said over the years:

> Art and music, when anthropocentric (involved in self-expression) seem trivial and lacking in urgency to me. We live in a world where there are things as well as people. Trees, stones, water, everything is expressive. I see this situation in which I impermanently live as a complex interpenetration of centers moving out in all directions without impasse. This is in accord with contemporary awareness of the operations of nature. I attempt to let sounds be themselves in a space of time. There are those ... who find this attempt on my part pointless. I do not object to being engaged in a purposeless activity.[1]

And what is your intention when you write music?

Cage: I am not concerned with intentions, but with sounds.

Which sounds?

Cage: I make them just as well if I sit still or go mushroom hunting.[2]

Like essentially all of my works since the late 40's and early 50's, these pieces (*Etudes Boreales*) are non-intentional. In writing them I gave up responsibility for individual choices by posing specific questions to be answered with the help of chance operations, according to the I Ching. In connection with my study of Zen philosophy with Daisetz Suzuki, I have used I-Ching chance operations in all my works, be they literary, graphic or musical, in order to free my ego from its likes and dislikes.[3]

Listen, if you can, to Beethoven and get something out of it that's not what he put in it. We must get ourselves into a situation where we can use our experience no matter what it is. We must take intentional material, like Beethoven, and turn it to non-intention.[4]

My intention is to let things be themselves.[5]

Nonintention in music: a relatively simple notion, but it turned out to be one of the most important simple notions in twentieth-century music. It is the basis of everything Cage has done, and many others have followed. But implicit in the idea of nonintentional music was another idea. If the music is nonintentional, shouldn't the performer, too, release some of his individual control? Shouldn't the interpreter also allow the music to follow its own intentions? Or the intentions of the I Ching? This is the real subject of our discussion, and this is not so simple. Did you ever try to play an instrument without intending to?

The question of how to interpret Cage's music has a long and troubled history. In fact, Cage has probably suffered more than any of his contemporaries from bad performances by unsympathetic or ignorant performers. During the fifties and sixties, on those rather rare occasions when orchestras or ensembles programed one of his works, it was often for the sake of adding a novelty to the program, and often the performers, or at least a large segment of the performing group, had almost no awareness of what the music was about. Often performances were intentionally camped up, intentionally gross in sound choices, or intentionally trivialized, and it was rare, except in those performances organized by Cage himself, and his closest colleagues, that one might have perceived that the main idea of the music was to be nonintentional.

In the intervening years, however, Cage's music has become much more widely and deeply understood, and today Cage interpreters sometimes produce truly exquisite musical objects, perhaps exquisite in ways that Cage himself never imagined.

Do they do so intentionally?

If so, doesn't that go against the basic intentions, or nonintentions, of the music?

What are the real intentions of a composer of nonintentional music?

What does nonintentional music intend to convey to the listener, and how can the interpreter help the message come across?

If a performer plays with great control, achieving exactly what he or she intends, does this contradict the nonintentions of the music?

The contradictions fold over one another endlessly, like one of those ever-confusing Zen koans, and we will never untangle all these ironies. But a few things should become clear if we consider some of the most satisfying Cage interpretations to be heard today. Several specific interpretations at the Cage 75th birthday festival in Cologne by the Arditti Quartet, Les Percussions de Strasbourg, and the violinist János Négyesy struck me as particularly clear examples, and certainly represent a vast development over the gross misunderstandings so common a couple of decades ago.

The Arditti Quartet plays Cage's *String Quartet in Four Parts* as if it were a Mozart quartet. There is a delicacy throughout, a care for each note, a subtle balance of voices in each harmony, and everything is immaculately in tune. One is not used to hearing the music of Cage performed so beautifully, and the effect is curious. Is this the music of a controversial American experimentalist? Is this the music that began a revolution in Darmstadt in 1958? One cannot help but notice a conflict between the music and the reputation of the music. Or is it a conflict between the nonintentionality of the music and the intentional delicacy of the performers?

The *String Quartet in Four Parts* was written in 1949–50, before any of the above quotations, and before Cage began to use chance decisions, though he was already strictly limiting his self-expression. The four movements express merely the qualities of the four seasons, as codified in Indian philosophy. The rhythmic structure follows the proportions 2½, 1½, 2, 5, 6, 5, ½, 1½, without exception, and the entire piece is to be played without vibrato. It would be almost impossible for a romantic melody or an expressionistic violence to break through this network of restrictions, and, without the possibility of vibrato, it would be very difficult for the first violinist to overlay a soulful interpretation of a melodic line.

The score must have been very frustrating for string quartets when it was first written. Even those quartets that played much contemporary music played mostly Bartok and Webern and had no experience with the sort of self-restraint called for in the *String Quartet in Four Parts.* By now, however, musicians like those in the Arditti Quartet have played many works by Giacinto Scelsi, Morton Feldman, and others, who have also reacted against expressionism. Thus the idea of restrained contemporary music is clear, and musicians know that some kinds of music simply come off better when they are not interpreted, not expressed, too much.

It is also clear that to do this is not so easy. Most violinists have trouble playing without vibrato for a long time; they forget, and they go back to their habitual way of playing. But the players in the Arditti Quartet don't forget. They don't swoon into little crescendos either. They remain always calm and controlled.

This kind of control is intentional. In fact, I would say that it takes much greater will power, stronger intention, for an instrumentalist to play in this way than to give vent to romantic interpreter expressivity. But since this control, this intentionality, has so much to do with *suppressing* expressive gestures, I would say that the interpreters here were fully in harmony with the music. Both the music and the interpretation had the effect of suppressing the ego, suppressing individual intentions.

Much the same could be said of the violinist János Négyesy and his interpretation of Cage's *Freeman Etudes,* but there are differences. The *Freeman Etudes,* written between 1977 and 1980 for Paul Zukofsky, are conceived as virtuoso pieces. Cage wanted to take the violin, and violinists, as far as possible into uncharted territory and unknown technical difficulties. Every note comes from another star, traced directly from astronomical maps, and almost every note has its own dynamic marking. The range goes higher than I have ever seen violin music go, and the notes/stars sometimes come in dense clusters. The pages of the score are sprinkled with many further complications, such as glissandos, harmonics, double and triple stops, and requirements to play certain notes on certain strings.

This is not the kind of music you can play without knowing what you are doing! The performer must know that every note will come out pretty much as intended, and when Négyesy played, I had no question about that. I loved the clarity with which he attacked short isolated notes, giving them just the sort of push or float or ring that he wanted. Even in passages where the notes came so fast it wasn't possible to hear exactly what was happening, I had the feeling that the violinist was playing the gesture just the way he always played it.

Négyesy continued like this through the whole set of etudes, playing for an hour or more, and he remained perfectly calm through all these myriads of technical difficulties. Perhaps this calmness was the secret. Perhaps that was why the music sounded so beautiful. Neither Cage nor Négyesy was getting excited or telling the music what to do. The music could just come out the way it came out.

Les Percussions de Strasbourg is one of the best contemporary music ensembles in the world and has a keen understanding of the music of Cage. The Cage work I heard them play was written for the Hans Arp centenary, and its title is a long quotation from a letter from the Arp Foundation:

> But what about the noise of crumpling paper which he used to do in order to paint the series of "papiers froissés" or tearing up paper to make "papiers déchirés"? Arp was stimulated by water (sea, lake, and flowing waters like rivers), forests.

This is one of Cage's less specific scores, with notation consisting of plus signs that mean to play in unison on at least two unspecified instruments or different materials, with circles that indicate "water sounds, paper sounds, or not easily identifiable sounds," and indications of duration. It's the kind of score that twenty years ago generally produced ludicrous shenanigans from baffled undedicated performers. By now, however, it has been demonstrated hundreds of times that sensitive performers can make wonderful music out of scores like this if they really want to. So for a group like Les Percussions de Strasbourg, that prides itself on doing everything well, the score is a chance to extend themselves and come up with something that has as much insight and invention and finesse as possible.

The six percussionists were distributed all around the edges of the hall of the Musikhochschule, and they played with extreme care and concentration. Each performer had a different kind of paper to tear or crumple, all six had original and ear-catching interpretations of the required unison sounds and water sounds, and no expense had been spared to acquire and transport the most effective possible instruments. One enormous water drum, which shimmered exquisitely under a special lighting, appeared to have been specially constructed for this piece. For about half an hour the music wafted beautifully through the space, reminding us of images from collages of Arp, and creating a lovely atmosphere. As in all good performances of Cage's works, the music drifted from one idea to another with a purposeless, unintentional effect.

But was it unintentional for the percussionists?

These six men, with their specially selected papers and specially constructed instruments, obviously knew what they intended to do, and did what they intended. Still, one could see that they were observing certain rules which they would not observe in most of the repertoire, and which are important in most of Cage's music. In a score like this, for example, each player must interpret his part as if he were all alone, without being pushed and pulled by what the other players are doing. The idea is to let your part play itself, not be affected by what the other musicians do, and, above all, never to coordinate purposely with the other musicians. Organized simultaneities spoil the nonintentional drift of this kind of music, simply because one can hear too much human manipulation.

Also important in the interpretation of a score like this is the way one handles the special paper and water sounds. Ripping or splashing cannot be completely controlled, and the players must be willing to let the music tear or rip or crumple or splash or ripple however it will. Les Percussions de Strasbourg seemed to understand this especially well. Several times during the performance I was struck by the concentration of one of the players as he just waited for his piece of paper to tear, however it was going to tear. The musicians were controlling the major parameters of the piece, but they were sensitive to the many details that they could not control and should not try to control. In such moments the music became nonintentional in a particularly literal and interesting sense.

But perhaps the interpreter who comes closest to achieving truly nonintentional interpretations is Cage himself. About the only performing the composer has done in recent years has consisted of reading the texts that he derives by chance from Thoreau, Joyce, names of mushrooms, and other sources. These works are largely nonsyntactical, and there seems to be much reluctance to accepting Cage into literary and poetic circles. But for me these pieces are pure poetry, and their author's style of reading them is also quite poetic. Particularly now, as Cage's voice becomes gradually frailer, older, he pulls me more and more into the words, the sounds, the implications of this unique phonetic music, somewhat like the way the recorded voices of Dylan Thomas or Carl Sandburg have drawn me into their work. There is no self-consciousness in Cage's reading, no desire to attract our attention or convince us of the quality of the work. The reading goes on almost despite the reader.

Following the reading of "Mushrooms and Variations" in Zagreb a few years ago, I commented to Cage that I particularly liked the mode of the pitches he had chosen for this reading, which in this case had been closer to chanting than to speaking. Much to my surprise he responded, "Was there a mode? I try not to think about things like that." This is not a case of naiveté. Cage could analyze the scale used in some melody as well as any trained musician could. Nor, in my opinion, was he teasing me or making a false claim. I am convinced that his technique as an interpreter simply functions in that way. He tries to focus all his attention on the text itself, to enter completely into the words and syllables, and to allow the pitches and rhythms to come out however they will. However *they* will. Not how Cage wills them to come out. And he can do it.

But of course, he did study Zen for a very long time.

If we stand back from these specific examples for a moment, however, it is not difficult to see that all good musical interpretation must be nonintentional to some degree. Did you ever hear someone *trying* to play Beethoven? If you have to *try*, you aren't doing it right. Your interpretation is necessarily confused and labored. Only at a very advanced stage is an instrumentalist able to play Beethoven in a way that strikes us as effortless, natural, organic, and smooth, and each of these adjectives, so abundant in positive reviews of classical music concerts, implies nonintentionality. A pianist who plays Beethoven "effortlessly" is a pianist who knows the music and the instrument so well that the will, the intention, the effort, all seem to have disappeared. It is as if the interpreter is no longer playing the music but rather being played *by* the music. The passive voice. The intentions of the music itself are realized, not only those of the interpreter.

And if the music itself has no intentions?

If it wants merely to drift through time nonintentionally?

In that case, the music is probably a composition by John Cage, about whom one could say the same thing: he doesn't write music, but lets the music write him. The passive voice. He composes as "effortlessly" as Horowitz plays the piano, and the works flow freely and generously from his pen. There can be eight or ten of them in a single year, and the flow continues—at the age of seventy-five. His work has changed the way composers compose, the way interpreters interpret, and the way listeners listen. Happy birthday to the man who has changed us all—nonintentionally, of course!

Notes

1. From a letter to the *New York Herald Tribune,* 22 May 1956, cited in *John Cage,* ed. Richard Kostelanetz (New York: Praeger, 1970).

2. From *Musik der Stille* (Silent Music), a radio work by George Brecht, directed by Brecht and Klaus Schöning; my translation.

3. From Monika Lichtenfeld's program notes for the *Nachtcagetag* twenty-four-hour Cage festival presented by Westdeutscher Rundfunk in Cologne, 14–15 February 1987.

4. From "Conversation with John Cage," in *John Cage,* p. 29.

5. From *Pour les oiseaux,* original French version, p. 235; published as *For the Birds* (John Cage in Conversation with Daniel Charles), trans. Richard Gardner (Salem, N.H.: Boyars, 1981).

A Conversation about Radio in Twelve Parts

Richard Kostelanetz and John Cage

HAVING already done distinguished work in music, in theater, in poetry, and in visual art, John Cage recently discovered, or rediscovered, a new medium to explore in radio.
Working with Klaus Schöning, a staff producer of *Hörspiel* (literally, ear-play) for Westdeutscher Rundfunk, he has produced a
series of ambitious *Hörspiele,* including *Roaratorio* (1979), *Ein Alphabet* (1982), *Muoyce* (1973), and *HMCIEX* (1984). Critically
speaking, these *hörspiele* represent an intermedium between poetry and music, drawing upon both, without falling into either.

For *Roaratorio,* subtitled "An Irish Circus on *Finnegans Wake,*"
Cage won the coveted Karl Sczuka Prize of German radio. The
citation read that, "Cage opens up an endlessly rich acoustic
world, although it is strongly rooted in literary and musical ideas.
It is a world made up of sounds, text and music, one of which the
listener is able at will to experience and at the same time is exposed
to sounds, which the radio, normally restricted to the mediation
of one-dimensional information, cannot normally offer." Three
years later, the German publisher Athenäum published a thoroughly bilingual package of the same title; in it are a book, a fold-
out score, and an audiocassette in which the entire piece is framed
by Cage and Schöning talking from and about it.

Behind these new Cage horspiels is a wealth of pioneering
experience with radio on the one hand and audiotape on the
other. As described by the composer William Duckworth in his
thesis on Cage, the latter's *Imaginary Landscape No. 1* (1939) "was
designed for performance in a radio studio, subsequently to be
recorded or broadcast. The score calls for four performers who
employ two turntables with Victor frequency records of constant
and variable frequency, a large Chinese gong, and a string piano.
The results of the performance efforts are picked up by two
microphones and relayed to an assistant in the control room who
controls the relative dynamics." Several years later, Cage created

in *Williams Mix* (1953) a pioneering audiotape mix, which has long been available on the three-record set, *A 25-Year Retrospective Concert of the Music of John Cage* (Avakian, 1958).

To explore these subjects, not covered by Cage elsewhere, I initiated our fourth extended conversation in the past two decades. The first, primarily about his music and theater, appeared in my documentary monograph *John Cage*.[1] The second, primarily about his poetry, was reprinted in my book *The Old Poetries and the New*.[2] The third, about his rewritings through *Finnegans Wake*, appeared first on a 1978 videotape and then in *The John Cage Reader*.[3] Now, focusing upon radio and audiotape (to the exclusion of everything else insofar as possible), we spoke in his New York City home over the continuous background sound not of radio or music but street traffic.

I

KOSTELANETZ: When did you first work creatively with radio?
CAGE: When I went to Seattle and took the job as dance accompanist for the classes of Bonnie Bird, I was attracted there in the first place by the presence of a large collection of percussion instruments; but when I got there I discovered that there was a radio station in connection with the school, like a big outhouse. The same building is still there, though now it's used I think for pottery. But then it was radio, and we were able to make experiments combining percussion instruments and small sounds that required amplification in the studio. We were able to broadcast those to the theater which was just a few steps away, and we were able, of course, to make recordings and, besides making records, to use records as instruments.
K: How did you use records as instruments?
C: Well, the record makes a sound and the speed of the record changes the pitch of it, and the turntables that we had then one no longer sees; but each one had a clutch: You could move from one speed to another.
K: What did you do in the radio station that you couldn't do playing the records elsewhere live?
C: Well, the turntables were in the radio station, they were not movable, and they had speed controls.
K: What could you do with these speed controls?
C: Well, when you change the speed of the record, you change the frequency of the recorded sound. I used continuous sounds that

were made for test purposes by the Victor Company, and they had both constant tones and tones that were constantly sliding in pitch through a whole range. Those records were used in the *Imaginary Landscape No. 1.*

K: Were the turntables played simultaneously?

C: No. That may have been the case somewhere in the piece, I forget; but they were played simultaneously with other instruments like cymbals, prepared piano and so forth. Generally, the record player would play one record at a time and then I'd change it and play another record.

K: So you could go swiftly from one record to another.

C: Not swiftly, but you could go properly.

K: Was the sound modified at all after it went into the microphone?

C: No, no, I've never done much with sound modification.

K: Why not?

C: I found the sounds interesting as they were.

II

K: Let me ask about your experience of radio at that time. What kind of radio did you listen to?

C: You mean when I listened to radio?

K: At that time, in the thirties.

C: I have no distinct recollection of ever listening to radio.

K: When you were young?

C: No, I do remember now. I can take it back a little bit. I had a tendency to listen to the news.

K: Did you like radio comedy?

C: No. My mother and father did, but I didn't. There's one thing you probably don't remember (or do you?). When I was twelve years old, I had a radio program. It was for the Boy Scouts of America. I rode on my bicycle from Eagle Rock, where we lived, over to KFWB in Hollywood. I told them that I had the idea of having a Boy Scout program and that the performers on the program would be Boy Scouts and that ten minutes of each hour would be used by someone from either a synagogue or a church who would give some kind of an inspiring talk, you know. I was in the tenth grade, and so KFWB told me just to run along.

So I went to the next radio station—KNX. It was nearby, and they liked the idea, and they said, "Do you have permission from the Boy Scouts to do this?" I said, "No, but I can get that." So I

went to the Boy Scouts and said that I had the agreement of KNX
to have an hour every week for the Boy Scouts and was it alright
with them? They said yes, and I said, "Well, will you cooperate
with me? For instance, can I have the Boy Scout Band?" And they
said, certainly not. They said you can do anything you like, but we
won't cooperate; so I went back and told the people at the radio
station. They agreed. Every Friday after school—I was still in high
school—I would go over to the radio station and conduct the
program which I think was something like four to five in the
afternoon or five to six. During the week I would prepare the
program by getting as many scouts as I could to play, oh say, violin
solos or trombone solos.

K: If this was in 1924–25, radio was still new to America.

C: Well, radio was very close to my experience, because my father
was an inventor. He was never given credit for it, but he had
invented the first radio to be plugged into the electric light system.

K: What was your idea for the show?

C: Well, what I told you: boy scouts performing and some ten-
minute inspirational talk from a member of the clergy. I no
sooner began the program than there was a great deal of correspondence, people writing in; and those letters would be read on
the air by me. I was the master of ceremonies. When there was no
one else to perform I played piano solos . . .

K: Of?

C: Mostly *Music the Whole World Loves to Play.* There used to be
these books with that title. They were on all the neighborhood
pianos. It's sad that we no longer have pianos in every house, with
several members of the family able to play, instead of listening to
radio or watching television.

K: How long did your juvenile radio career go?

C: That lasted for two years. Isn't that amazing? And it was so
popular that it became a two-hour program, and the Boy Scouts
became jealous. They came to the radio station and said that I had
no authority and no right to have the program. So, of necessity,
the radio station asked me to leave, and they accepted the real Boy
Scouts, because I was only second class. I was not even a first class
scout. They accepted the real ones, and the real ones used it in a
quite different way. They were very ostentatious and pushy. The
result was that after two programs they were asked to leave.

K: Was there a sponsor?

C: No, this was before the day of grants.

K: Was the program aimed at other teenagers, or was it for an
adult audience?

C: Well, the scouts all loved it and so, for instance, did very elderly women, who were at home listening to the radio.

III

K: What other radio experiences do you remember from the twenties and thirties? ·

C: I was very impressed by the Columbia Workshop plays; *that* seemed to be worth listening to. My mood for entertainment, when I was young, was satisfied by such things or by those beautiful Russian films, Eisenstein. Mostly I felt above Hollywood, where I was more or less living.

K: Did you hear music on radio that interested you?

C: I don't remember hearing music. We'd go to the Hollywood Bowl for that.

K: So, even into the late twenties, your experience of music came mostly from live music.

C: From piano lessons and so on. It was in church primarily. Aunt Marge had a beautiful contralto voice. I loved to hear her sing, always on Sundays in church and sometimes on weekdays at home. Then in college, at Pomona, I met a Japanese tennis player who had some kind of physical trouble as a result of playing tennis. So he was resting by taking a few classes at Pomona College. He was absolutely devoted to the string quartets of Beethoven, and he had as fine a collection of recordings of those as one could find. His name was Tamio Abe, and he played all those records for me.

K: The recording medium at that time was wire. Did you ever think of working creatively with wire?

C: I did some library research work in connection with my father's inventions. Because of that, when I became interested in recorded sound for musical purposes or even for radio plays, I then did library research for myself about the new technical possibilities; and they included, as you say, wire and film. Tape wasn't yet, in the early forties, recognized as a suitable musical means; but wire and film were.

K: Did you work with them yourself?

C: No, I just wanted to. I wrote letters, I think it was in '41 or '42, to corporations and universities all over the country trying to establish a Center for Experimental Music, and I didn't get anywhere. Well, actually, I got a little where. The University of Iowa's psychology department was interested through the presence there of, wasn't his name, Carl Seashore, who made many ways of finding out about intelligence and so on. He was interested in my project. Dr. Aurelia Henry Reinhardt, isn't that right, who was president of Mills, was interested. She was a very tall, big, imposing and brilliant woman. She had a great collection of Gertrude Stein books. So was Moholy-Nagy at the School of Design in Chicago. But none of these people had any money. They said, if I could raise the money to establish it, they would be willing to have it as part of their activities. For two years I kept trying to do that, and that's when I, so to speak, didn't get anywhere.

K: What did you imagine this center having?

C: Well, I was working with percussion instruments. One characteristic of percussion is that it's open to anything else than what it already has. The strings in the orchestra are not that way—they want to become more and more what they are; but the percussion wants to become other than what it is. And that's the part of the orchestra that's open, so to speak, to electronics or to . . . And so I thought of recording means as instrumental to percussion music.

K: "Recording means?"

C: Records, films, tape, wires, anything; so that a center for experimental music would explore new possibilities for the production of sound.

K: Isn't that "sound modification?"

C: No, it could involve new instruments like the instruments of Luigi Russolo. My letter, which I wrote and sent to all these corporations and universities, always began with the history of experimental music in the twentieth century and that begins, I think, with the work of the Futurists in Italy.

K: But that's the history of new machines for music . . .

C: Yes, new instruments; but, you see, machines are one thing and records are simply other kinds of machines.

K: You weren't interested in records for recording yourself as much as you wanted them as sound sources.

C: Right.

K: Because they had sounds that were not normally available to you?

C: Well, you can record any sound and then you can play any record and then you have an instrument.

K: Where did radio fit in this vision?

C: It had turntables.

K: Did these variable-speed machines we talked about before go from one predetermined speed to another, or did they have intermediate speeds?

C: They did; that was what was marvelous.

K: How could you do it?

C: Because, you see, it wasn't highly developed yet and you could go absolutely completely through the spectrum of possibilities from slow to fast. And it had clutches to go from one speed to another. The transition was not abrupt, but gradual, and produced amazingly interesting glissandi which you hear in my *Imaginary Landscape No. 1*.

K: What was your next radio involvement—the Kenneth Patchen project?

C: Yes, I always admired, as I told you, the Columbia Workshop play programs, and you remember the story of the play that had to do with the end of the world and how the entire country thought it was true; so that not only I, but many other people, were interested in the Columbia Workshop plays. I appealed to Davidson Taylor here in New York to let me make the accompaniment to a Columbia Workshop play. I explained to him that my view of radio music was that it should follow from a consideration of the possible environmental sounds of the play itself; so that, if it was a play that took place in the country, it would be natural to have the sound of birds and crickets and frogs and so forth. But, if it were a play that took place in the city, it would be natural to have the sounds of traffic. In other words, I wanted to elevate the sound effect to the level of musical instruments.

That appealed to him and so he asked me to suggest an author for the play. The first one I suggested was Henry Miller. I asked Henry Miller if he would write a play for me, and he said it would be better if I would first read his books. It was difficult at that time to read his books because they were considered pornographic, so he gave me a letter of special introduction to the New York Public Library when I was still in Chicago. I came to the New York library where he said his books actually existed, and I was able to read them. I didn't see the possibility of a radio play from those books and still felt that he should write something especially for the occasion. He didn't agree to do that. So Davidson Taylor said, well, who would be your next choice, and I said Kenneth Patchen. I had read and enjoyed *The Journal of Albion Moonlight* [1971].

I was now living in Chicago, and I'd made friends with the head of the sound effects department of CBS there. Since this was now a CBS Workshop project that had a particular date and deadline, I asked him what sounds I could use; and he said there's no limit to what you can do. (Musicians frequently say this to you also; they say, write anything you like and we will do it.) So I proceeded. I

used to go downtown into the loop in Chicago and close my eyes
and listen and I dreamed up through that listening all sorts of
requests which I wrote down verbally and musically; and when I
took them to the sound effects man, he told me, if you please, that
what I'd written was impossible.

K: Just as those solicitous musicians would tell you that the score
you'd just given them was impossible.

C: Right, so I said, what's impossible about it? He said it would be
so expensive. By this time the projected performance was only a
few days away and my whole score, which was for an hour, yes, of
music that I had written, was, he said, impossible. I had to write
another hour in just a few days, and I used the instruments that I
knew how to use—namely, the percussion instruments and records. The play that Kenneth Patchen had written was called *The
City Wears a Slouch Hat.* I stayed up about four days really without
sleeping, just napping now and then; and I wrote. I was married
then to Xenia Cage, and she would do the copying. We had the
musicians on hand to play and so forth.

K: So they would play the new score as you were writing it down.

C: Essentially yes. I would write it, she would copy it, and they
would play it.

K: Does that first score still exist?

C: No, I don't think so.

K: Can you reconstruct it? Could it be done, given technologies
available now?

C: It might be able to be done, but I'm not going to do it.

IV

K: Why were these early pieces called "Imaginary" Landscapes?

C: It's not a physical landscape. It's a term reserved for the new
technologies. It's a landscape in the future. It's as though you used
technology to take you off the ground and go like Alice through
the looking glass.

K: Were your other, later, Imaginary Landscapes likewise involved with radio?

C: They were involved with those turntables, but I didn't think of
them as necessarily being involved with radio, but rather as being
necessarily involved with new technological possibilities.

K: That were available in radio stations.

C: Or elsewhere, so that if I found something in a moving picture
studio, for instance, like a film phonograph, that would have been

suitable material for an Imaginary Landscape. Later, the *Imaginary Landscape No. 4* was for twelve radios, and *No. 5* was for magnetic tape.

K: How did you develop the notion of using radio as a musical instrument?

C: There was a tendency through the whole twentieth century, from the Futurists on, to use noises, anything that produced sound, as a musical instrument. It wasn't really a leap on my part; it was, rather, simply opening my ears to what was in the air.

K: Do you remember your thinking at that time?

C: Yes, my thinking was that I didn't like the radio and that I would be able to like it if I used it in my work. That's the same kind of thinking that we ascribe to the cave dwellers in their drawings of the frightening animals on the walls—that through making the pictures of them that they would come to terms with them. I did that later with the tape machine in Milan when I went to make *Fontana Mix*. I was alarmed over all the possibilities, so I simply sat down the first day I was there and drew a picture of the whole machine.

K: That dehexed it for you, so to speak.

C: Right, It's true.

K: Now why did you choose twelve radios, rather than just one, for *Imaginary Landscape No. 4?*

C: There're so many possible answers; I don't remember which one was in my head. One is the twelve tones of the octave, and the other is the twelve disciples, and so on. It seemed like a reasonable number.

K: It's said in the history books that when you saw them lined up, you said, "Ah, Twelve Golden Throats." Now I assume that's ironic.

C: No. This particular radio I was using was advertised as a "Golden Throat."

K: But did you think of them as "golden throats?"

C: Yes, because, when I was walking along one of the streets in the fifties near Radio City and these radios were in the window, they were advertised as "Golden Throats," and I immediately decided to go to the president of the company, or the manager of the store, and ask for the loan of twelve of them. I did that, and he gave me the loan.

K: So, with your exclamation of "twelve Golden Throats," you basically gave him free advertising.

C: Exactly.

K: Didn't you have two operators for each radio?

C: Right. One controls kilocycles and the other controls the tone control and the volume.

K: And what instructions did you give the performers?

C: The parts were written in what we call proportional notation, where the notes are at the points in space that they should be in time. However, this is written in a space which changes with accelerandos and ritards; so that it's at the cross between conventional notation and proportional notation. *The Music of Changes* [1951] is at the same point, so it's written in ⅔ or ¼. The space is observed, so that fractions of notes that are irrational can be placed in it by measuring them. Then I can go, for instance, from a note that's two-fifths of a quarter to a note that's one-third of a half, and so on, and measure each single fragment. In this case, because you're measuring, you need not add up to whole units; you can come out completely uneven.

K: Which is not so easy to do in straight musical notation.

C: No, but I was still using quarter notes and half notes, and half notes you see with fractions above them, very peculiar. Later due to David Tudor's studying a form of mathematics, to take the trouble out of my notation and doing it successfully, I dropped all notion of meter and went directly into plain space equals time, which has enormously facilitated the writing of new music.

K: Were those twenty-four radio performers musicians?

C: Yes, they were. They could all read notes, and there was a conductor who was beating ¼ time.

K: Who was he?

C: I was doing it.

K: My recollection is that there was something special about what time of day this performance was.

C: The first performance had almost no sound in it. Two friends of mine at the time, Henry Cowell and Virgil Thomson, both attributed the absence of sound to the fact that it was late at night—it was nearly midnight. However, I knew that the piece was essentially quiet through the use of chance operations and that there was very little sound in it, even in broad daylight, so to speak.

K: Because the volume levels would always be . . .

C: . . . always very low.

K: Tell me about your other works for radio at that time.

C: One is called *Radio Music* [1956] and what's the other one.

K: *Speech* [1955] "for five radios and newsreader," it says in your catalogue.

C: *Speech*, yes. Well, they're slightly different, but the radio piece was written more or less to please the people who were disturbed over the *Imaginary Landscape No. 4* because it was so quiet. I forgot what I did, but it can be played so as to be loud.

K: Your catalogue of twenty years ago says that in Radio Music "durations of tunings are free, but each is to be expressed by maximum amplitude."

C: It does. Well then it's obvious that that's what it was. If people wanted radios to be loud, that was the piece to play.

K: Is it basically the same piece?

C: No, it's relatively indeterminate.

K: It was a different score.

C: Oh yes.

K: But similar notation?

C: No, it's quite different. I haven't looked at it recently; it's really not very interesting.

K: In the catalogue there are no performances listed for *Speech*.

C: Well, it's been performed a number of times.

K: Can you tell me about it?

C: I don't remember it very clearly.

K: How did your writing these pieces change your attitude to radio, at least in your personal life?

C: It made it possible for me to listen to radio with great interest, no matter what it was doing.

K: And what did you listen to then?

C: Well, anything that I happened to hear. I didn't myself turn on a radio to listen to it; but when I was going through the streets or when a neighbor was playing the radio and so forth, I listened as though I were listening to a musical instrument.

K: Did radio become a favorite musical instrument?

C: Almost as favored by me as the sounds of traffic.

K: When you were driving the Cunningham troupe around the country in the fifties, did you have a radio in the bus?

C: No, we played Scrabble.

That must be the end of chapter four. This is like a novel.

V

K: When did you first encounter audiotape?

C: I must have first encountered it in Paris in the late forties, when I met Pierre Schaeffer who was the first to do any serious work from a musical point of view in relation to magnetic tape. He made every effort he could to get me interested in working along these lines, but I wasn't yet really ready. I was moving. . . . Well, I was writing my *String Quartet* [1950], and I had written *Sonatas and Interludes* [1946–48]. I was gradually moving towards the shift from music as structure to music as process and to the use, as a result, of chance operations in composition. I might have been more cooperative with Schaeffer, but I wasn't. It didn't really dawn on me.

K: Because of notational problems?

C: No, my mind was being used in a different way; so that I wasn't as open as I might have been to the notion of music on magnetic tape then. That's '49. In '52, when I worked with David Tudor and Earle Brown, we made several pieces—one by Earle, one by me, one by Christian Wolff, and one by Morton Feldman, with funding from Paul Williams. I made the *Williams Mix* [1953] then. All of that work was done with excitement over the possibilities of magnetic tape, and they were various. That's why I was anxious not to exploit them alone but with other people, because each mind would bring into the new possibilities a different slant; and that's certainly the case. Feldman was working with his early graph music, and it was just marvelous to come to a square on his graph paper with the number, say, 1097 in it. That meant that we were to chop up a piece of recorded tape so that it formed 1097 fragments and splice it back into the band, you know, at that point. I was very open at the time, and very interested in splicing tape and in making the music manually. I found various ways of changing sound not with dials but, rather, by physically cutting the tape.

K: Such as?

C: Well, the tape normally goes past the head horizontally; but if you cut it and splice it back diagonally . . .

K: You would have to cut it into such small pieces that, in effect, are no longer than tape is normally wide.

C: Yes, but you could get perfectly beautiful sounds by putting it at an angle to what it should have been.

K: That's terribly meticulous work.

C: Yes, and I was using chance operations, so that I was able to go from a vertical cut on the tape to one that was four inches long at an angle on quarter-inch tape.

K: It must have taken years.

C: Well, no, it took about a year with help to splice the *Williams Mix*, which was itself a little over four minutes of music; but we did other pieces. We did the *Suite by Chance* of Christian Wolff, and we did the *Octet* of Earle Brown and we did the *Intersection* of Morton Feldman.

K: Do all these works still exist?

C: I believe they do.

K: All I know is your *Williams Mix* from the Twenty-fifth Anniversary Record.

C: Earle's piece, the *Octet,* was made with the rubbish from the pieces by Feldman and Wolff and myself.

K: Using similar compositional operations?

C: Using his own composing means, but with regard to the sounds that were, so to speak, thrown away through the process of making other pieces.

K: You know that I regard the *Williams Mix* as your most neglected masterpiece.

C: Well, it's an interesting piece. One reason it could very well be neglected is that the score has nearly 500 pages and, therefore, it has not been reproduced. The original is at Peters, I think. It would be too expensive to multiply it; so I don't think many people are aware of it. I have illustrated it in the notes to the Town Hall program.

K: The Twenty-fifth Anniversary album.

C: People have seen one page that is like a dressmaker's pattern—it literally shows where the tape shall be cut, and you lay the tape on the score itself.

K: On the scale of one to one?

C: One to one, yes.

K: So the tape is, in effect, the length of 500 pages.

C: Yes, each page has twenty inches, two ten-inch systems, a little over a second in duration.

K: Which are, in the album illustration, reproduced on a single page, one atop the other. Your idea for this score is that it would be possible to reproduce the cuts with tapes other than what you used.

C: Yes. I labeled each entry in the score according to the categories A, B, C, D, E, and F and hoped with those categories to cover all possible environmental sounds. Then I took the various parameters of sound as little letters to follow those capital letters . . .

K: Of the categories.

C: So that you would know what kinds of transformations of those original environmental sounds had been made, whether the frequency had been changed or that the loudness had been changed and so forth; so if it was the same as it was originally, it was followed by a "c." If it had been varied, it was followed by a "v." So "Accv" would be a sound, let us say, from the country that had remained as it was in two respects and had been changed in a third.

K: And this "Accv" you would have gotten by chance operations.

C: Right. And then you could have a sound described as "Avvc" or "Bcvc" or their combination "AvvcBcvc," and someone else then could follow that recipe, so to speak, with other sources that I had to make another mix. It really is very interesting, don't you think?

K: Fantastic, yes. As you say, the score is like a dressmaker's pattern. You just simply lay it out and duplicate its cuts on your tape.

C: One of the pages has a hole in it, which came from a burn from a cigarette. I was a great smoker in those days.

K: To me, two of the special qualities of the *Williams Mix* are its unprecedented range of sounds and the rapidity of their articulation.

C: Right. What was so fascinating about tape possibility was that a second, which we had always thought was a relatively short space of time, became fifteen inches. It became something quite long that could be cut up. Morty Feldman, as I told you, took a quarter of an inch and asked us to put 1097 sounds in it, and we did it— we *actually* did it.

K: Within a quarter inch?

C: Which would be one-sixtieth of a second, you see, we put 1097 fragments.

K: Without mixing? You mean just little slivers of tape?

C: Little slivers of tape.

K: That's physically impossible.

C: No, no, we did it.

K: How?

C: By counting, and by hand.

K: You were crazy.

C: Oh, of course, it's crazy; but then don't you think it's true of both of us that we've been crazy all along.

K: Speak for yourself. I'm not that crazy.

C: Norman O. Brown told me once that any worthwhile activity is mad.

K: Or has a crazy element.

C: And the only reason it ever is taken seriously eventually is that one persists.

K: But, as you pointed out, even though you made for posterity a score of *Williams Mix* for others to realize, no one's ever done it.

C: But it's because the manuscript is so big and so little known.

K: What was your next involvement with tape?

C: *Imaginary Landscape No. 5* was for tape, and it was simply made for a dance by Jean Erdman. It was called *Portrait of a Lady,* and the dance had a kind of character that suggested popular music.

So I wrote a score that would make use of records—jazz records in this case, but they could be records of other kinds of music—treated as sound sources, rather than being what they were.

K: How long were those segments?

C: They were very short too.

K: Did you destroy any reference to their original sources? Was this collection as various as that for *Williams Mix*?

C: I don't recall whether I made the choice or whether Jean Erdman made the choice or whether it was made by the two of us; it must have had something to do with chance operations.

K: Does that tape still exist?

C: The score exists, and Jean probably has the tape. I don't myself know where it is.

K: What else did you do with radio between then and the late seventies?

C: One might consider the piece *Works of Calder* [1951] the recording or composition I made for that. I first went to the studio of Calder with the idea of recording sounds of the mobiles bumping into one another; this would be a proper accompaniment for a film about his work. I had two ideas in mind. One was that and the other was to write a piece of music, such as my *Sonatas and Interludes* or *A Valentine Out of Season* [1944] or *The Perilous Night* [1944] or something that would accompany the film that was made by Herbert Matter.

K: When you say something like that you mean . . .

C: A musical, so to speak—a more conventional musical . . .

K: But also something of some length—that would be elaborate within itself.

C: And that would take the structure of the film into consideration. I mean the story isn't being properly told because the piece for twelve radios actually comes after the *Works of Calder*, but *Works of Calder* includes the attitude that I had toward the sound being appropriate to the story or film, and that's why I wanted the sounds of the studio. What happened in the end was that the *Works of Calder* has both the sounds of the studio in one section and that it has, before and after that, more conventional musical accompaniment ideas.

K: The sounds of Calder's studio relate back to your idea of the sounds for the Patchen piece.

C: Yes. Since this film was about the mobiles of Calder, to go into his studio and tape the sounds of mobiles bumping into one another as the proper accompaniment for such a film.

K: And again to take those sounds straight—not to modify them in any way.

C: Right.

K: When did you first discover multitracking?

C: What do you mean "multitracking"?

K: Multitrack tape.

C: But my idea all along was to have each track be individual, so that the relation of the tracks could be independent of one another, rather than fixed in a particular scorelike situation.

K: But that wasn't possible with the *Williams Mix* because in those days you had only monophonic tape.

C: Well, it was, because we made the *Williams Mix* for eight separate mono tracks.

K: Eight separate mono tracks, to be played simultaneously?

C: Right, and they can't be fixed together, you see, in a particular way, though they are fixed that way for practical purposes, for Peters publishing them, for instance; but you can rent the single tracks, or tracks in pairs, or in fours.

K: You mean to say that the *Williams Mix* I hear on that twenty-fifth anniversary record . . .

C: Is a performance of eight separate tracks.

K: Eight mono tracks, played simultaneously within a period of roughly five minutes.

C: Four minutes and twenty seconds, something like that, or fifteen.

K: And you're saying that all eight of those tapes are autonomous elements of the piece.

C: They're parts, and there is a score—that dressmaker's score; but it isn't possible to get it precisely together.

K: A score for playing all eight tapes at once.

C: Well, to make them, to splice them, and theoretically, of course, they would all sound together; but the synchronization of eight things is not possible. That's why multitrack came into existence, sixteen-track machines and so forth; but I consistently refused to use it.

K: Why?

C: Because that would give *one* fixed relation to separate tracks.

K: So, therefore, the version on that record is not definitive.

C: I've all along spoken against records at the same time that I've permitted their being made and have even encouraged it; but I've always said that a record is not faithful to the nature of music.

K: Which can only exist in a live performance situation.

C: Right, right, right. I've always been a proper member of the musicians' union, in favor of live music.

K: And what is your instrument of virtuosity?

C: I'm listed in the union as a pianist.

K: This reminds me of the biases of your musical experience as a young man. I'm still going to ask you when you first used multi-track.

C: Every time that I've used it, I've been careful not to use it. Also that is to say all the individual parts can be separated from the congregation—the score of all of them together in one way. That's true of *HPSCHD,* which has something like fifty-six parts.

K: Fifty-six monophonic parts?

C: Right, and it's true of *Roaratorio.* How many parts does it have?

K: Over two thousand?

C: No, that's the number of sounds of something, but the number of parts is different.

K: How do you measure parts in *Roaratorio?*

C: Well, the number of individual tapes that could be used to make up the total. I don't think we've ever had a performance with more than, say, twenty-eight machines, whereas we had a performance of *HPSCHD* with fifty-six machines.

K: In Urbana, Illinois, where there weren't any multitracks either. What you've done, in effect, is made pseudo-multitracks. No, that's not quite the right word either. You've made choruses of autonomous monophonic tapes that cannot be synchronized.

C: Right.

K: In effect imitating the condition of the multitrack technology without taking advantage of its unique capability to organize everything.

C: Yes, I haven't wanted to fix the relationship of individual parts. And that continues and is in my present writing for instrumental music for the recent *Thirty Pieces for String Quartet* [1983], and with the *Music Ear* [1984], which is for anywhere from one player to, I think, eight now, where there's no score but there are all these parts that can go together in a variety of unpredictable ways.

K: And what is written on the parts?

C: Music.

K: Music with bars and staves and . . .

C: Well, sometimes in one notation, sometimes in another.

VI

K: Let me go back, because we're losing our thread here, which is your radio experiences.

C: The next time I'm conscious of radio is with the invitation from Frans van Rossum to make the *Sounday* in Amsterdam, and that was so extraordinary that I accepted it, extraordinary because it meant something like a twelve-hour broadcast with only an announcement at the beginning and one at the end and one in the middle. That was all. Otherwise, there was no interruption of the sound. So I put into the morning the pieces for Grete Sultan, the *Etudes Australes* for piano, surrounded by performances of *Branches,* the plant materials, cacti and all, and then I put into the afternoon the *Freeman Etudes* for violin.

K: Would these pieces be done simultaneously or alternately?

C: No, the morning consisted of *Branches* mostly, and every now and then the *Branches* would stop and you'd hear a piano etude. The image I had in mind was in a boat, and every now and then you'd see something lit up, some image.

K: But you didn't mix your pieces together, as some interpreters do.

C: No, and then in the afternoon the tunnel changed from being *Branches* to *Inlets,* the gurgling of the conch shells filled with water, and things that were heard changed from the piano etudes to the *Freeman Etudes* played by Paul Zukofsky, and then toward the end they changed to the voice of Demetrios Stratos singing the *Mesostics Re and Not Re Merce Cunningham.*

K: How much of this was live, and how much was prerecorded?

C: It was all live. The whole thing was a performance which could be attended through the whole day by people in Amsterdam. It was after that performance that I met Klaus Schöning.

K: But what made that radio experience of *Sounday* different from the live concert?

C: Well, the fact that you weren't there.

K: So radio was simply a dissemination medium.

C: Right, but you see it would have been unlikely then to think of giving a concert the whole day, whereas because of its nature of dissemination it was possible for Frans van Rossum to think of a broadcast that was uninterrupted.

K: Now one natural result of such a long broadcast, it seems to me, is that listeners can go in and out on it. Did you calculate for that fact when you chose your program?

C: I couldn't calculate anything. I could only be aware that people might tune in or out.

K: And in that sense programming for radio could be different from programming for a live audience.

C: Right.

VII

K: What happened with Klaus Schöning?

C: He had heard from Frans van Rossum that I had made a

Writing through Finnegans Wake, and he asked me if I would be willing to read it for his Horspiel program in Cologne, and I said yes. Then when I returned to the United States, I received a letter from him asking me if, since I was willing to read it, would I be willing to write some music to go with it, and I again said yes, and out of that came *Roaratorio.*

K: What were your compositional ideas here?

C: Well, the text is mesostics on the name of James Joyce. It's not my first *Writing through Finnegans Wake* but the second writing. It doesn't permit repetition of the same syllable for a given letter of the name. It was an attempt to shorten the first *Writing through Finnegans Wake;* and it not only does not permit repetition of the syllable, but it doesn't permit the appearance of either letter between two letters of the name, so that . . .

K: So that if the A in one line is that axis of "jAmes," that syllable . . .

C: Can't represent the A of another James.

K: Or the S, between the A and S of "JAMES." Did I get it right?"

C: No, between the J and the A you can't have another J or A, and the syllable that's used for the J can't again be used for the J; nor can the syllable used for the A appear again, and that ensures that the text will be shorter than the first one.

K: And by convenience one hour long.

C: I'm wondering, as I tell you all this, whether I'm telling you the truth. I think what happened with the second writing is just the following of *one* of those new rules, which is the nonrepetition of the syllable. It's in the third writing that I followed the new rule, which I call Mink's Law, because it was Louis Mink who suggested it.

K: That text, as you said, existed prior to your meeting Schöning, but the compositional idea for *Roaratorio* came when he asked you to write some music for it.

C: Then the question was what kind of music to write for the rest of that. I knew that reading the text by itself would take just about an hour and that was the length of program that he was interested in. So I decided to use my reading as a ruler, so to speak, through *Finnegans Wake* and that I would read the book to find sounds suggested in it. This goes back to my Patchen idea and the Calder idea, in other words to find the proper sounds for *Finnegans Wake* in *Finnegans Wake.* When a dog barked, if it barked, say, on page 23, line 10, then I would find where that was in relation to my mesostics, which were also identifiable by page and line, and that way I would be able to put everything where it belonged. So then not satisfied with those sounds going through *Finnegans Wake*, I then used Louis Mink's book, which gives a listing of all the places mentioned in *Finnegans Wake;* and I could go to those places and make recordings of environmental sounds and put these where they belonged in relation to the text. It made an enormous project that could take one's whole life or could at least take as long as Joyce took to write *Finnegans Wake;* but we did it arbitrarily in a shorter period. I wrote quite a number of people around the world to contribute sounds because I didn't plan to go to China. But I did go with John and Monika Fullemann to Ireland, and there for a month we collected sounds in places mentioned in *Finnegans Wake.* Then for a month in Paris at IRCAM, we put all those sounds together; so that my work and John's work at IR-CAM began on a particular day, and a month later it stopped. The people in charge of IRCAM were amazed, because they didn't expect us to start to work immediately, which we did; nor did they expect us to stop when we came to the end of the month.

K: In spite of the fact, known to all of us who have ever worked at electronic music studios, that nothing, but nothing, ever gets finished on time.

C: But we finished directly on time, and we used that as a way of stopping. We could have been going even now.

K: Didn't you use multitrack machines there?

C: We used not one sixteen-track machine, but we used multiples of sixteen tracks. I think it goes up, I don't know what it goes up to, but it's a large number, up in the fifties or sixties.

K: And then it was mixed down into a definitive form.

C: No, it exists in various forms. It can be played with all the tracks separately or in various combinations; so that it can finally be broadcast over the radio, or it can be stereophonic or it can be in four parts. It can be in any number of parts.

K: Can it emerge from 50 or 60 separate loudspeakers?

C: Yes, yes, yes.

K: So that puts you in the same territory as Edgard Varese's *Poème Électronique* [1958].

C: Yes, and I think it's a right place to go. One should go, as David Tudor goes in *Rainforest*, to a multiplicity of sound sources, rather than to a few.

K: I think of *Roaratorio* as being like *HPSCHD*, as both are pieces filled with an abundance of things, as opposed to your more minimalist pieces, such as *Empty Words*, your extractions from Thoreau; and what strikes me now is how similar *Roaratorio* and *HPSCHD* are, which is to say that the Irish music in the former has a similar structural function and weight as Mozart had in *HPSCHD*—both are always there in the background—in contrast to *Williams Mix,* in which the elements are always changing and nothing is continuously there. Why is that? Is that a structural accident, or does that reflect your method?

C: Well, you're quite right that there are certain ideas that one has that he can't be free of. Duchamp says this somewhere, that each person has in his life only a few ideas; and one of mine may be to make sure that everything holds together.

K: In spite of chaos.

C: Right, in my series of etchings called *Changes and Disappearances* the number of different colors is astonishing, but the thing that holds them all together is the presence, no matter how little, of some blue.

K: Hold on, that's really not analogous. Isn't the repeated presence of blue an accident?

C: No, it's analogous, because *Roaratorio* is held together, a) by *Finnegans Wake* . . .

K: By your continuous reading of *For the Second Time.*

C: More so even than the presence of Irish music, it's held together by my reading the mesostics on the name of James Joyce.

K: But in *HPSCHD* there is no analogue to the continuous text from *Finnegans Wake.*

C: The continuous thing in *HPSCHD* is the program which was made in collaboration with Lejaren Hiller. It's always present, and it's realized in fifty-six different ways, you see, for all those divisions of the octave; so that it is the octave which is the common denominator.

K: But can you hear the program?

C: I have never wanted people to know what they were listening to; I've always wanted the result to be mysterious.

K: But you haven't answered my question. Can you, John Cage, hear the program?

C: No.

K: Can anybody hear the program?

C: No.

K: So then it's not like the serial row.

C: And I *have* answered your question.

K: But one of the problems of the twelve-tone row, especially in its more sophisticated forms, is that you can't hear it, even though, in theory, you're supposed to hear, and appreciate, how the composer manipulates the row.

C: Yes, well, the thing there is that you could analyze it, whereas in my chance operations music I don't think you can analyze it.

K: Even in *HPSCHD* you can't discover the program extrinsically.

C: It's very curious. I'm wondering if it's just possible, because of the use of the computer, that a very bright programmer might be able to figure out what the questions were that were asked. Or maybe the use of chance operations is always somewhat perceptible.

K: To me chance operations are perceptible in the work's non-focused, nonhierarchic, nonclimactic structure, which indicates that its compositional program must have incorporated some scheme for realizing this quality.

C: You know that I now have a personal computer, and I now accept the use of the computer. For years I didn't and I acted as though I myself were a necessary computer, whereas now I know I'm no longer necessary except as the initiator of the program. I'm thinking that through the nature of computers or programming and so forth, into which my work falls certainly, that one can tell from what happens something about what was asked. For instance, if you see a graphic work that has white lines on a black field and none of the lines are curved but they're all straight or diagonal, and then you see another one which has nothing but curves or it has a mixture of straight lines and curves, you can begin to know what the questions were that were asked.

And what we would like to reach, knowing all that, in the use of chance operations, is a situation in which you could not figure out what was asked. Otherwise, we'd jump to the understanding of the work even before we use it; so that we have, so to speak, no use for the work if we can understand it before we hear it.

K: That reminds me of chess masters who can purportedly tell from the ways the pieces are now arranged where they came from, how they got that way.

C: What I think is so fascinating about chess is that, given the simple means of each person having sixteen pieces on a field of eight by eight, that no two games are the same.

VIII

K: Let me get back to our subject of radio art. Your next piece for Klaus Schöning was *Ein Alphabet* [1982]. Even though you speak disparagingly of it, I like it a lot.

C: You do?

K: Yes, an awful lot.

C: Well, I'm glad.

K: I like its radical relationship to the conventions of traditional radio drama, such as your having a language, in this case German, spoken by people who don't speak it very well, and then using sound effects that are so abrupt that they only sketch a setting, rather than, as is traditional, filling it in. What bothers you about it?

C: I think that the fact of its complexity together with its simplicity, the simplicity consists in being structured, divided that is to say into scenes and parts; and the complexity deals in the differences, abrupt differences, between one scene and the next; so that, so far as I listen to it, let me say this, I actually enjoyed making *Ein Alphabet* much more than I have enjoyed listening to it.

K: Making it with respect to writing or composing the program?

C: Well, in making the sounds, the sound collage and so forth, for each separate scene; but when I heard it all together, I found it difficult to listen to.

K: Why?

C: Well, the text is an attempt to revive one's experience of Joyce, Duchamp, and Satie and to add to the mystery surrounding their works, rather than in any way clarifying the understanding of their works.

K: And one quality that you found laudable in their works is precisely that they have resisted . . .

C: Being understood. So I used chance operations in order to find out whether they were all three together, or whether two of them were together, or whether one of them was alone.

K: With respect to?

C: A kind of imaginary theater.

K: But not in physical fact. "Imaginary theater" takes place in heaven.

C: Well, I was writing the text originally for a series of lectures at the Walker Art Center in Minneapolis, and they wanted to come to an understanding of the accomplishments in the twentieth century and I wanted to increase the mystery, you see; so I was writing a text that would last about a lecture length and which would present the work of Joyce and Duchamp and Satie. I decided to make a series of mesostics which would be quasi-theatrical. (I don't know how else to describe it.) I had a very curious experience writing the text. I wrote it in about four to six weeks; and in that period, more than any other time in my life, there developed a sort of correspondence or sameness between the night and the day; so that while I was asleep, I didn't have the feeling of being any different than when I was awake, and vice versa.

K: You hadn't done that before.

C: No, I hadn't done it, and it was delicious. I enjoyed it very much so that when I was asleep I was actually thinking in terms of the text I was writing, but I never got up to jot down an idea. I tried to remember how it felt to think that way; and then when I would get up in the morning, I knew how to think that way that I had been thinking at night and went to the table and wrote it. What I had to write, you see, were always mesostics on the names of Joyce, Duchamp, and Satie; so that I was guided by those limitations, mesostic limitations, to go through my day-night, night-day, I think. I was able to lay out the entire text—that was the first thing I did—and I was able to lay it out because I knew that they could all three be together or just two of them or one. That made a permutational situation, and I was able quickly to write well, for instance, all the places where they were alone, because those were nothing but quotations from their own writings. I had my notebooks, and each day these notebooks began to fill up at different points. I didn't write the text from the beginning to the end. I wrote it whenever I had an idea.

K: The concept of the imaginary conversation is clearly radiophonic. You can't do it live; you don't want to bring in actors to play the faces; you want them to exist only as voices.

C: That makes possible too the inclusion of the dead people and the mixture of life and death which becomes, I think, the subject matter of the whole thing, with that lovely conclusion coming from Suzuki that there's no difference between life and death.

K: And therefore sleeping and waking.

C: Right, it's so cheerful, isn't it. I haven't told you yet that the word *alphabet* becomes explicit in the composing means; so that the characters other than Joyce, Duchamp, and Satie are found by subjecting the alphabet itself to chance operations; so I was able to use the alphabet to choose sounds and the sound could be either relevant to the subject or irrelevant. I used that principle in *Empty Words* and in the *Songbooks;* so I used it again in *Alphabet.*

K: Where did you get the background sounds from?

C: Well, once I knew what kind of sound I was to get, then I went and got it.

K: Why did you decide to abbreviate the sound effects? Some of the settings were done with such quick sounds they really don't complete their scenes.

C: They had to be, because there wasn't any time and yet there could have been. You see, through chance operations quite a number of things had to happen in a particular scene. I knew the length of the scene and then I would get through chance operations the number of sounds, the description of the sounds, some of them were closely described and some of them were less closely described.

K: What bothers you about it now?

C: I haven't heard it very much; and each time I've heard it, it seems too complex to me.

K: Too complex, in what sense?

C: In the sense of also being too simple. There are those scenes and they're in a very simple way differentiated from one another. They don't overlap so that it's as simple as a work by Stravinsky, but within each part there's a great disparateness with the next part; so that the act of listening is very uncomfortable.

K: Yes, but it's also very radiophonic.

C: Okay, but my tendency in all my work goes back to the initial purpose for making music, which is to sober and quiet the mind, thus making it susceptible to divine influences. In this case, it's very difficult to maintain that attitude.

K: Well, that's because of the transitions from scene to scene.

C: There are no transitions.

K: That's true of *HPSCHD,* which has no transitions. *Roaratorio* is also a sustained piece of work.

C: Yes, but that doesn't have a structure; this one has a structure.

K: Such as a definite beginning and a definite end.

C: No, all those scenes have beginnings and endings. It's a multiplicity of beginnings and endings. That's what annoys me. I don't mind it as something to read; but as something to hear . . . I think if I were able to see it too.

K: Meaning?

C: Television.

K: You think it's a television piece.

C: Oh, I'm almost sure of it.

K: But how can it be, when you're dealing with the dead talking to each other.

C: With ghosts, and it could have been beautiful with Mount Fuji, and think of Joyce going into the whale like Jonah, and such.

K: What would the images be—these people, or actors playing these people?

C: Well, they could be anywhere from Wagner to Hollywood.

K: So you imagine actors playing these people on the screen.

C: No, you can imagine producing through chance operations quite a fantastic movie. Can't you imagine that?

K: You still haven't clarified for me what would be the images.

C: We wouldn't know, because we would be using chance operations. But we would find a way of . . . I don't know; it might make it worse.

K: If you redid it for radio in English, would you do it differently? Now, after all, it exists only in German—or mostly German.

C: That may be what disturbs me. It may be that I really don't have the experience of it, since I don't really know German.

IX

K: Even though *Muoyce* [1983] was produced by Schöning at WDR, it's not really a *horspiel* in the sense of your previous works. Or is it?

C: This is again *Finnegans Wake* and is the fifth writing through *Finnegans Wake,* which is like *Mureau* which was music-Thoreau. This is *Muoyce,* which is music-Joyce. It subjects all of *Finnegans Wake* to chance operations within a structure analogous to the original structure of *Finnegans Wake* itself, so that the proportions of the four parts are the same as the proportions of Joyce's original.

K: Except yours are far reduced.

C: Oh, it's much smaller, but the proportions are the same; so that there are eight chapters in the first part, four in the second, four in the third, and one in the fourth. And then I emphasized the differences between the books further by having the live voice and three tapes reading the same text simultaneously but with different timings and the timing differed for each line within a chance-determined range. The range was from six seconds through fourteen seconds per line. So that you have what Lou Harrison used to call a "Chinese canon" in which the imitations on the part of the second voice, imitations of the first voice are sometimes slower and sometimes faster and you don't know exactly where you are with respect to the canonic procedure.

K: Which is a device I heard you use before, when you read parts of your Thoreau text live against a taped accompaniment of your previous readings of the same text.

C: It doesn't ring a bell.

K: Really?

C: Anyway, in the second book there are three voices—one live and two recorded. In the third book, one live and one recorded, and then in the fourth book, which is only one chapter, there's only the live voice. All of them are whispered except when there are italics in the original text and those italics produce vocalizations. That vocalizing in a whispering situation brings about almost automatically a feeling of the church and of a bunch of monks who can't sing very well, don't you think.

K: In truth . . .

C: And the whispering too is like a confession.

K: I find this the hardest to listen to.

C: Oh you do?

K: Yes.

C: And, you see, as you found the *Alphabet* easier and I find it more difficult, I find this one easier. We have a different attitude. What makes this easy for me is that the quiet sober mind is assumed and is not disturbed, even by the lightning imitations which come through the loud interrupting sounds, because they don't really interrupt. Once they're gone, the whispering continues.

K: Is this a work that one is supposed to listen to from beginning to end? Or is it one you can return to?

C: Well, naturally, you can leave it because people *do*. Klaus Schöning told me of a performance he made in Frankfurt. He left the doors open, and people left; but about half of the audience didn't leave. So you could either stay or leave, and some of the people who left came back.

   I like it in the sense that I enjoy looking at, oh, the white writing of Mark Tobey, or I like it in the sense that I can look at some of my recent etchings, which to some eyes appear to have nothing in them, but to my eye give pleasure, because I know perfectly well that there's something there that just requires a particular kind of detailed attention to see. If you give that detailed attention, then you automatically fall into a field of enjoyment.

K: But the doors must be left open.

C: Yes.

X

K: How do you pronounce the title of your most recent WDR piece, *HMCIEX* [1984]?

C: "Hm siecks" is the letters H-C-E alternating with the letters M-I-X.

K: I pronounce it "H-C-E mix," because that's the best I can do.

C: Yes, that's good.

K: Thanks.

C: And it's Here Comes Everybody. It was written for the Olympics, and it ignores the fact that not everybody came. It uses folk music from all the various countries invited to the Olympics and then it uses the syllables of the names of the countries, both in German and in English. The German syllables are pronounced by Wiltrud Fischer.

K: Who has a great voice.

C: Yes, and I pronounce the syllables in English and the syllables are placed in meter through chance operations, so that there's a kind of Yin/Yang or male/female dialogue that acts somewhat like the mesostics through *Finnegans Wake* to hold all the various folk musics together.

K: I was struck here by your use of larger fragments, longer fragments, than you're accustomed to using. What was the reason for that?

C: Well, that comes down to the nature of the questions asked and the gamut within which the durations played was from quite short to longer. I thought, you see, originally that it was going to be performed, rather than spliced. Had it been spliced, I would have consistently made the durations shorter, as I did in the *Williams Mix;* but thinking that it would be performed I admitted the possibility of longer durations.

K: Performed and recorded live from that performance?

C: I thought it would be an hour long and I thought it would be practically produced in a single session in the studio. The reason I thought that was that on a previous visit to Cologne I had very quickly responded affirmatively to a request to use chance operations with respect to a large body of recorded material on a program called Your Choice of Classical Music—*Classische auf Wunsch*—or something like that. And that included brief quotations from *Finnegans Wake* in a dialogue between Klaus and me. Anyway, all of that went very well and easily, and there was no rehearsal.

   When Klaus proposed doing *HMCIEX* in Cologne, I assumed that it would be performed live and that each person would have a stack of records beside him and he would put them on and off. I made longer durations so that people would have time to take the record off and put another on.

K: That sounds reminiscent of *Imaginary Landscape No. 1.*

C: You see that's why it has longer quotations. However, when we

got into the studio, Klaus had not foreseen my desire to repeat the
Klassische auf Wunsch situation. He had fewer technicians on hand,
and he had a studio in which the possibilities we'd had for the
Klassische auf Wunsch were not available; so that it simply couldn't
be done. It became a time-consuming job for which we didn't have
the time. So the first thing I did was to . . . Well, we worked like
devils. Some dear friends of mine, who wanted to see me in
Cologne, couldn't believe it when they saw how I was working. I
couldn't even say hello properly.
K: What strikes me, when I hear this piece, is how close it is to
Stockhausen's *Hymnen.*
C: How close is it?
K: Much too close.
C: Bet you he doesn't have anything like those two voices going
together.
K: No, of course he doesn't; but the similarity comes in the use of
extended quotations and then the international repertoire of
those quotations.
C: But wasn't he more interested in certain centers, whereas here
you have a real presence of the Third World, don't you think.
K: That's true. At each of the four so-called centers of *Hymnen* is a
Western anthem—French in the first, German in the second,
American in the third (which he dedicated to you), and the Swiss
in the fourth.
C: Whereas here you have really a feeling of the Third World, and
very little of a feeling of Europe—a little bit, but mostly the
atmosphere is that of the Third World.
K: So therefore more . . .
C: Or more . . . I don't know what.

XI

K: *Muoyce,* it seems to me, should become a record, because it
should be listened to again and again in ways that your other
radio works need not be listened to again and again. The questions then are how does radio differ from records, and when in
the current situation are records more appropriate than radio? A
related question is when is radio more appropriate than live
performance?
C: If you're thinking from the point of view of the use of it on the
part of the listener, I'm not a great listener to radio; I pay little
attention to television. Merce Cunningham loves to look at televi-

sion, less so now than he did formerly. He's beginning to feel more the way I do, but what he enjoys about radio or television, I think, is that he can change the station whenever he wishes. And he does that frequently; and these modern devices of control from a distance, remote control, facilitate your changing whenever you feel like it. I don't know quite what to say in relation to radio, records, and television and the differences between them, because I don't play records for my enjoyment, and I don't listen to the radio, except for the news and the time, now and then, and the weather; and I don't look at television at all.

K: Even though, in your house here, it sits in the middle of a corner room that overlooks both the avenue and rooftops.

C: I look out the windows. On the other hand, I was deeply influenced, I can even say, or deeply encouraged by the work of Marshall McLuhan, who paid attention to the differences of those media with some precision and insight and all of that. When I found out what insights he was having, they mostly corroborated feelings that I had independently of those media in relation to the art of music.

K: But we agree that a record is different from radio, and I think I was trying to suggest that one of your recent works was really far more suitable for records than radio.

C: You mean in the case of a record that you can come back to it whenever you wish, whereas in the case of radio you're listening only then.

K: Radio imposes itself on you in its time. There's a certain surprise factor involved that is, as well, of interest to me.

C: I don't know how I could feel if I, say, had not made *Muoyce* or *Alphabet* and I turned on the radio and there was the experience. Klaus tells me that Hans Otte turned on *Muoyce* and then just afterward called Klaus to congratulate him on having made something that he enjoyed so much. I remember once happening to listen to the radio when I lived out in the country and I left it on rather than turning it off, because the performance was very good, a piece of orchestral music. I'd always been very critical of the work of Leonard Bernstein, and I thought that this was very well done; and, if you please, at the end of the broadcast, they said that Lennie had been conducting.

K: That's an example of the surprise factor again. You didn't know in advance who was conducting. If you had, you might have turned away. If you saw the same piece in the record store, you wouldn't have bought it.

C: I wouldn't have listened to it.

K: I listen to radio all the time, to music most of this time. What makes the experience so extraordinary to me are not only all the good things I hear, but that so much was previously unfamiliar to me. WNYC here, in particular, gives you the news of new music in a way you're not going to get from going to concerts, because when you go to concerts, you tend to pick things you already know. Radio becomes our principal medium for musical surprise.

XII

K: Has your work in German radio taught you something you didn't know before?

C: I don't know that the connection with Klaus has been instructive, but it has been stimulating. He's an extraordinary . . . He's insatiable.

K: His enthusiasm seems insatiable.

C: Yes, absolutely, and he feeds himself things that make him think of other possibilities that he's yet to see realized, and he's able to prod people; so that the field of radio has in it other things than it had before he did all this.

K: Before I came here I thought I would say that one charm of German radio is that it enabled you to realize the definitive versions of your own pieces in a way that hadn't been true before. That perhaps accounts for why I like *Roaratorio* so much.

C: No, I think that that is true.

K: If that is true, you're not making scores for other people to use; you're not acting as a composer as much as acting as a producer for your own work.

C: Well, no. In the case of *Roaratorio,* the composition of *Roaratorio* is not called *Roaratorio.* It's called "blank blank Circus on blank" [written out as "(title of composition) (article-adjective) Circus on (title of book)]. I wrote the score for *Roaratorio* after having performed it with John Fullemann at IRCAM, [Institut de Recherche et Coordination Acoustique/Musique] and I generalized it so that it could be performed by someone else in IRCAM or some other studio with respect either to *Finnegans Wake* or some other book.

K: That score is printed in the back of the *Roaratorio* book as, simply, a three-page outline.

C: Yes, but briefly, it shows all the work that we did from the writing of the text, which becomes the ruler for the performance, to the listing of the sounds that you found in the course of reading the book and going to the places mentioned in the book and making environmental recordings and putting them where they belonged with respect to the ruler.

K: So *Roaratorio* represents your own realization of your composition, or compositional prospectus of a "Circus," which could be realized by other performers, in drastically different ways. Much of your *Roaratorio* results from your selection of *Finnegans Wake* as your text.

And this way of working, John, recalls your statement on the flyleaf of the hardback edition of *Notations* [1969] about what constitutes a musical score nowadays.

C: Yes, why don't you print it here. It's not available anywhere else.

The reading or memorizing of something written in order to play music is an Occidental practice. In the Orient, music by tradition is transmitted from person to person. Teachers of music require that students put no reliance on written material.

Western notation brought about the preservation of "music," but in doing so encouraged the development not only of standards of composition and performance, but also of an enjoyment of music that was more or less independent of its sound, placing qualities of its organization and expressivity above sound itself.

Furthermore, as the permissions to reprint in this book testify, music, through becoming property, elevated its composers above other musicians, and an art by nature ephemeral became in practice political.

In any case, until recently, notation was the unquestioned path to the experience of music.

At the present time, however, and throughout the world, not only most popular music but much so-called serious music is produced without recourse to notations. This is in large part the effect of a change from print to electronic technology. One may nowadays repeat music not only by means of printed notes but by means of sound recordings, disc or tape. One may also compose new music by these same recording means, and by other means: the activation of electric and electronic sound-systems, the programming of computer output of actual sounds, etc. In addition to technological changes, or without employing such changes, one may change one's mind, experiencing, in the case of theatre (happenings, performance pieces), sounds as the musical effect of actions as they may be perceived in the course of daily life. In none of these cases does notation stand between musician and music nor between music and listener.

Asked to write about notation, André Jolivet made the following remark: "One hundred and fifty years ago, Western musical writing acquired such flexibility, such precision, that music was permitted to become the only true international language."

François Dufrêne, replying to a request for a manuscript, wrote as

JOHN CAGE AT SEVENTY-FIVE

follows: "I am not in a situation to give you any kind of score, since the spirit in which I work involves the systematic rejection of all notation. . . . I 'note' furthermore that a score could only come about after the fact, and because of this loses from my point of view all significance."

The book, then, by means of manuscript pages (sometimes showing how a page might leave its composer's hand in its working form, sometimes how it looked in its working form as he used it, sometimes finished work) shows the spectrum in the twentieth century which extends from the continuing dependence on notation to its renunciation.

You see, I'm still very much involved with writing music.[4]

Notes

1. This monograph, published in 1970, is still available from RK Editions, P. O. Box 73, Canal Street Station, New York, N.Y., 10013; part of this initial conversation appeared in my book *The Theatre of Mixed Means* (1968), which was reprinted in 1980 by RK Editions.

2. See Richard Kostelanetz, *The Old Poetries and the New* (Ann Arbor: University of Michigan Press, 1981).

3. *The John Cage Reader* (New York: Peters, 1983).

4. The original transcription of this conversation was prepared by Benny Tao, a film student at New York University. The production of this text was partially funded by a grant from the New York State Council on the Arts.

Notes on Contributors

NEIL ANDERSON is a painter who is best known for a series of works he calls *Ground Paintings*. His paintings are in the collection of the Museum of Modern Art, the private collection of John D. Rockefeller IV, and the corporate collections of AT&T, Prudential Insurance, and Xerox Corporation, among others. He is represented by the Fishbach Gallery and lives in New York and Lewisburg, Pennsylvania, where he teaches painting at Bucknell University.

GENE BAGNATO, a photographer from New York, specializes in portraits of artists and entertainers. His series of portraits of contemporary American composers was exhibited at the Vincent Astor Gallery at Lincoln Center in 1982. It was subsequently purchased by the United States Information Agency and has since been exhibited throughout the world.

WILLIAM BROOKS composes and writes in Savoy, Illinois. He is particularly interested in the intersection of music and language, and many of his compositions involve the voice. His scholarly work centers on the history of American music, particularly in the twentieth century; he has written extensively about Charles Ives, John Cage, and American vernacular idioms. Future plans include a series of pieces based on *Finnegans Wake,* a monograph on three works by John Cage, and continued study of the history of twentieth-century music.

NORMAN O. BROWN is Professor of Humanities Emeritus at the University of California at Santa Cruz. He has been a scholar of the Classics, author of *Hermes the Thief* and *Hesiod's Theogony;* a philosopher, author of *Life Against Death: The Psychoanalytical Meaning of History;* a poetic visionary, author of *Love's Body* and *Closing Time.*

DEBORAH CAMPANA is Public Services Librarian at the Northwestern University Music Library where she directs reference and circulation services, is the bibliographer for music books, and edits *NU Quarter Notes,* the quarterly publication of the Music

Library. She earned a Ph.D. in music theory from Northwestern University (her dissertation was titled "Form and Structure in the Music of John Cage") and a master of arts in library science from the University of Chicago.

WILLIAM DUCKWORTH is a composer, author, and teacher. His best-known composition is a one-hour work for piano titled *The Time Curve Preludes.* Selections from this work have been performed on four continents, including Carnegie Hall in New York, the Darmstadt summer festival, and the People's Republic of China. He is currently working on a book of interviews titled *Talking Music: Conversations with 5 Generations of American Experimental Composers.*

TOM JOHNSON is a composer/performer who currently lives in Paris. His work includes several operas, of which the most famous is *The Four Note Opera,* which has been produced over fifty times, in French, German, Italian, and Polish, as well as in English. Between 1971 and 1982, he was the principal critic for new music for the *Village Voice* in New York.

RICHARD KOSTELANETZ has authored many books of poetry, fiction, criticism, and cultural history. More recently, he has been composing his own horspiel for German radio stations, and for this work he has received grants from the NEA and ASCAP. He is also working on a book of essays about alternative radio.

JAMES PRITCHETT is a doctoral student in musicology at New York University. With the assistance of a fellowship from the American Musicological Society, he is currently completing his dissertation on John Cage's chance compositions of the 1950s. His research on Cage's *Concerto for Prepared Piano,* the result of the discovery of previously unknown Cage manuscripts in the possession of David Tudor, has been published in *Perspectives of New Music.*

ARTHUR J. SABATINI is a writer, critic, and university instructor. He is also Special Projects Director for Relâche, the Ensemble for Contemporary Music. Through 1987 he worked as the General Editor and Coordinator of the New Music America 1987 Festival in Philadelphia, produced by Relâche.

MARGARET LENG TAN, from Singapore, is one of Asia's leading pianists and a foremost exponent of New Music. The first woman to graduate with a Doctor of Musical Arts from The Juilliard School, her awards include the Van Cliburn Scholarship, a National Endowment for the Arts Solo Recitalist Award, and an Asian Cultural Council Grant to research contemporary music in Japan. Miss Tan has presented New Music to audiences worldwide. She participated in festivals honoring John Cage's seventieth and seventy-fifth birthdays, and presented his *Four Walls* in its New York premiere. Her recordings include *Litania: Margaret Leng Tan Plays Somei Satoh* (New Albion) and *Sonic Encounters: The New Piano* (Mode) featuring two first recordings of music by Cage.